FUNDAMENTALS OF
ART THERAPY

FUNDAMENTALS OF ART THERAPY

By

SHAUN McNIFF, PH.D.

Professor of Expressive Therapies and Dean
Institute for the Arts and Human Development
Lesley College Graduate School
Cambridge, Massachusetts

CHARLES C THOMAS • PUBLISHER
Springfield • Illinois • U.S.A.

Published and Distributed Throughout the World by
CHARLES C THOMAS • PUBLISHER
2600 South First Street
Springfield, Illinois 62794-9265

© *1988 by* CHARLES C THOMAS • PUBLISHER
ISBN 0-398-05388-X
Library of Congress Catalog Card Number: 87-17956

With THOMAS BOOKS *careful attention is given to all details of manufacturing
and design. It is the Publisher's desire to present books that are satisfactory as to their
physical qualities and artistic possibilities and appropriate for their particular use.*
THOMAS BOOKS *will be true to those laws of quality that assure a good name
and good will.*

Printed in the United States of America
Q-R-3

Library of Congress Cataloging in Publication Data

McNiff, Shaun.
    Fundamentals of art therapy.

    Bibliography: p.
    Includes index.
    1. Art therapy. I. Title.
RC489.A7M37   1987   616.89'1656   87-17956
ISBN 0-398-05388-X

FOREWORD

I BELIEVE THAT all therapies and therapists participate in a shared dialogue which is expanded and deepened through the arts. Although I make use of rhythmic sound and movement, objects, enactment, poetry and other artforms, the visual media of painting and drawing as presented here, have been my principle artifacts within an image-centered therapy. *The Arts and Psychotherapy* (1981) introduces the vision of a pantheon of creative arts therapies and the integration of the arts in therapeutic practice. The book defines the arts in psychotherapy as contemporary manifestations of ancient and indigenous healing practices. *Educating the Creative Arts Therapist: A Profile of the Profession* (1986) was the first book to deal with the training of creative art therapists. In addition to reviewing the history of education in all of the creative arts therapies, it presents an 'artistic theory of mental health and therapy.' The call for theory indigenous to art is consistent with my search for the archetype of the creative arts therapist in the person of the shaman. I have encouraged creative art therapists to build our profession through close cooperation between the different artforms and with theoretical principles that are native to art and our different cultural histories. The two previous books establish the context for the more focused treatment of art therapy in the present volume.

The search for "essential elements" runs through all of my published writings on psychotherapy. This book began with the title, *Fundamentals of Art Therapy,* and my desire to write a comprehensive manuscript on what I do within this discipline. The title is an expression of intent and a desire to become aware of the elements of art therapy as they manifest themselves in my work. I am committed to the "artistic fundamentals" which distinguish art therapy from other modes of psychotherapy. I do not wish to imply that I am going to present the definitive essence of art therapy as experienced by all people. A task of this kind is beyond the reach of a single person, or even a group of writers. Art will always surprise us with alternative forms and different ways of interpreting what we do.

In 1804 Jean Paul Richter in his *Vorschule der Aesthetik* said that "The essence of poetic presentation, like all life, can be represented only by a second poetic presentation." He felt that aesthetic experience is to be described with images that "mirror kindred life." I wanted to write this book in a form that embodied what I do. In keeping with Richter's advice I have tried to create "a second poetic presentation." The first poetic experience is art therapy itself. Since my work is a process of continuing dialogue with colleagues, students and images, I have described it within this form. The dialogue is also a classical and proven form of philosophical inquiry. It has allowed me to get as close as it is possible within the format of a book to the phenomenon of art therapy as I have experienced it within a particular context, and during an actual period in my life.

We have not begun to imagine how great the soul of the art therapy profession is. In order to do this it is necessary to re-imagine the nature of art in our society and the traditions of mental health and psychotherapy. We have given considerable attention to how the conventions of mental health institutions discourage imagination from transforming the entire scenario. I am becoming increasingly aware that the same can be said of artistic conventions. If only we could be capable of continuously taking a fresh look at everything that we do and starting anew each day. I am convinced that revolutionary transformations must occur on a daily basis. Those transformations that are sympathetic to the human soul, to its life rhythms, will survive. Change is helpful when it takes us toward the fundamentals and when it improves life for many people. There has to be a sustained commitment to the cause and a trust that useful things will sustain themselves. Art operates in this way.

Thanks to Paolo Knill, Jill Goldman, Catherine Cobb, Janice Shapiro, Kit Jenkins, Leslie Powell, Hadass Shlagman, Helen Landgarten, Louis van Marissing, Annette Brederode, Klaus Boegel, Baruch Zadick, Phillip Speiser, the Lesley community, Payne Thomas and the staff at Charles C Thomas, Publisher.

CONTENTS

FUNDAMENTALS OF
ART THERAPY

I. Ideas and Process

EMERGENCE OF IMAGES

L ISA IS A former professor of art education who is trained to be an art therapist. I am her supervisor. She is now working with children in a community counseling center, and she is struggling with how to involve them with art materials.

"I have worked for so many years as an art teacher," Lisa said, "that it seems impossible for me to go into an art therapy session without an exercise for the children that has been planned in advance. And I know that the structure that I create will bias what the children express. Judy Rubin writes about how her psychoanalytic training has helped her to allow spontaneous expression to emerge with art materials. I realize that I use art exercises because I am afraid of losing control; I fear chaos and empty space. The need for 'lesson plans' is not unique to art teachers. I see it in myself and other art therapists. I always sensed that there is 'more' going on in the children's artwork than what we teachers planned."

"This question about how to work with art materials is one of the most fundamental issues in art therapy," I said. "My nine-year-old daughter surprised me one day when I referred to myself as a teacher.

Daddy, you're not a teacher, she said.
Then what do I do?
You talk to people about their ideas.
And what does a teacher do?
A teacher tells people what to do.

"In her simplified way my daughter had defined one of the primary differences between what teachers and therapists have become in our society. The learning dialogue has moved from education to therapy. It is quite possible that it may return to education, at least I hope it does. I think that the movement we see from art education to art therapy has to do with a need to understand what is happening inside the people we work with and ourselves, how we affect others and how they affect us, what the images are saying to us, and so forth. Art therapy is an expression of our desire to know more about images and people and to do more with them.

"The principles of dialogue, whether in words or images, are concerned with exchange and opening to whatever presents itself. The early psychoanalysts tried to further expression through free association and by encouraging people to say whatever entered their minds. They were not afraid of chaos because there was a purpose to what they were doing. They were looking for themes and messages in what would at first seem to be a fragmented fomentation of thoughts and images."

"What do we do with the person who is incapable of speaking or who chooses not to speak and will not take any initiative with art materials? Isn't it necessary for us to structure the situation for them?"

"With some people structure increases freedom. The specific task, whether it is making a picture with scribbles, straight lines or a combination of both, or painting with the drips from a brush, gives the person something to relate to. The 'assignment' provides intentionality. It can be designed in a way that minimizes fears of failure and embarrassment. The person is given the opportunity to act, to choose and to respond to whoever is suggesting the particular activity. If we are working in a group, a common task may generate a spirit of cooperation and collegiality. It is necessary to accept the person's handicap and do something about it. When I first started to work in a mental hospital with severely handicapped people, I carried on long internal arguments with myself about whether or not my 'structures' were restricting the freedom and choice of the people I was working with. As the weeks went on, many of the people continued to sit motionlessly with a blank piece of paper in front of them. The demands of this environment ended my abstract deliberations on freedom. I was close to a staff person who had worked at the hospital for over forty years. She was an old-fashioned 'attendant' and she had no formal therapeutic education. She dressed in spotless white every day and had a sarcastic response for every situation. When I described my dilemma about freedom, she said to me: 'These people aren't here because they have flat feet.' Her comment, as derogatory as it may sound, helped me to accept their disabilities and my role at the hospital."

"Wasn't that a time when mental health systems were being severely criticized?"

"The system of institutionalized mental health was mad, abusive and terribly confused. Yet, at the same time, I liked my job and I enjoyed working with my colleagues. We were all critical about 'the system' but we tried to focus our energy on the patients in the hospital and what we could do for them. I had been hired to get them 'involved' in art and not to deliberate on the politics of artistic freedom which seemed to matter little to everybody but myself. I am sure now that my internal dialogue at that time was more concerned with my insecurity, my inexperience and my complete lack of understanding of what to do.

"It never felt correct for me to take other people's art recipes and apply them to the people I was working with. I had to find out for myself, through my own experimentation, my advances and my failures."

"This is the area I have the most difficulty with as a trainer of art teachers," Lisa said. "There is always such a hunger for 'techniques' that can be used immediately in the classroom. I have encountered few students and teachers who are willing to find out for themselves. They see me as the person who is supposed to 'tell them,' as your daughter says. I became good at telling them. My classes were lively and they left with pages of recipes. I enjoyed it in the early years because their need for me and their responsiveness was affirming. But I soon discovered that there was an absence of depth to my teaching. I was not taking risks and I was protecting my students from risk. The process lacked dynamic creativity. I was repeating myself year after year and operating within the fixed script of lesson plans. But aren't you contradicting yourself when you say that structure is necessary?"

"Perhaps. Therapy and life are packed with contradictions that make it impossible for us to operate according to road maps, unless we happen to be driving in cars. The psyche is not as predictable as the highway. It is not fixed in material forms."

"How can the beginning art therapist begin to grasp these contradictions?"

"I encourage therapists, and myself, to concentrate on what presents itself in the situation before us. Everything depends upon the context and what people are capable of. Diagnosis and assessment are ongoing. They never stop and settle into fixed labels. Our observations, what we see before us, and what we learn from experience and our reading, are merged within the practice of therapy. Theories are important as guides but generally give way to disciplined instincts when we are working with people. This flexible and adaptive responsiveness to what presents itself within the situation is the essence of clinical practice. 'Clinical' performance applies as much to the making of art as it does to medicine.

"If I had suggested to many of the people that I was working with in the mental hospital that we were going 'to paint from within' we would have continued to have weeks of blank paper. I had to intervene with specific suggestions and materials. This engagement of both materials and emotions is what defines art therapy. We begin by making physical contact with materials. In the case of one man who never touched a brush for months, I learned that it was necessary for me to begin by holding his hand and painting together. This is an example of how the smallest movements in art therapy can also be seen as dance therapy. The perception of what we were doing as dance gave it additional meaning and relevance. This kind of painting can also be used in depth-oriented psychotherapy. Everything depends upon what the situation calls for. Perhaps all roads lead to the same place."

"Did you fall into routines in terms of what you did with people?"

"Absolutely! The rhythm qualities of the routine were actually pleasant for the people I was working with and myself. It can be likened to a family that likes to eat certain things for breakfast and agrees on plans for evening meals that are repeated over a period of time. The routine also increases predictability and a sense of control and safety. I have discovered that a feeling of safety is generally necessary if people are to take risks and open themselves. For example, theatres are constructed in a way that strives to maximize concentration, enclosure and the elimination of distractions. I have also found that routines generally change over time and provide for the introduction of new elements, diversifications of menu.

"My difficulties with the routine came when I moved to a radically different context, like your moving from the 'culture' of art education to art therapy. Today, I am engaged primarily in doing depth-oriented psychotherapy with people who respond very well to the suggestion that they 'paint from within,' allowing whatever they feel to emerge. They want the freedom to engage what is relevant to them at the moment and to work thematically with their art over a period of time."

"When I worked as an art teacher I protected myself from risk with clearly defined plans for what the children were to do. I was in an elementary school where one of the teachers ran an informal classroom with an art corner where the children could go when there was an opportunity. It was difficult for me to accept that the images produced in that classroom had more vitality and imagination than what we did in the formal art class. The art area in the informal classroom came much closer to a real studio environment, whereas the art class began to feel more like an assembly line. Teachers observed individual children in the art corner and listened to the stories they told about their pictures. The process closely corresponded to the way I imagined art therapy taking place. That particular art corner was the beginning of my disenchantment with the way we do art education in America, where roving art teachers work with hundreds of children each week with predesigned lessons and little opportunity to engage the children in serious dialogue about their work. When a teacher is responsible for hundreds of children, sometimes as many as five hundred each week, then it is inevitable that everything is focused on the planning of materials and virtually no attention can be given to the individual child. It was difficult for me to accept that my most cherished values of artistic expression in childhood were being realized by that classroom teacher and not by me. The children did not have to be told what to do. They just went to the easles that were equipped with brushes and large bottles of tempera, and began to paint. I noticed how they looked at each other's work and influenced one another. Individual styles emerged and it was not difficult to determine who made a particular picture. Expressive and sensitive pictures were being created by all of the children. It was a fourth-grade class and the teacher had equal success with previous groups of first-, second- and third-graders.

"In some ways that art corner was the most exciting and authentic studio environment that I had experienced. I began to realize the large impact that context has on art. It was not necessary to tell the children what to do. The classroom teacher was not trained as an art educator and I think that was her greatest advantage. She went to a liberal arts college and majored in anthropology and literature before going on for a masters of education degree. She had an excellent eye for design, color and other visual principles and was enthusiastic about what the children did. Art works were hanging everywhere in the classroom. In our training of art teachers there is so much emphasis on methods initiated by the teacher, too much I think. In this way we will build-in the expectation on the part of art teachers, other educators, parents and the children, that the teacher will be telling the children what to do. The orientation is so ingrained into our school programs and our educational history that it is nearly impossible to go contrary to it. I think it has even influenced art therapy, unless the difficulties I am experiencing are unique to me."

"What were some of the factors that influenced the quality of art being expressed by the children in the art corner?" I asked.

"There was an unspoken environmental emphasis on the emergence of images rather than art instruction. It was assumed by all of the children that they could paint and they did, naturally. In my art classes everything was focused on methods presented by the teachers as well as correct and incorrect procedures. So much of art education is far closer to industrial assembly than the atelier. Educational environments are in this respect projections of our social values.

"Children in the art corner had a freedom of time and space that corresponds more to the working dynamics of the artist. They had access to art materials when they felt the urge to work, and they had the time to complete their pictures or to work on a series if they were inspired. There was little flexibility of time in our formal art classes."

"Is your art therapy appointment schedule, within the time limits of one-hour sessions, more like the formal art lesson than the art corner?"

"Yes. But there are so many differences between what I am potentially able to do in the art therapy sessions than what characterized my experiences in the classroom. I can work with small groups, families and individual children on a consistent basis, with time being given to me for case conferences, supervision and writing progress reports. Those are the most striking differences. I also sense that I have the opportunity to form an entirely new way of working with people and images. The fact that we are scheduled to meet together within a particular frame of time is one of the features that does make the art therapy work more like what I did as an art teacher than what I saw happening in the art corner. Perhaps it is this formality of professional roles that makes me think that it is my responsibility to get things started by defining what we are going to do."

"What are the problems that you have with getting started?"

"At times I feel as though I am running an exercise class rather than a therapy session. I am so afraid of the open space, losing control and failing. I am making some progress, in that I am relying far less on prescribed art methods and I am beginning to adapt the spontaneous art techniques of other art therapists to my work. I use the scribble technique in my individual sessions and Hanna Kwiatkowska's exercises with my families. But the scribbles produced in art therapy sessions are looking too much alike. Art therapists relying on them seem to be generating endless amounts of art therapy art. The family art therapy exercises have been helpful. When families come together, the specific instructions to draw both individual and group pictures, drawings from scribbles and abstract family portraits, are in some ways liberating. But I have trouble having to rely on 'instructions.' To me psychotherapy is more concerned with finding the structure that exists in the moment and engaging whatever needs to emerge. What do you think?"

"We do not give enough direct attention to *what we do* in art therapy and how we are similar to or different from art education and other forms of psychotherapy," I said. "Scribbles exercises and other methods are not invented by individual people and forever ascribed to them. I think that we repeat certain methods because they are useful and because they become part of the routine of a profession. Rather than just assuming that 'the scribble' is the primary method of the art therapist, it might be better to inquire into those qualities of the scribble that make it useful. Knowledge about the materials we use and the process of working with them helps to avoid feelings of emptiness and fear. Experience, understanding of the work context and disciplined instinct enable us to respond and adapt to whatever presents itself. I have learned that the oracle, which offers messages and counsel, often speaks in strange and unexpected ways. If we are only looking for that which we plan to see, we can miss the message which can sometimes disguise itself and challenge our sensitivity and adaptibility. At other times we are so busy looking for hidden meanings that we cannot see what is before us. We do not want to use techniques like the scribble purely out of routine and without understanding why we are engaging them at particular times, with a specific person or group. What are some of the qualities of the scribble that account for its usefulness?"

"It helps us to subdue the harsh critic within ourselves."

"Do you mean that the scribble supports spontaneous expression?"

"Yes. It provides an alternative to the cliches that people have in their minds. . .the house, the tree, the flowers, the dog, the horse, the automobile."

"I would like to come back to those images, but let's stay with the scribble for now. What does the harsh critic do to you?"

"It immobilizes me and takes away my self-confidence. It devalues whatever comes out."

"Is it the scribble or the art therapist that helps people to deal with these things?"

"Both, I know that part of my job is to be affirming. You have spoken in class about D. H. Lawrence saying that the job of the artist is to transmit life. My years of teaching have confirmed how important this is. I am realizing how necessary it is to be inspirational. You have spoken about the contagious vitality of art and creating a context in which the person realizes that the worth of a black dot or single line depends only to the value that we attach to it. So, maybe it matters little whether we make scribbles, dots or gestures with paint."

"I think it matters, Lisa. Materials and images are our associates in art therapy. We do not want to establish hierarchical or one-dimensional attitudes that promote the interpersonal relationship at the expense of image making, or vice versa. It is through materials, images and the process of art that art therapy expands the shared psychotherapeutic dialogue. I think we have to be sensitive to how scribbles, dots and gestures with paint are different from one another. This differentiation is part of our clinical intelligence. So let's go back to the properties of the scribble. In addition to assisting us in achieving higher degrees of spontaneity, what else can it do?"

"As you suggested, the scribble serves as a form of movement therapy. There are also many different kinds of scribbles: large, small, fast, slow, aggressive, delicate. . . . A wide range of feelings can be expressed through the scribble. This mode of expression is not dependent upon planning and it is closer to emotion. The scribble can be cathartic, a mode of release and ventilation. It is adjustible to a broad range of human capabilities, from the severely handicapped person who is learning how to hold a crayon or pen, to the person who chooses to scribble with eyes closed in order to experience the movement qualities more fully. The spontaneity of the scribble may stimulate corresponding inner feelings and healthy adaptability. Forms *emerge* from scribbles. The lines build things up as well as cover up. Pictures can be shaped from what would appear to be random movements. Accidents and surprises reveal possibilities that would not manifest themselves through carefully planned exercises. You are always saying that 'expectations can be blindfolds.' Inhibitions of people who are not familiar with drawing and painting are often related to expectations. They feel that their images do not correspond to standards of art. They typically have an image in their minds of what they would like to do and this image becomes an obstacle to expressiveness. Experienced artists know that images emerge from the properties of the material and their movements which give them something to relate to and build with. Perhaps the scribble is fundamentally an artistic vehicle of emergence. But it is just as much connected to action and feeling. Children typically scribble as an early form of expression. They are learning how to use a tool and put their mark on the world. Art therapists have used the scribble as a projective vehicle. The truly 'free' scribble is the antithesis of conscious planning. Stories and images are constructed in response to what the scribbles suggest. They provide easy access to fantasy."

"Excellent! Are there also some potential problems associated with the scribble?"

"I imagine that it can become too much of a routine. Art therapy does not want to be perceived as just scribbling. Too many people adopt the 'technique' attitude, and the projective qualities of the scribble are turned into a test situation in which there is an absence of art and depth."

"Yes. There are many other materials and techniques that can be similarly useful and which might expand upon what the scribble offers. For example, with paint we may lose some of the precision and control achieved through the crayon, pen or pencil, but we gain flow, mass, and texture. All of these properties evoke feelings and stimulate imagination, usually in different ways. Rather than starting with our emphasis on 'scribbling,' we might think in terms of movement and touch as fundamental elements of the 'visual' arts. The process of making a picture depends on the teaming of these senses with sight. There is also a profound dramatic dimension to both the making and viewing of a picture. The 'visual art' concept is in this respect misleading. Presenting a person with the opportunity to 'move' with lines or paint can sometimes be liberating, in that it sidesteps inhibitions that may be attached to painting and drawing. 'Action painting' can be as useful to art therapy as it was to art history. Scribble stereotyping may be eliminated by thinking about art as movement and action, and not just scribbling. Art therapy will benefit from the introduction of more varied movements of the body and the emotions. It can be helpful to stand while making art. This allows us to put more of our body into the picture. A large surface for painting and drawing will also encourage body movement."

"Do you have a standard technique for positioning the body while making art?" Lisa asked.

"No. I generally work with what is possible and most comfortable in relation to the characteristics of the physical space and what benefits the person. In training groups I give people considerable freedom in 'setting up.' In ongoing one-to-one sessions we generally work and sit in the same place. This becomes part of our ritual."

"These ritual aspects of art therapy probably make it easy to fall into the repetition of standard techniques with both clients and techniques."

"You are perceptive. The danger that faces art therapy involves giving too much attention to 'the technique' and its standardized repetition as contrasted to sensitive clinical judgments and intuitions. We are overly involved in the invention and following of methods. Both can be attributed to our ego needs. Inventing is associated with achievement and recognition, whereas the need to follow is motivated by fear of emptiness, uncertainty and failure. We should be concerned with determining what is happening in a given situation and acting according to what we think is needed. Standardized art activities may be useful as research tools that tell us something about human variations and commonalities. Recipes, technical routines and the preparation of lesson plans prior to engaging a person or situation do not advance the clinical expertise and depth of our profession. It might be argued that a particular routine or plan may be part of a clinical prescription, but this approach supports adjunctive roles. We also know that routines have many useful functions even within the most adventurous art therapy processes. The ritual dimension of repetition illustrates this, in that routines can help to invoke the positive aspects of predictibility such as trust and relaxation. So, it is not a matter of simply yes or no with regard to repetition and technique. This illustrates the intricacies of clinical work."

"You seem to be more interested in the phenomenon of scribbling and what it does in art therapy than the universal use of the scribble technique."

"Yes. And I encourage a similar inquiry into every material that we use. There is so much going on at every moment. We cannot take anything for granted. Comparative studies are useful, in that they highlight the qualities of materials through an investigation of similarities and differences. We did this briefly with our comparison of scribbles and movements with paint as contrasted to pencils. I have found that the adoption of standard techniques limits this phenomenological inquiry into the nature of different art materials and processes. It is interesting that many art therapists do excellent work within radically circumscribed techniques. Limits sometimes sharpen concentration. Although operating within tightly drawn boundaries can be advantageous to individual therapeutic practice, it is not recommended for the profession as a whole where we need to encourage diversity."

"You sound like an anarchist."

"I have been called an anarchist many times. The positive elements of the philosophy of anarchy are always overlooked. People think only of chaos, and the loss of control is one of the biggest fears in our culture. The anarchist believes that the structure should fit the particulars of the moment."

"Would you say more about 'structure' in an art therapy session?"

"I have discovered that there are major misconceptions about what is structured and unstructured in both therapy and education. Structure and form are always present in any life situation. However, I accept that people are not always capable of seeing it. Therapists in training want structure. They generally think that it is their job to 'give' the structure to a person and the therapeutic context. This imposition can at times go against the inherent structure of the situation. I think that my job is one of helping people to see the structure of the moment and of the past. The psychotherapeutic structure is whatever is needed in the moment. If possible, there is more of an emphasis on inner direction as contrasted to environmental manipulation. The term 'non-directive' can be misleading, in that it often refers to situations that respect inner direction and the complexities of structure. If we are working in a group, the presentation of a single structure by a teacher or leader can be useful, in that it provides the group with a common focal point and shared purpose. Yet, at the same time, the complexities of the inherent structure of the situation are magnified tremendously in groups, families and communities. In my experience, the strongest groups have acknowledged and supported the revelation and realization of variety. This tolerance enables them to move freely from private to shared experience. Sophisticated and subtle forms of leadership inspire inner direction and acceptance of differences. The direction cannot be contrived.

"This issue of structure, as it relates to what leaders or teachers tell groups to do, has caused me to do more soul-searching than any other aspect of my clinical and educational work. It has produced more conflict in groups and more pain for me than any other issue. I have concluded that conflict is the subject matter of our work. I do not believe in contrived conflict, but I certainly feel that I should not be avoiding it when it presents itself.

"Bruce Moon, when he was serving as the president of the Buckeye Art Therapy Association, told me that we grow during the painful times. That's when we have to reach out, and in, for help and clarification. During a difficult period I wrote in my journal 'we make our mark in the dust and go on.' It may sound trite, but there is nothing more important than going on, the humbler the better. The more open we are to the structure that is present, the better. This is what the people we work with want: an ability to meet them where they are. The 'giving' of structure is often a symptom of not doing this, of making people go to where we are. In the realm of diplomacy, whether with international relations or in community business dealings, it is a sign of respect to visit people, to call on them, in their place, rather than expect them to come to us. I do not like educational models that present the teacher as the authority who establishes the structure that everybody is expected to follow. Too much is lost. I find it better to respond to individual interests and common goals that emerge from our experience together as well as the demands of the world.

"The inherent structure of a situation is all too often one of conflict and we have to learn how to engage it, or better yet embrace it, lovingly. I have repeatedly discovered that depth and commitment come after the transformation of conflict. There is an inevitable testing that we go through with the people in therapy. They want to know whether or not we can accept their anger, rage and confusion and create a safe community. The Jungians would say that these conflicts are not 'their's' but they belong to all of us and that healing involves the acceptance of this universality. Any help we can get to remove the crippling possessiveness and insecurity of the ego ought to be cherished.

"In art therapy, structure is always present in the form of the materials we use. Whatever we make available, whether it be paint, clay, drawing materials, video, sand, wood or stones, structures the context. This innate structuring of art materials and process accounts for why beginning creative arts therapists will often start their work with clients with paint or clay. It provides something tangible to work with and there is generally a clear outcome (i.e. a blank page to an image). In my opinion, whether or not we recommend what people do with these materials depends on their needs for guidance. I will only suggest a theme or task when I believe that the person is incapable of working without my intervention. I have consistently found that freedom and choice are prerequisites for depth."

"I think that these principles apply to the education of children, especially the need for inner direction, freedom and choice," Lisa said. "Depth of learning depends upon the arousal of interest, some degree of personal focus and an ongoing exchange of inspiration between children and teachers. What we describe as the 'open education' movement of the late 1960s and early 1970s is terribly misunderstood. Open education was in my opinion concerned with studies of how children learn and how they need to be active rather than passive, finding things out for themselves with the guidance of instructors. Teachers encouraged individual choice and instruction within a community environment. They designed environments that facilitated active learning, movement and a

multiplicity of projects. Unfortunately, most people could not see beyond the removal of the rows of desks which they associated with the re-
bellious spirit of that time. Many teachers thought that by removing the
desks they would achieve the objectives of 'open education.' Chaos naturally ensued in many classrooms and schools, and 'open education' was
dismissed. There has been little attention given to how the chaos was a
result of the teachers' inability to work within an open environment, to
individualize instruction, supervise simultaneous projects and keep pace
with the children's learning. The schools went back to the conventional
model which requires the children's learning to keep pace with what the
teacher is capable of presenting. This is another example of our cultural
dependence on the model of the authority figure being responsible for
the presentation of structure rather than the situation where teachers
and students cooperatively create the structures that they work within.
We are so afraid of losing control that we limit the creative dialogue and
rely too much on prescriptive cliches."

"Yes, Lisa, but we should talk about 'cliches,' how we define and relate to them. The subject came up earlier when we were talking about
trees, houses, flowers, horses, automobiles, and so forth. Excessive prescription and control will produce cliches, things and expressions that
can be described as trite, lifeless and stereotypic. Yet, at the same time,
folk art is often characterized by traditional repetition, uniformity, rules
of procedure and more emphasis on the communal rather than individual characteristics. But when we look at a fine piece of highly uniform
folk art, there is a sense of character and soul to the image; we get a feeling for the way it was made; the personal handicraft element is accen-
tuated; there are often individual signatures within the uniformity.
These elements do not characterize the cliche which can best be
described in terms of the absence of imagination and soul. As an art
teacher, I might become depressed if surrounded only by cliche images,
because my job, the standards of my profession and my personal values
would be oriented more to soulful imagery. But, as an art therapist, I
have learned to engage the cliche as the form that is presented. It may be
the only thing that we have to work with or the best that a person can do.
The cliche is a starting point. My acceptance of it can be expressive of a
willingness to accept the person and the context with its particular limitations. I might even get excited about the cliche, especially if the person
who made it seems enthusiastic about it. We can respond imaginatively
to it and infuse soul into it with our associations and stories. Through
our interactions we can learn more about the nature of the cliche and

why it is so commonly used by people. What we label as a cliche might be an archetypal image of a house, tree or human figure. The cliche problem may be attributed exclusively to the stereotypic response that the art therapist might have to the image. It is our job to respond sensitively and imaginatively to whatever manifests itself. This use of imagination also relates to the issue of structure that we just discussed. What we present as problems of structure may be described as problems of the teacher's imagination. Our methods have some responsibility for the existence of cliches."

"How do you relate to the way children express images of contemporary television shows and movies?"

"When I was working in classrooms, children and especially boys were always drawing pictures of the current child-culture obsession. . . *Jaws, Star Wars.* At first, I saw them as cliches and stereotypes. But, in time, I realized that the children were celebrating mythological themes that were the basis of the appeal of the films. I gained a deeper appreciation of the sharks and the sinister figures of the 'dark side' that were emerging in picture after picture. The children were involved with emotional engagements and dramas that we adults completely overlooked because of our obsessions with the cliche status of commercial film content. I am becoming increasingly protective of the cliches. Perhaps we negate them because we have become so dependent on constant change and 'originality' for stimulation.

"The pictures of trees, houses and flowers are always relevant. As art therapists we sometimes feel disappointed when we do not see images loaded with rage, turbulence, depression or other forms of psychic action and excitement. . .stabbings, mutilations, screams! When we speak about avoidance and defenses against revelation, we are perhaps revealing our professional impatience and personal needs for stimulation. We are sometimes like movie audiences desiring sex and violence. A review of art therapy P.R. materials from around the world will show that the profession is a lot more interested in the upheavals of the underworld than trees, houses and flowers. I am keenly interested in the underworld and in sexual imagery and do not want to sound puritanical. What I have to guard against is the possibility that my interests and preoccupations will get in the way of being open and receptive to what the client presents. Art therapists doing research exclusively focused on a particular image or theme have to be extremely careful in their clinical practice where there may be an unconscious tendency to bias the client's expression toward their research. The same applies to any therapist attempting to prove a theory.

"The tree, flower or house might be intended as a healing image."

"But if it is presented as a cliche response because the person cannot make contact with something more vital, we can still go to work with the image through dialogue. Trees, houses, flowers, animals, and even automobiles are archetypal and universal images that embody vast cultural resources. I believe that art therapists will gain more from the study of the mythological and symbolic histories of images of trees, houses, animals and human figures than from the psychopathological cliches of psychiatric drawing tests that have mystified the profession for so many years. Perhaps we see trees and houses as cliches because we are ignorant of their psychic implications and histories. We have so thoroughly internalized the attitudes of the drawing tests that we see images within their frameworks."

"How do we get beyond these habits?"

"I am becoming convinced that the intellectual and philosophical range of art therapy can be dramatically expanded. We can do it ourselves. If we envision ourselves as a noble, intelligent, soulful and necessary profession, we will become this. Our vision will take shape in life. If we let the vision emerge, it will become a material fact. Art therapy is limited only by its vision of itself and its ambition. We have everything that a profession of the soul needs. We have inherited the image, symbol and materials of art together with the inner dialogue and process that accompany them and we have not realized this. We place ourselves within the confines of the psychopathological diagnostic drawing test cliches because we fear what we can be, what we are not."

"Are you suggesting that art therapy does not know what it is?"

"I would like to imagine that what we see of art therapy today is only a partial manifestation of what is possible."

TALKING IN ART THERAPY

"I HAVE HEARD many art therapists describe how they talk during their sessions much more than people realize," Lisa said. "Because the visual imagery associated with our profession and the art-making process are so distinctive, we sometimes think of ourselves as a 'non-verbal' therapy. Art therapy can of course work on a purely non-verbal level, and there are times when words are not necessary. The creative arts therapies can provide a relief to excessive talking. I understand how spoken language can become chatter, going over and over the same material without insight. Imagery and the process of making a picture often provide a stimulus that lies outside old patterns. They offer something fresh and unfamiliar, and in this way they evoke new responses and different ways of envisioning our lives. It is unquestionable that art therapy operates effectively on this level of unspoken artistic process. But in my personal experience I have discovered how it is necessary to name something, to talk about it, to hear what others have to say, in order to be aware of what is taking place. In my formal art training, student colleagues discouraged talking about pictures. There was a feeling that what we were doing was 'beyond words.' We felt that words, talking and analyzing took us away from the images. We were studying art to learn how to look and paint and not to talk. Our artistic values were visual and not verbal. Many of us were involved with art as a meditation, a sacred pursuit, away from the 'noise' of the world. There was a sense that the wise artist 'sees' and the dilettante 'talks.' But we were always talking to one another socially and about what we were doing in the studio. Talking is just something we do as human beings. But in the art studio it seemed secondary, or in service of visual expression."

"These are excellent distinctions that you are making, Lisa. A colleague of mine in the Netherlands, Marijke Rutten-Saris, described to me how she rebels against the work being described as 'non-verbal.' 'It is not verbal,' she said. When we describe it as 'non-verbal' it is cast in the negative, and it is still defined in relation to verbal expression. Why not call talking 'non-visual' communication. It is a subtle dominance. Yet we need words. Please continue."

"As I review the history of the arts in psychotherapy, there is a tendency in the writings of some people to approach pictures as resources for verbal psychotherapy, providing images that are talked about. This seems to be the case with the early psychoanalysts who were essentially verbal therapists with an interest in visual images. There is also the psychological diagnostic tradition with both standardized and informal approaches to giving fixed meanings to images. The culture of the art studio that I was a part of in school did not think highly of either of these methods, both of which they thought degraded art and made it adjunctive to something 'more important.' I think that if the arts do not explain themselves and articulate what they do, then they cut themselves off from the world. When serious artists became involved in the practice of psychotherapy and when art therapy established itself as a profession, we see the beginnings of collaboration between the purists of the studio and the verbal traditions of psychotherapy. To me art therapy is a new, or very old, integration of the histories of both the visual arts and psychotherapy. As we bring these elements together, nothing has to be lost or compromised. We amplify the resources of therapy and create new combinations.

"I have been able to work this out in my mind from my readings and on the basis of my life experience, but I have not even begun to imagine how I am going to pull it all together in my art therapy work with children. There are so many things to potentially say to the children, many of which relate to what I have read, that I feel awkward, uncertain and incompetent in their presence. Do you understand what I mean?"

"Yes," I replied. "You have become inhibited by thinking that there is a 'right thing' to say in every situation. Do you also fear that what you do say might be harmful?"

"Of course, I fear that I will misuse powerful experiences that will turn against the people I am working with. I am often trying too hard to be clever and to make perfect clinical statements. When I try too hard to say the right thing or to avoid saying the wrong thing, I become anxious."

"You probably lose your spontaneity and find it difficult to be your-self. Do you find yourself preparing in advance what you are going to say to people?"

"Yes. I even imagine what they will say to me. But it never works out as I planned and I become more insecure. I can spend days and even weeks going over what I said in a session or in one of our classes here at the graduate school thinking how I could have said it better and won-dering what other people thought."

"It sounds exhausting."

"I can get so involved with my deliberations about what I should be saying that I lose contact with the person before me and this makes me feel even worse. At these times I am grateful for the art which is always there when the words are not working. I get confused about whether I should be talking about the art or about the person. I have gotten into even more trouble when I try to use psychotherapeutic techniques, like mirroring back the words of people. Last week, a twelve-year-old boy asked me if I was an echo. I felt ridiculous, devastated. I could not even respond to his humor because I was not myself. I had become the tech-nique, a clinical strategy without a personality."

"These preoccupations are exceptional opportunities for learning. You are quickly discovering what you do not need. Techniques are use-ful only when they are completely incorporated into your way of being. Otherwise, we give the impression that we are operating out of an in-structional manual. I have yet to meet an excellent therapist who did not go through the confusion and doubt that you have described. It is the essence of our initiation. We improve through honest assessments of our performance. All of our studies, experiences and years of super-vision bring us right back to ourselves but hopefully with a deepened understanding of what we do and say. There is no way to learn how to walk in this profession without falling, repeatedly. A major difference between experienced therapists and beginners is that they know how to fall, and in many cases our falls present opportunities for even greater depth in the therapeutic relationship. I would go so far as to say that when the panic comes, and it does present itself to all of us, that it may be necessary to die symbolically in order to realize that we will come back to life, sometimes better equipped from the experience. In order to survive, and better yet flourish in this work, we need to be able to 'eat' pain and conflict, to take nourishment from them, but also let them go. I try to do the best I can and muster up enough strength to return after a failure. The 'eating' metaphor has been attractive to stu-

dents over the years because it is primal and expressive of the way we carry problems around in our stomachs, intestines and other parts of the body. Its appeal is also due to the fact that it is difficult to let things go. It amazes me to think of why we choose to carry so much unnecessary 'baggage,' excessive burdens that exasperate us and cause terrible psychic indigestion. The world, our profession and ourselves will be much better off if we let them go. The redeeming part of holding on is that the process can be expressive of a desire to improve our performance. It might also help our learning to see that we become human, vulnerable and perhaps more lovable to people when we demonstrate blind spots, impatience and imperfect judgment. I wonder what it is in us that creates the belief that therapists and teachers are to be omniscient. This is not what people need from us."

"What do they need?"

"That depends on the specifics of the context, but generally they need us to be fully present, open and responsive to them. Inner dialogues about what should and should not be said can be forms of avoidance. They take us away. I have learned that when I am with another person or group, that particular engagement has to be the most important thing in my life at the moment. I have to learn how to let go of the previous session or what happened to me earlier in the day. People quickly sense when we are not present. Our bodies can be there while the soul is absent. I think it is part of our animal nature to make judgments as to the presence of soul. . .perhaps with our eyes, ears, smell and body feelings.

"No matter how good we become at making transitions between people and situations, there will always be instances when we are taken by surprise or when just too many things happen at once. There have been many times when I have had as many as three separate crises erupt simultaneously as I was preparing for an appointment. I just tried to do my best. I know from experience that I must get whatever is not concerned with the person before me out of my mind and out of my body. I have found that it is not a good idea to ventilate what I am trying to get away from to the person I am meeting with. That generally prolongs and amplifies its hold on me, sometimes even distracting me with an added element of guilt. If I am asked, 'How are you?' or 'What's going on?', then we may have to spend a few minutes on it. I have also discovered from experience that a high level of emotional distraction before a session begins can be useful, in that it propels me into concentration. If I am able to be present with other people, then the words, what needs to be said, will always emerge. I have learned to trust in this. It is remarkable how the words take care of themselves. Our preparations cannot be focused on words, what we are going to say."

"Then how do you prepare?"

"I am realizing that preparation has more to do with emptying than filling. In therapy we want to be alert, ready and open for what presents itself. Even though I love my work and I have been doing it for years, I am always feeling resistance. I think this is natural. When we are involved with the depths of the soul, it takes discipline to leave a situation or person or image and go on to the next, completely present. I am always saying that resistance is the gate and a sign that we are getting close. When the gate presents itself, I make the choice as to whether or not I will pass through. In my work I am usually against the idea of 'closure.' I can never be open enough. Life provides more than enough limits. I am talking about a state of disciplined openness, not chaos. I work constantly at opening and receiving rather than infusing others. I have found that this is what I have to work toward in both professional, personal and family relationships. I am not against having a personal influence on another human being. I have actually discovered that if I am being open and receptive, then my influence increases."

"But I think that I have to work more on having something to say. I have trouble speaking up."

"Do you think that you are open in situations where you have trouble expressing yourself?"

"Probably not."

"Opening to the other can be frightening. It can be difficult for experienced therapists to look into the eyes of another person."

"Have you struggled with this?"

"I think that a primary element of training involves observing other people in action. We can benefit from evaluating what we admire and dislike in others. One of my most important professional lessons came through watching my colleague Paolo Knill work. In spite of my good intentions, I knew that there was something big missing in what I was doing and that it had something to do with me as a person. I was in my early thirties and frantically busy. Paolo was older and perhaps this had something to do with what he had to teach me. When he sat with a person, not only his eyes, but his entire body was attentive; it was as though he transformed himself into a cat when he met with people. He was relaxed and totally accepting. This was liberating to the people with him and it was not happening in my relationships. I could say that I was an 'open' person, capable of saying whatever I felt and capable of listening to whatever people said to me or to each other, but there was not the openness of soul that I observed in Paolo's work. As it turned out, I received plenty of criticism that I did pay attention to. However, the ability to take negative feedback is a different kind of openness, perhaps just as important, but they had to be distinguished from one another. Your difficulty with having something of value to say is yet another dimension. Is all of the attention that goes into thinking about what you are going to say an avoidance to opening?"

"I think so. It is good for me to look at this situation from a different perspective. What you are saying about how clear and sensitive conversation emerges naturally when we are open and relaxed is helpful. It is the opposite of what I thought I had to do. I imagined that the words were outside of me, out of my reach, and that through training I would 'acquire' them. When I have soul-to-soul talks in my personal life, there is always something to say. The words come freely and with depth. I cannot imagine these personal dialogues going according to a script that is planned in advance. I think that this is what Moreno was exploring in his 'theatre of spontaneity,' an immersion in the pure present. Actors know how easy it is for the soul to be absent when operating within a script. Your image of Paolo as a cat is challenging. It is a more artistic and imaginative way of looking at a role that too often gets tied up with professional formalism. What is it that allows me to speak freely with close friends and not with people that I work with?

"You have to respond to that."

"It is probably professional responsibility and role expectations. I do want to be professional and responsible but not 'tongue-tied'."

I asked Lisa to describe qualities of professionals that she admired.

"They do not have the split that I am afflicted by. They are able to integrate personal and professional dimensions of themselves. One of my motives for choosing art therapy is a desire to use my sensitivity to help others, to communicate. But I do not trust these natural abilities, because I am always thinking that there is something more, a repository of professional knowledge that I have to obtain. The more I read, the more confused I become, and watching excellent therapists in action further undermines my self-confidence, because I think that I will never be able to be as good as them. I find it easier to be around people who I feel superior to. I tend to affirm myself through the realization that I can do a better job. I am realizing now that I am too involved with myself. Now you see how my obsessions get in the way of being with other people."

"We are also defining what you need to do."

"What do you mean?"

"Only through experiences of this kind can we reach an in-depth personal understanding of what we need to work toward. I could have told you in advance, and maybe I did at the beginning of your training, that 'you' are one of the primary instrumentalies of art therapy, but this would have been just another example of something coming to you from an outside source. Right now, we are working on a core element of psychotherapeutic training that we have to learn from ourselves, over and over again. We cannot find out for ourselves unless we have the experience. The degree of learning is always proportionate to the degree of conflict. That is the encouraging part. Do you see what it is that you have to learn?"

"It has something to do with respecting my instincts or, better yet, letting my instincts operate. I am discovering that therapy has more to do with instincts than I realize. Through experience, I will discipline my instincts and bring them to a new level of awareness."

I began to think about how words become expressions of our insecurity when we are in unfamiliar situations. I also realized that Lisa and I needed to be more specific about what it was she was saying to people. I said that when I observed her working in art therapy groups she appeared to be clear and articulate. When we recreated her conversations with children, there did not appear to be difficulties. She was being too hard on herself. A tendency toward self-criticism is certainly more desirable than the attitude that there is little that one has to learn, but Lisa was going too far. She was becoming overly conscious of herself. We began to look at the experience of the children she was working with.

"It now occurs to me that the children are probably having a more difficult time speaking to me. A lack of self-confidence and resistance to opening are major themes in our work together. I have already noticed that artworks are tremendously helpful in freeing up our conversations. The art gives them something to relate to imaginatively. It helps them to be less self-conscious about what they are saying. Most of the children are completely resistant to the type of direct soul-to-soul presence that we were discussing earlier. They hide their fear by mocking that kind of relationship. But we can be intimate in other ways, through spontaneous play in particular. I am noticing that the children carry on dramatic and imaginative conversations when I sit next to them while they draw or paint. The stories they tell are as much a part of the artistic expression as the pictures. Art therapy gives enough attention to its dramatic and storytelling nature. This is the type of thing that was not possible when I was an art teacher working with large classroom groups. How do you dialogue with the children about their pictures?"

"The children talk spontaneously through their stories and dramatic enactments. Often, I will just listen as they paint and talk. If I am going to initiate a conversation, I am discovering that imaginative dialogues work best. If the stories do not emerge spontaneously, I will ask the children to tell a story about their pictures. As we spend more time together, they begin to realize that our sessions are concerned with both painting and talking and our dialogues happen naturally. I sometimes talk about what I see in their pictures. . .colors, images, movements and compositions. I tell them how the pictures make me feel. If I do not understand what is going on or if I feel confused, I am learning that it is best to either say nothing and let the situation work its way out, or I may tell the child that I do not understand. I am certainly listening more and I worry less about what I say, about being trite. I am trying to be myself. I am already discovering that when my relationship with a child is working, there is a sense of communion between us, the words flow naturally and with perfect timing. Even the silences and the sounds that are made in the room are part of the dialogue. Everything fits. Pictures motivate conversation, and what we say in turn generates a deeper involvement with materials and the image."

THE NATURE OF ART

"HAVE YOU defined art in relation to therapy?" I asked. "What are the materials of our profession?"

"When I was studying aesthetics I felt that there were no limits to what could be perceived as art. Art is whatever manifests itself, whatever we give aesthetic value to. The world can be perceived as an immense force of transformative action. God is referred as 'The Creator.' But aren't these just esoteric preoccupations that have little to do with a child in crisis or my working with a depressed person with art materials?"

"Not at all. These questions help us to define the instruments of art therapy. It has amazed me how little attention the profession has given to philosophical inquiry into the nature of art. This is perhaps largely due to the fact that people are so busy doing art therapy, and I support this primary orientation to action. There are pragmatic opportunities in philosophical reflection. The creation of an aesthetics of art therapy will guide and illuminate action. Complacent and stereotypic definitions of art do not expand the breadth of the profession. Art is inspired by what exists outside its boundaries. As an artist I find all of this talk in psychotherapy about creating boundaries distressing. In my personal life I work at being more open to people and sensitive to what is outside me. Boundaries are colossal illusions of the ego that limit us. The vicissitudes of life cannot be contained within them. I think it is better to learn how to respond and adapt to whatever presents itself within the open field of life. We need enclosures and sanctuaries, safe and quiet places to go to for rest and contemplation. Protection, caution and good judgment are also necessary. I like these words much better than our changing psychological jargon. It is the tone of the boundary talk that I object to, the overemphasis. It feels like the psychic equivalent of the Berlin Wall, 'Step over my boundary and I will shoot you!' These fortified walls are expressions of insecurity and overprotection. They are manifestations of distrust and anger toward other people. Perhaps we are living in an age where there is little safety on the street, on the job and even in the home. In therapy or with students, I do not advocate tearing down the walls. There has to be respect for differences. There may be a sickness in the world today with its distrust of people and excessive self-protection. This is one reason why people come to therapy: to let down the walls and engage their vulnerability with a person who will be worthy of their trust. Art is also restricted by too much self-protection. We might say that in our age art needs therapy and vice versa."

"I remember hearing some prominent art therapists strongly demand that art therapy limit itself to drawing, painting and sculpting with clay."

"This is an example of how rigid boundary making operates. There are also the inevitable traces of distrust and overprotectiveness. Ultimately, these attitudes restrict depth. In *The Apocalypse,* D. H. Lawrence said that the forms of art increase in variety the deeper we go. As I mentioned before, I am not against people who choose to work with only one form of art for the rest of their lives. But do not try to construct professions around these limitations. Right now, I am working extensively with painting and drawing in art therapy. There are endless possibilities within the media. I am interested in what colleagues are doing with other materials, and my work also integrates rhythmic expression, storytelling and performance art. Everything is focused on the act itself, in whatever form it happens to appear in a particular moment. I am interested in Grotowski's reference to the 'holy actor.' There is a religiosity that is associated with an interest in the life of the moment and making it sacred. Do you find that the forms of art multiply when there is a depth of feeling?"

"It goes both ways with me. There is an abundance of imagery and possibilities when I feel vital, and a blank emptiness and immobility when I am depressed."

"But doesn't depression also have a tendency to generate aggressive action and outbursts?" I asked. "It is good to have art around to embody the explosions that follow the dormant periods."

"I guess that is what art therapy is all about. I have noticed how when I feel depressed going into an art therapy session, I often feel much better at the end. Other art therapists have told me that this happens to them, too. Why does this happen?"

"It is probably attributed to the contagious vitality of artistic energy. The images and feelings of the other person fill the emptiness of our depression. They recharge us. The exchange of artistic energy in therapy between client and therapist can be perceived as a charge and counter-charge. The dyadic dimensions of transference and countertransference between clients and therapists can be amplified through the imagery of art therapy. If we personify images, there are many more entities in the room. The aesthetic stimulation animates us. Art therapy imagery provides opportunities for multiple relationships within the single client-therapist relationship. It is invigorating."

"Do you think that all of the different uses of pictures and images in the mental health field today can be called art?"

"Certainly not! If I am feeling magnanimous about the inclusivity of art, I would say they are bad art. The prescribed drawing tests used by both psychologists and art therapists are graphic exercises rather than artworks. Sometimes, people will create dynamic pictures in spite of the standardized tests. When I say that something is not 'art,' it is because there is an absence of aesthetic intent connected with the action. The 'test' is not motivated by artistic values. Art is the antithesis of a standardized series of prescribed actions. Art desires to increase rather than limit variability. It is interesting to look at the pictures drawn in these testing situations to see how a person's artistic instincts prevail in spite of the standardized format. The tests are not constructed to measure soul. I have actually observed many situations where art therapists are involved in something other than art. The work of art is intended to express and embody soul, and its materials are limitness. Artistic perception sees soul in the objects of daily life, in nature and imagination. It is this ensouling dynamic that distinguishes art from the exercise or test format. There is definitely a correspondence to Mircea Eliade's distinction between the sacred and the profane. At the end of his life, D. H. Lawrence described art as a religious activity. I agree and I think this is why I am involved with art therapy."

"What do you mean by ensouling?"

"Literally, it means to give soul. Art is a matter of intent. What is perceived as art depends upon the attitudes and values of the person. Anything, a found object, or a series of lines can become art. The only limits are the range of the artist's perceptions, available materials and imagination. The artist 'gives soul' to materials through both expression (i.e. putting paint on paper with aesthetic sensibility) and perception (i.e. being able to see the soul of an already existing object or .he emerging shapes in a painting)."

"The artist who *gives* soul begins to take on godlike characteristics."

"It is an interesting point that you raise. J. L. Moreno and other writers have stressed the godliness of each person. If we approach the issue more modestly, we can say that the artist 'transmits' and 'perceives' soul which is constantly manifesting itself in the world. The artist is a person who looks for it."

"How does this apply to therapy?"

"As an art therapist I begin by looking at all of therapy as an artistic context. Otto Rank asserted that the therapist is a new 'artist type,' and Steve Ross emphasizes how the primary artistic instrumentalities of therapists are their personal resources. These ideas by no means belittle pictures and images. I think that an artistic philosophy of therapy adds soul to all dimensions of the work. Under no circumstances do I want to perceive art as 'adjunctive' to another theory of therapy. I am an artist involved with art and therapy, and I feel it deepens the significance of what I do to approach everything, including life itself, as art. Does this sound too esoteric?"

"No, not at all," Lisa said. "I find it liberating to think in this way. When asked how art is therapeutic, I am noticing that many people, and especially artists, will say that it gets them out of themselves and into contact with the world. We want to encourage contact with the world in as many ways as possible."

"The arts keep us close to physical things and our senses. They do the same thing for therapy. In an essay on 'The pantheon of creative arts therapies,' I spoke of this expansion of the artistic act and how the idea can be threatening to those who are committed to the 'container' functions of the profession. If everything can be perceived as art, then who are the artists and who are the art therapists? In the essay, I say: 'The rationale for the existence of the profession does rest fundamentally in its use of materials with the skill and discipline associated with the fine arts. Virtually every creative arts therapist works with art materials as a principle focus of clinical practice. We will not lose our identity or adeptness with materials through the expansion of the artistic community. It is critically important to include those who work with art ideas. They complement and give philosophical depth to work that is done with traditional art materials.' "

"How does the art idea appear in the physical world of therapy?"

"Through performance. Intentional acts. Therapy is a performing art. How do you think this relates to the children you are working with?"

"Anything I do to make their actions more intentional is of use. I imagine that 'performance' can help them to be more aware of what they do, more sensitive to how they effect others and more responsible for their actions. And they need the attention that the performance 'scenario' brings. Perhaps we all do.

"Young children perform for their parents," Lisa continued. "I performed for my parents. We perform well or poorly in school, on our jobs. Then there is sexual performance. Maybe performance is the active, intentional part of living, making something of our lives. The arts heighten or deepen experience. The 'life as a stage' metaphor helps me to see how artworks lead back to the life process from which they emerged. Your idea about therapy being a performing art fits what we do in art therapy because everything is always *live*. We are not just working with materials, pictures and images but with the people before us. And I do not think we can avoid the value giving side of performance assessment, whether a particular incident worked or did not, whether it felt right. Supervision concentrates on performance and how we operate. But many of the children are in therapy because they need a place where they can be themselves without having to perform, where they can 'just be,' without performance anxiety, or stage fright, or critics. They are afraid to fail. Maybe there are some problems with perceiving therapy as a performing art."

"Every metaphor or attempt at description has its shortcomings when attempting to describe something as complex as therapy or art. That is why we need many metaphors, artforms, perceptions, therapies and points of view. But let's stay with the performance idea and see if it can still be useful.

"I think that we go into therapy with a desire to perform, but within a new context, where we will be safe, accepted and affirmed, where we know that criticism will be given in the interest of our well-being. Performance can be what we make of ourselves or of a situation. Let me try to describe what I mean by performance in terms of the process of art therapy. The creation and emergence of imagery within the realm of visual art materials is the core of art therapy, but we are distinguished from colleagues in art education and studio art through what we do with the images, materials and ourselves. Within both dyadic relationships and groups the picture or image becomes another presence in the room. We engage it in our dialogues and it communicates with us. The art therapist engages the same art experience as the art educator and the studio artist but within a healing context where the therapeutic properties of art come forward.

"In my art therapy training sessions that meet for weekend or weeklong sessions, we make art in a free studio environment, with conventional painting, drawing and clay materials, for one to three hours. I present the studio as offering an opportunity to go into our private dramas, journeys and meditations with art materials. After this studio time we work verbally with the pictures. The students call the process which follows art making 'sharing.' It is a term used by Moreno to describe what took place after a psychodrama. To me, the sharing time is just as much of an art event as the private work with materials. As a therapist, it is the time when I am 'on' and more directly engaged with the person and the group. It is a continuation of the therapeutic studio in which the individual is given the opportunity to take the work further through stories, dialogue with me and the group, or through a performance in which the person and the group intentionally become part of the artwork. In one-to-one relationships, the structure of making art and sharing is usually quite different. Sometimes we talk together while the art is being made, especially with children. There are few fixed operational patterns in my work. It is more important to let structure emerge in relation to the needs of the situation and the styles of the people I am working with.

"The sharing time in art therapy can be viewed as a performance that concentrates on 'being.' I do not think that the two have to be separated. Actors tell us that the more they let the role emerge from within themselves, the better they perform. This is 'acting' at its best, action in the world. Negative associations to 'acting' refer to something else that is contrary to 'being.' In art therapy we try to be ourselves as fully and as authentically as possible. In our groups, an individual places one or more artworks in the center of the circle and the dialogue goes on from five minutes to two hours, depending upon what is needed and what the person asks for. I try to help the person in the center to take control of the time element as much as possible, stopping when it feels right to do so.

"Some people want to tell their stories through images, others ask the group members what they see and listen to what is said before responding. There are many ways of operating. I usually try to sensitize group members to the importance of timing and the need to relate to the differing rhythms and styles of those who are in the center. When the pace is too fast or when group members talk frantically out of anxiety, I bring them back to our responsibility to the person in the 'center' who is working with us.

"A psychiatrist colleague in Sweden told me about how he sees a correspondence between the therapy group and the theatrical chorus of ancient Greece. The group accompanies and supports the performance of the person in the center by asking questions that open up new insights or they listen and witness compassionately. The group tends to act in unison when affirming the person in the center who is taking risks for the sake of their common experience. This unified action can be likened to what Harry Stack Sullivan described as 'consensual validation.' When we work in groups or in one-to-one situations, I think that the primary motive of the person who is performing is to do something useful and significant in that moment. In groups, the person in the center acts as much for others as for the self. The reality of action in the moment strengthens our therapy as performance metaphor. Performance is a process that is totally in the present and connected to the social situation. Therapy operates in this way. Even our excursions into the past take place in the present.

"We put on performances of soul. Through artistic expression we project our souls into the world. My experience indicates that healing takes place when expressions of soul are taken into the souls of other people and when these people give us back responses from their souls. This inter-soul exchange activates our experience of the soul of the world. There is a release of captured, imprisoned or abducted soul. It flows into the world, is received and transformed through other people and flows back again. The process goes on and on through varied transformations. Otto Rank and Nietzsche suggest that soul consists of energetic power. I have found that this soul energy and dialogue need to be initiated by someone. It is generated by purposeful action, what we are describing here as performance. The artistic action is an opening to soul, an invitation for it to manifest itself. In addition to having someone who opens the energy, the person in the center of our training groups, we need others to receive it and begin the inter-soul exchange which opens us to a yet larger sense of the world soul, something that all human beings share, something that heals.

"A native American healer told me once that a person must first ask for help before healing can begin. I support this completely. Asking for help is the first opening. I do this too as a therapist and teacher. I am always asking for help, telling people when I do not understand a situation and need assistance. Asking for help can be cleverly disguised as with aggressive adolescents who are literally screaming for attention through their desperate acts."

"Can you give me an example?"

"I am referring to the actions that we describe as self-destructive and anti-social. We can learn from art that destruction is a necessary part of change. The transformation can begin, even in the most intimidating situations, if we therapists take these expressions into ourselves and give back something that enters the soul of the troubled person. Entry into these heavily guarded, turbulent souls is an element of our art, our performance."

ANIMISM AND ART

"THERE SEEMS to be increasing talk about soul in psychotherapy today," Lisa said.

This idea pleases me. Otto Rank described how the early psychoanalytic therapists revived the dream but suppressed the soul. There were at least two primary directions in the early psychoanalytic work. The dominant group, led by Sigmund Freud, wanted to use a secular, medical science as the basis of psychoanalysis. This tradition still has institutional control of the mental health field throughout the world. The second direction is committed to soul. The soul-work tradition has been carried on by the Jungians and especially by James Hillman. There is also Ludwig Binswanger, a friend of Freud's to the end, who believed that religion, culture and art cannot be reduced exclusively to hunger and sexuality. Within the original psychoanalytic circle, it was Otto Rank who spoke on behalf of the soul and therapy as art. He was sharply critical of the pseudo-scientific aspects of psychoanalysis and the emphasis on standardized techniques, methods and universal theories, all of which take us away from the person before us. Rank said that in spite of the 'famed passivity' of analysts, they were always in the center. He was more interested in his responsibility to the person in therapy. In *Will Therapy*, he said: 'In each separate case it is necessary to create. . .a theory and technique made for the occasion without trying to carry over this individual solution to the next case. . .one must learn the speech of the other, and not force upon him the current idiom.' The heightening of variability over replication is what distinguishes the artistic method of therapy. The imaginative science envisioned by Einstein and others does not separate itself from art. There is an openness to whatever works best in both art and imaginative science. The presence of soul is characterized by awe and wonder, sensibility and imagination, rather than logical analysis with a single theoretical framework."

"You mentioned the importance of variability. But isn't repetition also essential to the arts?"

"Thank you for mentioning this. It is fundamental to folk art, and we also have rhythm and its repetitions in dance and music. Vincent Ferrini says that 'Repetition is the pleasure principle.' "

"Do you think that soul has a chance within our mental health systems?"

"The artistic, soul-oriented psychotherapeutic tradition is on the rise today. The creative arts therapies are one of many manifestations of this phenomena. I realize that the majority of our colleagues probably operate within the medical science idiom. The irony is that Freud just replaced one religion with another, and it was psychiatry which carried on in-depth psychological investigations during the first half of the twentieth century. Virtually every prominent psychiatrist that I have met has had vital artistic instincts. I have referred to this as the 'artistic soul of psychiatry.' We are much closer to the souls of psychiatrists than we realize, and I wish that they would let their artistic instincts be more of an integral part of their professional image."

"How does soul relate to illness?"

"I found a connection in my studies of shamanism. Indigenous cultures in all parts of the world and in different historical epochs define illness as a loss of soul. I agree completely with this principle. The loss of soul is particularly relevant to depression. The idea can even fit with biological constructs. Acute psychosis is to me a manifestation of not only soul-loss but motion sickness. In psychosis, we lose our ability to respond rhythmically to life situations. The shaman's job is to go in search of the person's abducted soul and bring it back so that it may be reintegrated with the body. Soul is a term that is deeply lodged in our culture and our psyches. The suppression of soul within the mental health field manifests a tacit complicity with illness. We want it back. I know I do. Our contemporary music suggests this. What is more fundamental to art than soul? The arts bring back the abducted souls and infuse life with their energy."

"Do art objects have souls?"

"They are soul. Soul is not something separate from us, an invisible entity distinct from the body. And it is not something that we 'possess.' I do not think that a person 'has' a soul. The same applies to artworks. This implies that the 'possessor' is more important than soul. For me, soul is an essence of every physical thing. Art helps us to engage soul as material. It can be experienced if we have the ability to see. This is why the classical philosophical tradition has emphasized 'seeing.' It is up to us to perceive soul. We determine whether or not everyday objects are illuminated. Soul lives in the exchange, the dialogue. We need physical things to experience soul. The particulars of experience are the carriers of soul. The separation of the soul from the body is a denial of eros and a deprecation of the body. We have to reclaim the word soul and revive its old meanings. In the United States we are fortunate to have Afro-American cultural traditions which demonstrate how soul is something visible, tangible and very much connected to the body.

"The psychological community is often disparaging in its response to anything that has to do with soul. I have observed how many people are resistive because of what they perceive to be the negative influence of religion on society. Soul is a highly charged word which they associate with repressive religion. It is considered to be delusional or 'magical thinking.' The extremes of a soul in the heavens ideology has produced an equally extreme materialistic reaction. One of my colleagues, a psychologist who was trained in Freudian analysis, was a guest in our home. Late at night, I was asking whether or not pictures have souls. He thought this was nothing but projection and superstition. The next morning he came to breakfast and said that he did not sleep well. Before he went to bed he had locked all of his windows for fear that the dead souls would come to punish him for insulting them."

"Psychology has placed almost exclusive emphasis on what the person projects into the picture."

"Rudolf Arnheim has been the leading exception. He takes us into the image and describes how its physical qualities determine its expressiveness. Arnheim's life work can be perceived as illuminating what belongs to the image and how *it* influences the person who looks at it. He is so helpful and refreshing in showing how artworks and images have lives of their own. Pictures and other art objects are sources of the energetic power described by Rank. They are more than what we project onto them. The tranquility of the Leonardo's *Mona Lisa* is sharply distinguished from the aggression of Picasso's *Guernica*. A Georgia O'Keefe landscape of the Southwest generates something very different from an urban scene by Hopper. I like the word soul much more than creativity. It is more archaic, closer to the religious consciousness that art and psychology are part of, and it is more descriptive of the spontaneous emergence of imagery in the arts. Of course, there is nothing wrong with 'creativity' and there are many people throughout the world doing important work under its aegis, and our profession is called creative arts therapy. But the idea of creativity has been overanalyzed by psychology. Perhaps whenever we have too much talk about a concept as opposed to acting on it, we make cliches. Creativity as an idea has lost soul. Maybe it will return. It can be said that the same thing happened to soul within our western religious traditions."

"Can we measure soul?"

"I think we can if we have the right attitude. If we approach soul technically as a statistican, we will not even be able to see it. But if we are motivated by artistic desire, we will be able to determine which images move us more than others. I would define measurement of soul as the evaluation of an emotional or aesthetic response. We can assess emotional vitality in a painting, song or enactment. To the extent to which soul is an attribute of physical things, it does make itself accessible and visible. We have lost soul by describing it as something distinct from the physical. I prefer to see soul as the essence of any physical object, that which makes it distinctly itself. This can be measured or perceived through direct observation, comparison with other things and by the feeling that it arouses in us. Soul is more particular than general. This is another reason why the arts are carriers of soul. For me, the concept of 'tone' is descriptive of soul. I respond to the tone of a person or artwork. *The American College Dictionary* defines tone as 'any sound considered with reference to its quality, pitch, strength, source. . .a particular quality, way of sounding, modulation, or intonation of the voice as expressive of some meaning, feeling, spirit. . .an accent particular to a person, people, locality (I would add thing). . .tension or firmness proper to the organs or tissues of the body. . .state of the body or of an organ in which all of its animal functions are performed with healthy vigor. . .healthy sensitivity to stimulation. . .normal healthy condition of mind. . .style, distinction. . . .' See, we can even find soul in the dictionary.

"Pictures and sculptures can be perceived in relation to tone. What are their distinctive accents, styles and qualities? What feelings do they transmit? Are their physical features in tone? Are they vigorous and expressive of our instinctual sensibilities? We can certainly add these soul-oriented qualities to assessments of pictures which have historically been more concerned with some form of psychosexual pathology. Images and pictures may also express an absence of soul, and perhaps this is an indication of illness as suggested by the definition of health that I have given.

"What distinguishes the creative arts therapies in the mental health world is their tone. We share the fundamental clinical concerns of all of the therapies, but we add something that is unique to us: the physical qualities of the arts. I hope that we heighten rather than 'tone down' these contributions."

"How do we work with soul?"

"Much of it has to do with our attitudes and values. We begin with a sense of reverence for the other person, the images and the world. Perhaps everything that we have said in these discussions has to do with the evocation of soul. It is essentially a commitment to energizing whatever we do, working passionately. The experience of soul is highly contagious. We inspire it in one another. Art objects do this to us, too. Artistic soul-work involves a desire to relate things outside of ourselves to the depths within.

"Plato described how Socrates spoke to the youth Charmides about healing. He criticized the medical people of his times for trying to cure the body without the soul which is the source of both sickness and health. 'For this is the great error of the day in the treatment of the human body, that the physicians separate the soul from the body.' The cure of all ailments according to Socrates must begin with the soul. The condition of the whole determines the well-being of the part. Perhaps soul can be defined as the experience of a particular moment, place, person or thing. Our souls are those energies that draw upon all of what we are. Soul can then be measured by the extent to which we are engaged in an experience. The method of healing that Socrates described to Charmides involved the use of 'charms,' words or images of well-being, that once infused into the soul 'overflow' to the whole body. Do you think this has any relevance to art therapy?"

"Yes. Assagioli has said that images have 'motor elements' within them," Lisa replied. "The image directs the process of change. It stimulates an inner transformation that corresponds to its physical properties. Meditation on a restful landscape can bring piece of mind. Native Americans use sandpaintings in the manner that Socrates described. Art activates us. If we have soul music, there is no reason why we cannot have soul painting. Although I have not been trained to look at art in this way, there does seem to be soul energy associated with pictures that inspire me. I have experienced these feelings of soul strongly in relation to places in nature. My question about measuring soul makes me think of how indigenous cultures give careful consideration in determining where and when rituals are to be conducted. For the druids, the full moon, oak trees and running water were important. They built their sanctuaries in places where they experienced energetic powers, what we are describing as soul. I have found that many people respond negatively to the word 'power.' Have you also experienced this?"

"Yes. Power has for many people been associated with the forceful domination of others, might, machines. . .power drive! Nietzsche's work has been terribly misunderstood because of this. I perceive power as vitality, soul energy, the ability to live fully. Perhaps power can be best understood through its opposite condition. How would you describe that?"

"Sterility and the inability to act."

"Do you experience this condition in the way children sometimes respond to their art?"

"I do. This is one of the major problems that I face in my work, barren images and the lack of responsiveness in the children. Soulfulness is probably the opposite condition. I notice that when we begin to talk about the pictures and give them attention, the depressive feeling begins to lift. What might first appear to be an empty picture, stimulates an emotional story. Afterward, we not only feel differently but the picture itself is transformed. This is why it is so important for me to talk to the children about their art. I am seeing that the energy of the talking and storytelling is an infusion of soul. In my own art I am discovering that feelings of depression, and depressed images actually bring me to the depths of my emotions. Perhaps this is also true for the children. But they need help in dealing with the immensity of the emptiness. Art therapy might be one way of showing them how something can emerge from it."

"When depressed, I do not take life for granted," I said. "The word 'animate,' to give life and make alive, is again descriptive of soul and what it does in art therapy. Artworks and our responses to them give life, they animate, fill us with soul. As Socrates said, soul overflows from them. The close relation of 'animate' to animism helps us to define soul as giving life and vitality. This validates Rank's definition of soul as energetic power. The word 'animal' is also close to 'animate.' It is interesting how people can view animals without souls, since the word is derived from 'anima' (soul). The sensory vitality of the animal may help to illuminate what soul is. Severe depression is characterized by the absence of vitality, and in psychosis vitality is misdirected, turned against itself.

"The process of art therapy, the physical work with materials, the emergence of form and the ensuing dialogues with the images can be perceived as 'animating,' making alive and infusing with vitality."

INTENTIONALITY

"**I**S THERE one particular area where the children you work with in art therapy have the most difficulty?"

"Motivation and inner direction are probably the most consistent problems that I have seen in both art therapy and art education. The absence of self-confidence is part of it, too. The major problem seems to be one of getting going and feeling good about what is done. Some of the children lack inner controls and act randomly with a brief attention span. The depressed or withdrawn child is afraid to move. All of these conditions are directly reflected in how they approach the process of art. I find that getting the children motivated and involved in a sustained art process is often both the means and the end of therapy. When they are making art in this way, they are solving problems, expressing themselves, relating to something outside themselves and commiting themselves to a course of action. For me, these are primary objectives of art therapy. My role as a therapist and as a teacher is to help motivate, or better yet inspire, the children. I am finding that the most effective way to arouse interest is through my attitude and personal involvement in the art experience. It is often necessary to give children something to relate to, an idea or material that inspires them. I find that the therapy generally works best when they have the desire to draw or paint and I accompany them in the process."

"What is it like when the process is not going well?"

"I feel directionless, immobilized and nothing therapeutic is happening."

"The lack of movement might be perceived as a soothing stillness. The condition can be auspicious, depending on our intent. In *Being and*

Nothingness, Sartre says that 'action is on principle intention.' Intentionality applies to both you and the people you are working with. You will not be lost in your sessions if you are able to grasp the therapeutic intentionality of your own actions while also being able to understand and give meaning to whatever the child may be doing. I do not think that it is always so much of a problem with the children's motivation as it is an inability on our part to find intentionality in their actions, to be affirming and thus strengthen their self-confidence and understanding of what they are doing. In therapy, we work with whatever presents itself and inquire into its intentionality. What does it feel like when you are immobilized?"

"I'm afraid, in panic sometimes. I lose contact with what is going on."

"Can you describe a situation for me?"

"In the art therapy training group where I am a participant, one of the women was working on how she frustrates herself with her lack of authentic expression. She was talking about how she often feels like a cyclone inside but presents a consistently placid face to other people. I told her that it sounded like she was trying to get beyond her mask. She began to cry and said: 'Am I wearing a mask? Can't you see me? Won't you take me seriously?' I realized that I had hurt her and I panicked. I couldn't believe how insensitive I had been. My statement was just too strong. I began to talk about how the mask was getting in the way of her feelings. Then the leader said that it seemed like I was judging her, that the mask was my image and not her's. I must have been going blank, because the leader asked me if I was alright and if I was afraid. Other people in the group sensed the confusion and a number of them tried to intervene with suggestions. The leader then talked about how when we are afraid there is a tendency for people to jump in and try to fix the situation which results in even more confusion. This brought us all back to the woman that I had upset. The leader was trying to help the two of us to talk to one another, to share and clarify our feelings and perceptions of the situation. She told me that I had hurt her very much, but she also thanked me for opening up the problem so that she had the opportunity to work it through. I became increasingly preoccupied and unable to relate to her. It was only after the group that I realized that I had been terrified throughout the incident. The leader saw this and tried to help me, but I was unable to respond. If I had been able to tell the woman that I was afraid, then we could have communicated more clearly. She wanted to be authentic and was. It was me who was blocking an authentic dialogue in that moment, and there I was evaluating her. I find it painful to miss these openings for soul-to-soul communication that is intensified when two people are honest with one another. But it does feel better now to have a sense of direction about what happened. I can vividly feel what you mean by intentionality. I have it now, afterwards, with regard to what was needed in that situation."

"This is what happens when we do not say what we are feeling at the moment. An inner confusion occurs and we lose the ability to act with full intent and conviction. Something is being held back and other people sense this. In this situation you stepped out of the dialogue because of your fear. I think that if you told the woman that you were engaged with that you were afraid because what you said might have been too harsh, then this expression of vulnerability on your part might have made you stronger, more present. The French concept 'esprit d' escalier,' sagacity after the fact, is related to this inability to participate fully in an event. When I have the aesthetic feeling that something worked out well, I rarely have these afterthoughts about what I might have done differently."

"I took a first step toward being honest when I said something negative to the woman. This was a big step for me, something I do not normally do. And since the woman thanked me for saying it, the risk seems to have worked. I could not take the second and larger risk of exposing my confusion and fear. I really lost my way. A purpose of therapy seems to be to make things clearer. I also lose my way when I try to operate according to a theory of what should and should not be done. Clear intent seems to have a great deal to do with personal strength and the ability to follow instincts in the moment."

"If I am able to tell someone that I may have said the wrong thing or acted improperly, what might have been an insensitive statement actually serves as a breakthrough and sometimes that takes us in to authenticate communication. This is why I am always saying that it is more important to stay with the other person, openly, than it is to make judgments about what may be right or wrong. But we just cannot let go of the harsh evaluator within us that stops movement toward open expression. I have discovered how important it is to slow down when emotions become agitated. It is remarkable how my authority can be furthered by my saying that I do not understand or that I am confused. This gives people the opportunity to explain and to listen to one another as opposed to feeling an independent responsibility for making things right."

WHAT DOES IT MEAN?
INTERPRETATION AND
IMAGE ABUSE

"ART THERAPISTS have been known to take on the role of clever interpreters who claim to *know* what images mean. I think that our profession is obsessed with meanings. I have never been able to know what an image means, to fix a label to it. D. H. Lawrence spoke of how single meanings cannot be ascribed to symbols. Yet, interpretation is always taking place in art therapy and in life. In *Human, All Too Human,* Neitzsche said 'there are *no eternal facts.'* Life is a process of ongoing interpretation. Life is an artwork to be interpreted over and over again. Nietzsche also said that even a painting is constantly changing 'and therefore should not be considered a fixed quantity.' In art therapy I have observed how our interpretations of images change."

"How do you define interpretation?" Lisa asked.

"The traditional definition of interpretation has to do with explanation, elucidation and giving meaning. All of these elements are important to me, but I see interpretation as offering more. When my colleague Steve Ross heard that I was lecturing on interpretation in art, he was puzzled and thought that perhaps I was changing my attitudes about the abuses involved with fixing diagnostic labels to artworks. He said that the word 'interpretation' threw him off because of its history in art therapy and that on one level he would have preferred me to invent a new word. He was describing the non-verbal awe that he experiences in front of a great work of art. In my opinion his experience resulted from his interpretation of the artwork on a purely visual level. Interpretation does not have to be verbal. I think that Rudolf Arnheim's writings on visual thinking demonstrate how we perceive and respond to artworks through the senses. Interpretation is both intuitive and intellectual, verbal and non-verbal. Art interpretation is sensual and imaginative. I see it as the process through which we relate to the image while we are working and when we look at finished pieces. For me, it includes both cognition and perception. It is certainly more than an oral explanation as we can see from the painter who interprets his subject's appearance in a portrait, the singer who provides a personal interpretation of a traditional song. With pictures, the primary interpretation is visual. We use words to communicate what we see to others and to expand the scope of the picture with our stories. Naming and verbal explanation are only one part of the interpretative process."

"How do you approach the interpretation of art with people in art therapy?"

"As a dialogue with the image."

"Do you mean that you actually talk with pictures?"

"We often do that. Please, pardon the verbal connotations of the word dialogue. I think it is a useful term because it suggests ongoing communication. Although the dialogue can be silent and without words, I think that we art therapists are concerned with how to use spoken language in our work. Even though my sense of the word 'interpretation' may include all of the senses, I think that Steve Ross is right, in that most people will associate the interpretative experience with verbal language. So, maybe this is part of the reason why I like to refer to what we do as dialogue. In my experience with art therapy people have always had a need to talk about what they do. The picture has something to say and we respond to it. By describing interpretation as dialogue, there is an implied respect for the image. This contrasts to labeling and the process of fixing meanings which imply that we know more than the image. Personifying images helps us to consider their existence as separate from us. We are less likely to abuse them."

"How does this dialogue relate to diagnosis and the clinical responsibility of the art therapist?"

"This question is one of the most important issues in the profession of art therapy. It relates to our history, professional image and future vitality. It will take me a few minutes to answer it. My personal history in art therapy began with two primary feelings. The first was positive and concerned the boundless potential of art and healing. The second feeling was one of outrage at the 'image abuse' that has characterized many of the psychiatric and psychological approaches to art within the twentieth century. I would like to concentrate on the second feeling here.

"I realize that the use of art for psychiatric or psychological diagnosis is generally motivated by a desire to understand a person and to find out what is going on, especially in situations where people cannot or will not tell us, where it might be too painful or threatening, where there may be too much to tell, or when we are simply not aware. The arts definitely expand the range of materials for diagnostic review. The essential problem of the diagnostic history of art has to do with frameworks of knowledge. Within the mental health community there are different theoretical constructs and systems, each of which share common beliefs. For example, there is a widely held belief that what we do in the present is determined by what happened to us in the past and that our emotional conflicts originate in our infantile experience. With psychiatric diagnosis, artistic imagery has been consistently taken out of its own framework and evaluated within another which typically is far more concerned with psychopathology. Art is not evaluated on its own terms. It can be likened to evaluating a Democrat on the basis of Republican values."

"Do you believe that art and psychiatry are opposed to one another like different political parties?"

"Absolutely not. My analogy is used to show how there are different operating principles and values in art and certain psychiatric theories. These can be viewed as cultural differences. There are many psychiatrists who share my artistic values and who do not operate within the infantile psychopathology model that I presented. And in general art therapists and psychiatrists work within a context of profound cooperation. In order to avoid the abusive analysis of art by theoretical systems that do not correspond to the dynamics and values of the artistic process, it is necessary for art therapy to create its own psychological theories of interpretation, hopefully with the cooperation of psychiatrists, psychologists and other therapists who practice art therapy."

"Can you give me some examples of what you mean by 'image abuse'?"

"There is a pervasive tendency to look negatively, suspiciously at pictures. The abusive approach assumes that the message is hidden and that the real meaning is something other than what is presented. For example, I have heard people say that a boy's drawing of a person pushing a lawn mower suggests castration fear rather than the experience of cutting grass. It may be that the boy has insecurities related to his sexuality and these fears may in fact be tied in with lawn mowers, but it is perhaps more likely that the picture relates to cutting grass. The castration interpretation belongs to the interpreter. I would be interested in seeing how often this particular interpreter makes judgments of this kind with the pictures of other people. If the interpreter in question is constantly seeing castration in anything to do with cutting, oral deprivation in vacuum cleaners, sexual repression in 'x' configurations, and so forth, then we have a revealing profile of the interpreter. The pattern of these interpretations generally reveals what theoretical framework the interpreter is working within. The abuse of images and artworks has to do with the implied negativity of the interpreter and the inability to approach the art object for what it is. My colleague Steve Levine urges us to complement suspiciousness with generosity when interpreting artworks. I feel that it is essential to have more respect for the image and the person who made it. When the interpreter is invested with omniscience, we have established the foundations of abuse. The image becomes an object for the interpreter's gratification and power over others. This is a strong way to present the problem, but I think it is necessary. I have seen too much abuse of artworks in clinical settings. The problem is magnified to epidemic proportions through the publication of interpretation catalogs which actually tell people what a particular image means. The catalogs inevitably embody the psychopathological conventions of a particular era. As in other situations of abuse, the problem is largely one of ignorance. People are unaware of what they are doing. What harm are we doing to images and the process of art with our projective and negative interpretations?"

"But isn't all interpretation a process of projection?"

"I think so. But let's be careful with omniscience and be more aware of our personal projective patterns. This is why I find the process of dialogue so useful. It assumes intersubjectivity, an 'I-Thou' relationship, between the images and us. I believe that psychotherapy has always been committed to the values of dialogue. The abuse of artworks came through the assumption that verbal communication was higher than visual; through the evaluation of art according to theoretical frameworks that did not understand its nature; the standardization of diagnostic drawings tests according to these psychological frameworks; and the widely held assumption that fixed psychological meanings can be given to images and artworks."

"Do you think it is impossible to give a fixed meaning to a picture? What if the interpretation happens to correspond to what the artist intended?"

"Artists have the freedom or the right to give titles to their work, and perhaps this is as close as we can come to fixing a meaning. Other people looking at the image then have the freedom to see whatever they can. Our perceptions may be strikingly different from those of the artist. The process of fixing meaning raises the eternal issue of where the painting came from. Are we having the dream, or is it having us? History reveals how the values of our epoch or culture will influence what we see. Yet, there are structural elements of an image that transcends epochs. Rudolf Arnheim's writings demonstrate how the dynamics of visual perception influence how people respond to artworks. If the artist and an interpreter see the same thing in a picture, that is wonderful, but this shared experience does not necessarily 'fix' the meaning.

"My experience in doing art interpretation with groups of art therapists in different parts of the world clearly indicates that people tend to have many differing interpretations for images. Even the person making the artwork will generally tell varied stories about what it may mean. It might be said that the expectations of the group or my values encourage this multiplicity. There will always be some biasing of this kind taking place, so we can support our position by looking at the history of art interpretation where the same multiplicity will be seen. The use of projective tests like the Rorschach in mental health systems again offers evidence supporting multiplicity in our interpretive responses to visual stimuli. It is necessary to distinguish the storytelling dimension of interpretation from the more factual structural analysis of what we see before us. If we are working with a picture of a red table in a white room, then we can assume that many people will give a similar description of what they see before them. Although experiments in visual perception repeatedly show that even the most basic configurations will stimulate varied descriptive responses, it is when we ask people what the picture of the red table in the white room 'means to them' that the endless varieties of the storytelling response is activated.

"I have learned from my experience with art interpretation in groups that there can never be a fixed meaning or story 'behind' a picture. I have yet to see it happen. The image arouses our imagination, and our interpretations are stories that may change whenever we tell them."

"Once again, it might be said that you are advocating clinical chaos?"

"Chaos comes when we do not understand what is happening, when we lose self-confidence and the sense of intentionality that I described earlier. In response to the fear of chaos, people have established rigid systems of interpretation which give standard meanings to drawings. Yes, I experience chaos and I would rather not live in it for prolonged periods of time. When I try to penetrate to the essence of what is going on in a relationship, in a picture or in myself, I often lose my way. But I want to keep looking and not settle into a prescriptive system. My experience as an art therapist repeatedly reveals how we give multiple meanings to images. I have profound respect for what takes place in groups when we interpret artworks. This multiplicity is multiplied by the members of the group. The group has an interpretative intelligence that far exceeds that of an individual person. The group often functions as a single being, with great sensitivity, and a broad range of interpretative insights. I try to encourage art therapy to avoid clinical deception, which occurs when we cover up interpretive multiplicity and the inevitable variety of meanings and replace them with a judgment that serves the purpose of the interpreter."

"Are some interpretations better than others?"

"Yes."

"Can bad interpretations be therapeutic?"

"That is possible, since there is such a high degree of subjectivity involved. There are many people, both colleagues and clients, who want art therapists to fix meanings to pictures. Clients may expect us to tell them what something means and employers might see it as part of our job description. I personally value the ability of an image to generate many different responses. I think that this multiplicity of response is a tribute to the image and it reveals how people operate. Yet, I know that people can leave a therapy session feeling much better after a therapist has told them what their drawings mean. They feel that they got something for their money and that it helps to put their lives into better perspective. Clinics might feel better after fixing psychological meanings to pictures. The process affirms their sense of competence. There are no limits to what can be therapeutic and this is what causes confusion. If we believe in a therapeutic procedure, it will make us feel better. Therefore, a system of therapy that abuses images may in fact produce results that many people are happy with. My goal is to encourage therapy to make people feel better within a context which also respects the integrity of the artistic image.

"An art therapist that I was working with told me how important it was for her to have a place to bring her art, dreams and stories. By making art, telling her story and hearing the different responses of people, she saw life vividly. The multiplicity of our interpretative responses corresponds more to life, and for me therapy affirms life."

"Do you follow a guide to interpretation?"

"I am always making notes of those things that I have learned from my experience that help to describe what I am doing and what I believe. The list is always changing, but there are some things that survive. Most of what I have discovered can be found in the writings of others. James Hillman encourages us to withhold meanings; stay with the image; let it speak; try not to insult it; get the ego out of the way; spend time with the image; and respond imaginatively. St. Augustine and the phenomenologists speak of illumination, letting experience shine. All of these suggestions recommend opening to the image and dialoging with it. I try to discourage formulas of interpretation; respect my instincts and common sense reactions; listen to what other people have to say; encourage a Socratic emptiness in terms of preconceptions; respect multiplicity and paradox. All of these guides to interpretation are elements of a good relationship. One person cannot be in control.

"Viewing interpretation as storytelling has been the single most important aid for me. I have also realized that the process takes time. I have attached a taboo to hasty interpretations. The process is always subjective and the image, as Rank suggests, can only be further interpreted. The same applies to dreams and the stories of our lives. As art therapists, we have to be keenly aware of how images are formed through the specific properties of materials and how media will influence what we see. The flow of paint, hardness of stone, stiffness of wood, the pliability of clay, the textures of oil crayons, charcoal, pencils or acrylic paints will determine the expressiveness of the image.

"I also keep in mind some eternal principles of interpretation such as reversal and correspondence. Freud and Jung were masters of the reversal principle and they used it constantly. For example, small size may be indicative of a high level of emotional attachment and big objects may not be so important; a negative image of a person may suggest that they are actually quite important to me; and so forth. There is some truth to things not always being what they appear to be, and we do avoid what we do not want to see. The reversal principle is useful to me as a way of opening up the range and variety of my responses to an image. Abuse occurs when the principle of reversal is used dogmatically and when interpreters use the metaphoric language of dreams only to promote their positions. When images and objects substitute for one another and change places in dreams, it is not possible to prove the validity of an interpretation.

"I learned about the principle of correspondence from my studies with Rudolf Arnheim, and I researched its use within indigenous healing traditions. It is based upon the premise that what we see outside influences what we feel inside. The formal qualities of the external image will shape the quality of what we feel. Our inner feelings will also affect what we see. And from dreams I have learned that the events of the day, and the structures of our lives in the present, will influence the content of our imagery. I have experienced extraordinary parallels between the process of dreaming and art. Work with dreams has deepened my understanding of art. The two go together well. Rank spoke of how animistic cultures interpreted reality according to the dream. Perhaps I am a primitive, animistic man."

"I am intrigued by your references to Rudolf Arnheim."

"He helps us to see what is before us. I know that I continuously need help in being more visually aware. Increased sensory awareness can in itself be a fundamental objective of art therapy. When I am working with a painting I tend to think in three different ways about its interpretation possibilities. The first concerns our personal responses and the stories we tell. The second way is archetypal. If we are looking at a tree, we consider the universal, historical and cultural significance of the image of the tree. The archetypal dimension takes us outside ourselves and it complements, and sometimes validates, our personal stories and responses. Arnheim's work with the structural and formal qualities of visual configurations brings us right back to the material presence of the artwork. For me, this is a third and necessary element of interpretation. We can get lost in our fantasies about the image without this emphasis on the thing itself, its specific qualities."

"Arnheim's work also has a strong process orientation. We might consider this as a fourth way of approaching art interpretation."

"Thank you for this insight. It amazes me how easy it is to overlook process. I was just lecturing at the art therapy academies in Holland on the subject of interpretation and they kept emphasizing the material and process dimensions of art therapy and how art making is itself an interpretative process. Arnheim's writings take us close to the experience of the artist. He describes how children and master artists solve problems of perspective and representation. He is concerned with motives, social environment, history and all dimensions of the psychology of art. His writings helped the world to understand the visual language of cubism, expressionism and abstract expressionism. In this regard his structural studies enabled us to see the poetic and dramatic dialogues between colors and shapes. There is a depth and passion to his commitment to the image and visual thinking. He shows me that understanding cannot be achieved without an awareness of what is physically present. Arnheim's writings apply to the complete range of art therapy applications—from our attempts to increase the sensory awareness of severely handicapped people to the use of art in depth-oriented therapy."

"He has helped art educators to become more intelligent about what they do. When I was training art teachers, Arnheim was our most important resource in explaining the cognitive and expressive elements of art. I believe that he can do the same thing for art therapy."

"This discussion about the artwork as something distinct from the person raises an important issue for art therapy. Is it possible that the 'person-centered' contributions of our profession are damaging art?"

"Art therapy can be viewed as placing more emphasis on the life of the person than on the image."

"The profession is an expression of our era's more pervasive tendency to focus on the person rather than the object. In *The Arts Without Mystery* (1973), Denis Donoghue criticizes 'the flight from the work of art to the artist.' In his essay, 'The zealots of explanation,' he describes how our reductive analyses deprive art of its mystery. He suggests that we are unable to accept 'the sacred object.' I am supportive of these positions, and I think that art therapy can benefit by opening to the 'mystery' of the art object. Our interpretations are the responses that we have to the image. They never offer definitive explanations but rather contribute to the mystery."

"You are suggesting that psychotherapy is a religious experience."

"Psychotherapy can be defined as providing something that is missing in our daily lives."

"It seems that people seek out psychological help in order to receive explanations rather than mystery."

"I have found that we often search for the reverse of what we really desire. I also think that mystery and explanation complement one another. The same applies to the dichotomy between the person and the image. Art interpretation can include all of these things."

As we continued to elaborate on issues of art interpretation, Lisa became frustrated. "What can I do when I am working with children in a short-term, assessment-oriented clinic? Parents and school systems want an immediate diagnosis and explanation. We do not have the 'time' you talk about for the telling and retelling of the story."

"What I have just said about interpretation can only be used as a guide and, perhaps in the case of short-term diagnosis treatment, as a caution. When we see a child only once or twice for an hour at a time, then we do the best we can within that context. Our job is to report what we see and make recommendations for the future. When we are only seeing a child for one or two hours, then it is important to consult with colleagues, parents, teachers and other people who have a more extended relationship. But we cannot avoid interpreting the art in the situation you describe. It is our responsibility to use every resource we have to help people understand the situation better. Let's look at the drawings you brought today."

"I saw two seven-year-old boys this week in diagnostic sessions in their school. The clinic sent me out to determine how they performed within the classroom milieu. In both cases, the clinic staff suspects that there is some form of abuse taking place at home.

"The first picture (Fig. 1) was done by Jimmie. He was referred to the clinic because of his aimless and wandering behavior in the classroom. Jimmie said that his drawing shows his friend's father coming after the friend with a knife. The boy is the small figure in the upper right and the father is the large figure on the left. The father is smiling, wearing pajamas and pointing the knife at his son who is in bed. Jimmie drew the image a second time, just below the first, 'to make it better.' He said that it was a dream. He then started to talk about monsters and how they frighten him and run after him in his dreams. I asked him where the monsters lived in the dreams and he said 'down under the ground.' He started to make monster noises. Then he described a 'good' dream that he had about going to the circus where the woman gave him 'lots of free tickets.' He seemed to enjoy the session. He talked freely with me, and he worked seriously on his picture.

Figure 1

"The staff at the clinic responded quickly to the picture with interpretations. They focused on the knife, seeing it as a penis suggesting some form of sex abuse. The staff also spoke of the father's smiling face as an indication that something was done for his pleasure. They noted how the boy's face is barely discernible and does not clearly express emotion. The fact that it is a drawing of something that a friend's father is doing to a friend in a dream was perceived as distancing from what might actually be taking place in Jimmie's home. By drawing and telling this story about his friend, he was able to get it out. If this is actually taking place in his home, it might be too threatening for him to describe. They saw his drawing the scene a second time as a repetition compulsion, that reinforces the significance of the scene."

"How do you relate to the drawing?"

"I can only see it within the context of my relationship with Jimmie, brief as it may have been. The drawing is part of the story that he told me and it represents an effort on his part to communicate with me. He actually related to me quite well. And he seems capable of acting on his feelings. I see the therapeutic value of his expressing himself in pictures, telling stories, describing dreams and using his imagination. If the monsters are threatening to him, then I feel that it is good that he is able to identify with them in his dramatizations and have some control over the situation. I also see the drawing as an indication of his ability to work on a problem or fear, to put them down on paper and get them outside of himself. When interpreting the picture, I tend to identify Jimmie with the man with the knife. It is something he drew or something that came through him. I imagine him having a fear of doing something harmful to himself or to another person. And I tend to agree with the people at the clinic in terms of his repeating the theme. The repetition may be an indication that he is drawing something that is important to him. Rather than looking to the drawing as 'evidence' of what is wrong with Jimmie, I see it as an indication of his ability to express himself within a context where he is asked to perform for a new person. Yet, I do not want to deny that he is having difficulties."

"It seems that you are being protective of Jimmie."

"Well, of course, isn't this part of our helping role? It upsets me when I do not feel this compassion in the other staff."

"What do you think of the smiling faces?"

"It is quite possible that they are nothing other than a standard child's representation of a smiling face. It is important to keep these drawing conventions in mind. The more obscure faces of the smaller figures may be due to the fact that he was trying to make small details in a tiny circle with a large crayon. My experience with children's art makes me think that the moods we see on the faces are often due to drawing conventions and materials. What do you see in the picture?"

"I start with what is there in front of us, a larger figure on the left with a smiling face. There is a smaller figure on the right in a 'bed' and a triangular shape that Jimmie calls the 'knife' between them. It seems to be pointing at the boy. The image is repeated below. However, the two lower figures are closer to one another and the triangle or knife is pointing above the figure to the right, or perhaps it is being held over its head. It is a dynamic picture which depicts action and something that is taking place between two people, or perhaps different parts of the same person.

"The knife is prominent. It is in the center of the picture and seems to be a connecting link. When I see the knife I think of its archetypal meanings and its associations with power, pointing, cutting through, separating and its relation to killing. In mythological language, the knife is often a symbol of the intent to cut off desire and longing, or to cut away and prune excessive or uncontrolled growth. The combination of the knife and father does seem suggestive of authority, but all of this is totally projective. Some people and cultures will not see authority in either the knife or the father. The large smiling figure appears to be standing up and the smaller one is apparently lying down on the bed. One is dominant, pointing the knife at the other figure which is passive and in a far more vulnerable position. The bed is suggestive of vulnerability. The larger and more dominant figures have big smiles in contrast to the lack of expression on the smaller figures. I see this as suggestive of the fact that an experience, and a picture, can have many sides, smiling together with fear and pain. The same juxtaposition is expressed by his telling you the circus dream together with the story about the father and the knife. These different elements can exist together. They do not have to be perceived as conflicting realities. Children show a constant ability to go from one to another, from monsters and the underworld to circus animals and 'lots of free tickets.' They are all part of life, and perhaps the child is closer to their existence than us.

"Returning to the knife again, it is so large that perhaps it might be a sword. In myths, the sword is often associated with spiritual energy or a positive force that is reaching out and into the world. It can be related to aggression and 'lower' desires. In the broad archetypal sense the sword and the knife are more likely to be associated with discipline, skill and control of the instincts. In most warrior cultures the skillful use of the sword is one of their highest attributes. Thousands of years of this history cannot help but leave traces in the psyche. The sword is active, willful, physical, empowering and expressive of conflict between differing positions. In our history the sword is 'the decisive factor' and a symbol of judgment through combat. Although our myths may not suggest that the sword is a penis, I have seen many drawings where it is intentionally used as an object of penetration and sometimes explicitly as a penis. Women often associate it with the painful dimensions of the male sexual organ, how the penis may not only penetrate the vagina but the body and the psyche as a whole, right up through the mind. Whenever someone tries to label the sword as male, I mention Joan of Arc or the great female warriors of Celtic mythology. So, we can have eternal speculations about what this single image of the knife may mean in Jimmie's drawing. I think that it is necessary to speculate but to make sure our deliberations stay close to the life and presence of the person who made the picture. The interpretative process is a means of getting closer to Jimmie, increasing our empathy for him."

"How do you relate to the smaller figures below?"

"As I look at the second drawing of the father pointing the knife at the son, it seems less threatening. Maybe he was trying to de-sensitize the image. The first one might have been too strong, too hot. Jimmie's effort to 'make it better' may be an attempt to say, 'Well, it's not quite that bad' or 'It's bad but I do not want to show it for what it is.' He might have been frightened by the first image or if we believe what he said, he was just trying to improve the drawing. Or perhaps he is afraid of failing and this is why he is 'aimless' and 'wandering' in his schoolwork. He does not want to commit himself to a situation that might result in disappointment. The large figure pointing the knife might represent these fears and how they control him. All of these interpretative possibilities are especially useful if the client is interested in hearing what the image provokes in other people. In my work with adults, there is a hunger for this as long as the environment is safe, compassionate and totally focused on the well-being of the person whose work is being interpreted. We have a similar respect for the image itself. A child who is hurting can be relieved if we understand the cause of the pain without it having to be spoken. I believe that most attempts to interpret children's art are motivated by a desire to understand what may not be able to be expressed in words."

"The hands of the boy in the bed are large."

"I am sure that there are some therapists who might suggest that the large hands of the boy lying in bed suggest that he is masturbating and that the father is catching him and pointing the knife of authority at him, perhaps representing punishment," I replied. "Or maybe he was just trying to draw hands within the limits of the space in the picture and the materials. By focusing on the hands with a big crayon, they are likely to be large since they require more details than an arm or a leg. The knife, a symbol of 'cutting away,' may be an expression of castration anxiety according to the classical psychosexual theories. Or if we consider all of the figures as portraits of Jimmie, then maybe the large smiling face is an image of himself enjoying what is going on, and the knife pointing to the smaller figure is his guilt. Maybe it is a masturbation picture, or maybe it is something he saw on the television. Most definitely, these responses are the fantasies and fictions of interpreters. The consideration of all of these possibilities can be useful to us. The problem comes when somebody says authoritatively that the picture 'means' masturbation guilt or some such thing. Poor Jimmie may not have even discovered these things yet, or maybe he is trying to tell us something along these lines. Or maybe the picture is expressive of his feelings for you.

"We can interpret pictures with more clarity when we see patterns emerging over periods of time, when we have more information about what is going on in the person's life and when the images correspond to the stories that the child tells us."

"We seem to be demonstrating the endless interpretative possibilities for this picture," Lisa said.

"Exactly, and we are affirming the power of Jimmie's picture to stimulate imagination."

"But how do I go about making an assessment of him for the clinic staff?"

"All you can do is follow your instincts and what you believe is going on in this boy. Tell them what you see in him, how he handled the meeting with you which is a testing situation in its entirety. Describe what he did and what he said in a summary manner. Express the essence of what you observed. Be clear about your bias, how you were responding to him personally and how this in turn influences what you observe. Address what the clinic wants to hear, so that you can all fulfill your responsibilities. The best assessments are ultimately cooperative and involve collaboration with other staff. Do not overdo it and feel that you have to figure it all out for yourself. Talk to colleagues about your doubts and questions. The ultimate value of your work in art therapy is its ability to expand the resources for assessment not only through the content of the picture but through your description of how he engaged you and the art materials."

INTERPRETATION AS THERAPY

"CHRIS IS THE other seven-year-old that I saw this week. As I told you earlier the staff at the clinic is questioning whether or not he is being abused at home. He did this picture of a tower-like house that is on fire (Fig. 2). To the right of the building a fire engine is putting out the blaze."

"Did you ask him to draw a particular theme?"

"No, with both Jimmie and Chris I sat down with them at a table and they went right to work, choosing the materials and the theme."

"What did he say to you about the picture?"

"When he started to draw the house he said: 'I'll make my house.' As he drew, it became 'Bob's Steak' (spelled 'stake') house where he said he goes with his parents to eat. As he was completing the house, he began to draw the fire. He then added the 'hook and ladder and hoses' and became excited. His teacher told me that Chris has difficulty staying with a consistent theme. He is always changing his story in relation to his mood at the moment. The teacher had the feeling that he is constantly fabricating answers. Although she respects his imagination, she is frustrated with his inability to stay with tasks and relationships."

"Children's drawings rarely have one fixed story attached to them. This house might begin as Chris' home, turn into a restaurant and become his house again. The same applies to Jimmie's picture of his friend and the friend's father that might also represent Jimmie and his father as well as different aspects of Jimmie. In this respect, the process of the child's associations to a drawing closely parallels the multiple possibilities for interpretation. It is questionable whether there is ever a single meaning. Changes in his story about the drawing are not necessarily

59

Figure 2

pathological. But it seems that he does not tell a consistent story about anything in his life."

"That's right. He misrepresents everything that happens to him."

"Did he say anything else about the picture?"

"I asked him: 'How did it burn?' And he said: 'Someone was careless. They found a clue in the ashes.' I wanted to know if anyone was hurt and he said: 'No, there was no one there.' "

"The house is surrounded by red lines, fire, and inside the windows it is bright yellow and there are shapes in the lower section of windows that almost look like figures. Did he say that the red was fire?"

"Yes."

"What did the staff at the clinic say about the picture?"

"It must have been hard for them not to say something about the phallic shape of the house," Lisa replied. "They focused on this and spoke about how he might be telling us there is something wrong in the house. They saw connections between the fire and aggression, possibly violence. The fire engine was considered an expression of his need for help. We discussed the sense of urgency expressed by the picture, since the fire seems overwhelming. The fire truck doesn't appear to have much of a chance. There is no water that we can see and the ladder does not reach the house, furthering the impression of being trapped inside. One of the staff commented on the constancy of phallic forms in the house, the hoses, chimney and the smoke coming out of the chimney in the shape of a projectile. This was related to masturbation, sexual guilt and extinguishing passion. They saw the absence of people as an expression of his disassociation from others and his lack of trusting relationships. I spoke about how perhaps the picture did not need people and that sometimes decisions are made for purely aesthetic reasons. The tall 'phallic' house might have been the result of his drawing the image on a vertical page. But he could have drawn the picture horizontally."

"You seem to be coming to the rescue again."

"Maybe I am the fire engine."

"This identification with Chris and his imagery is what therapy is all about. We are fire engines from time to time, if the situation calls for this kind of action. At other times, we are the match or the fire, igniting action, change and the destruction of bad habits. What strikes me about his picture is the dominance of the fire, the intensity of the passion."

"One of the staff spoke of the phallic house, the red color, the large irregular windows and the fact that the hoses are connected to the house as possible signs of incest. The fire truck which is supposed to be a helper looks like it is feeding the fire."

"What do you think?"

"In this case, I am giving careful consideration to what the staff saw in the picture. I do not have any evidence at this point of incest, but I do think that there may be considerable aggression in the home. Chris is constantly pushing and hitting other boys in the classroom, and he does not appear to have consideration for the feelings of others. This may very well be due to the way he is being treated at home. On the positive side, his energy and creativity are expressed by the picture. He also shows an ability to express his feelings, to make a spontaneous, lively and well-organized drawing. Perhaps he is expressing his need to keep his emotions under control. He seems to have succeeded in this instance, and it might be a good idea for him to continue in art therapy. It could be especially helpful to record his changing stories so that he can see them for himself. How would you approach the archetypal elements of this picture?"

"This picture, as with every piece of children's art, and every artwork that we adults make is full of archetypal imagery. The archetypal psychologist might encourage us to look at the picture as a phenomena unto itself and not make too many connections to the particulars of Chris's life. Our interpretations of what is happening in his personal life are projections that we make, and he will tell us his interpretation. The image on the other hand has a life of its own that can be interpreted completely on its terms. I find this archetypal perspective useful. Relating to a picture in this way broadens my understanding of both the image and Chris. We are all separate entities, you, me, Chris and the image. I want to understand what you think about it, your story, his story and my personal reaction. But I also want to look at the picture as something separate from all of this. This way of looking increases the importance of the image and its value to us. It is a therapeutic strategy in itself. We need to separate, distinguish, understand differences, what is mine, what is your's, what is his, what concerns our relationship, what belongs to the image and how we are going to relate to this multiplicity in a way that works for ourselves, others and the world. When we become overly involved in a single point of view, one story, one meaning and one therapeutic objective, we lose this interdependence that is necessary for a healthy life.

"Chris needs to know about the opportunities in life as well as his responsibility. Therapy is concerned with clarifying differences, learning how to act, having trusting relationships with other people which will hopefully inspire greater confidence. Psychopathology is closely connected to problems with how we relate to ourselves, other people and the world. Things go wrong when we are so overly preoccupied with our obsessions, fears and guilt that we see everything in life from this distorted perspective. It is a problem of too much self, exaggerating our personal influence on people and situations, and not being able to open to the many different elements of any given situation, different points of view, different values. Everything does not have to pass through us. Imagine the congestion. Attitudes of this kind, trying to control everything, are doomed to fail. By relating to the image as something distinct from us, we can begin to implement a more healthy and cooperative way of operating. I find it useful to spend as much time as possible with an individual picture. I like to look at the picture as a whole, in terms of how it is put together. I am also interested in details. A careful review of parts can deepen our understanding of the whole."

"It seems that you are recommending that we carefully consider the more universal, symbolic qualities of pictures as distinct from the person and then apply them to the particulars of a given situation."

"The terms 'symbol' and 'image' can be easily confused. The symbol is generally more concerned with 'meanings' associated with images and can be perceived as a 'meta-image,' in that it refers to something other than what is immediately present. The term 'meta' suggests transcendence, something beyond. I do not think that one is higher than another. If I have a preference, it is for the physical presence. Sometimes, the symbolic view takes us away from the art object. Although image and symbol are often interchangeable, I think that 'image' is descriptive of the phenomena itself, the particular thing and its material qualities, whereas symbol is more directed to both personal and universal meanings. When I see an apple before me or when an apple appears to me in a dream, it is in the form of an image. When I think about what the apple means to me personally or in a more universal, cultural sense, then I am transforming my image of the apple into a symbol. The 'sign' is a symbol which means one particular thing, whereas symbols that appear in art have multiple meanings. The diagnostic history of art in mental health has been more concerned with developing systems for decoding 'graphic signs.' These practices demonstrate how symbols can be reduced to signs. However, I am more interested in doing the reverse, heightening their symbolic power. What symbols do you see in the picture?"

"A house, fire, a door, windows, a ladder, a tree."

"Let's look at each of them. Although there are general symbolic meanings attached to each of these, there are many different kinds of houses, fires, doors, windows, ladders and trees. Let's do an archetypal review of the images in this picture in order to learn more about this dimension of art therapy. What do you see as the archetypal meanings of the house?"

"The house can be symbolic of the body and also of the soul. It is an enclosure. I think of homes, safe houses, a place to sleep. Rooms in the house are symbolic of different parts of the self. This house looks like a tower which makes me think of elevation, climbing, a view from the top, jumping."

"The black smoke on the right side of the picture is falling in a spiral pattern. I respond to the smoke with images of density, bad air, being driven away. How do you relate to the door?"

"I see the door as expressing passage, entrance to different realms," Lisa said. "I think of the shaman's doorway through which access to the realms of the spirits is gained. But I do not get a sense of passage from this door. It is closed, colored blue and tucked off to the side. It does not seem accessible or welcoming. There is no path leading up to it. It feels more like a barrier than an entrance."

"The windows?"

"In myths, windows are symbolic of opening and illumination. The window is an image of the soul being connected to spiritual realms. Chris's door is shut tight, but his windows are large, open and beaming with light. If the house is perceived as a portrait of him, then there really appears to be something going on inside that he wants us to see."

"The fire?"

"For me it represents desire, passion and energy. In this picture it seems to be associated with destruction, danger and alarm. Yet, when I look at the picture, the house is intact. It is glowing with the flames, radiating energy both inside and out. It is interesting to consider the house as a symbol of the self which is packed with inner energy that is also expressed externally. This seems to offer a good portrait of Chris."

"Heraclitus praised fire as the essence of life. The Holy Spirit is associated with fire, together with love and purification. Hell fire represents the darker side, guilt, atonement and suffering. The fire is a dominant image in this picture. As I look at the picture, I also sense great energy, burning inside and out. How do you relate to the ladder?"

"The ladder is typically a symbol of ascent and the progressive steps of spiritual enlightenment and self-improvement. Buddha is sometimes pictured as sitting atop a ladder with the earth below. In this picture, I see the ladder as part of a rescue theme, or perhaps escape. Ladders help human beings; they enable us to gain access to places that are either difficult to reach or hard to get out of. As I look at the picture, I have a strong sense of the ladder's inability to reach the building. There is fire between the two."

"And how do you respond to what appears to be a tree in front of the fire engine?"

"It is a very small tree?"

"Maybe it is a bush."

"Perhaps. It is a vivid green, full of vitality. The tree is also a symbol of the human being. It is a nurturing symbol when it is full of life as this one is. The tree bears fruit. It is the tree of life, aspiration, understanding and stability. I can easily imagine Chris as this small tree being overwhelmed by everything around him. His rooted tree life is quite small compared to the passion and turbulence of the house on fire. Yet, the tree stands at the front of the picture. It overlaps the fire engine and it is connected to the earth and the green grass that he has drawn below."

"Let's think about the grass for a minute."

"It can be soft, burned out, full of weeds. This grass looks lush and supportive of life. It is symbolic of growth from the earth."

"And the apparent absence of water?"

"It's good that you mentioned the water. I think of water in terms of survival, cooling, putting out the fire. It is one of the essential elements of life. Chris does not seem to have any water in his picture. Perhaps he does not have what he needs to deal with the fire. There are not any people that we can see. The fire engine appears to be without water and people, and the ladder seems too short. I can imagine myself making up a story for Chris, a fairy tale, in response to this picture."

"This is what psychotherapy is all about, an exchange of stories. You and Chris get to know one another through your stories. Is the therapist supposed to be a passive listener?"

"The classical image of the therapist guards against projection."

"We are seeing that every interpretation, no matter how guarded, is a projection."

"Some therapists think that the systems that they work within are transpersonal and that there are universal truths of psychological causality."

"If we are interpreting according to the rules of a system, we may as well keep a catalog in front of us. Ultimately, issues like this make us define our personal therapeutic values. The Swiss psychiatrist Medard Boss in his book *Psychoanalysis and Daseinsanalysis* said that if we interpret a situation according to a theory of interpretation, then we do not encounter experience. He calls this 'umdeuten' instead of 'deuten,' 'deviated' vs. 'direct' interpretation. People who follow Freud interpret like him as opposed to finding their own way. We can see from the many varied interpretations that just the two of us are making in response to the pictures of Jimmie and Chris that there can be no single 'objective' interpretation."

"I once thought that the therapist should know all of the possible interpretations."

"All of us get stuck in this position from time to time, thinking that we have to know all of the answers. Maybe what we have to know is that interpretative possibilities are defined only by the limits of the imagination. The process of interpretation is a fundamental indicator of our human variability. We seem to be much more accepting of multiple interpretations in politics and the world of art than in psychotherapy. Perhaps psychotherapists have to be perceived as possessing all of the shortcomings, idiosyncracies and differences that we expect from politicians and artists."

"But what does the therapist have to know?"

"I keep returning to the old philosophical axiom, 'Know thyself.' We should be able to know our projections and why we are having them and how they might be of use to others. If I am going to understand the person I am working with, I have to understand my experience, which is not the same and cannot be the same as the experience of the other person. Therapy is essentially concerned with knowing these differences and how we can communicate with one another about them. But we must also know what is separate from both of us. This applies to images and artworks which tell their story within the language of the particular medium. As art therapists we have to know the properties of our artistic medium, we need to know something about others, about the history of therapy, about images."

"Some might say that the person making the picture is the ultimate authority when it comes to interpretation."

"Yes and no. The picture is distinct from the person. There are no ultimate authorities when it comes to the interpretations of images, only endless interpretations. I think your concern about who is the authority has more to do with therapeutic values and style. Some therapists are only concerned with what the client says about the picture and they withhold personal interpretations. However, I know that I am never fully aware of what I am doing when I make a picture. Too much awareness can be crippling. Sometimes, it is important to just act. There are therapists who are more concerned with their interpretations and the standards of the system that they might be working in, than the interpretations of the client. Others see the therapeutic dialogue as an exchange of interpretations. I am inclined to go with the exchange, what the phenomenologists call 'intersubjectivity.' "

"I do not think that discovering the problem can be a cure in itself."

"As soon as we resolve one, another will spring up, or maybe two or three. I see therapy as a process where people travel together. There is continuous motion. The scenery is constantly changing and there are always surprises and new problems. We might never discover why we are on the journey or why we choose one another. The therapy involves learning how to travel and how to be with another person.

"As soon as we fix a meaning to a symbol or to a picture, it is likely that another one will emerge. I have an image of psychological labels or fixed interpretations as attempts to patch a hole in a dike or a dam. I think of the little Dutch boy who stuck his finger in the hole to stop the water. The Freudians will see something altogether different, of course. The water behind our concepts is too big for our little holes of thought. That is why I like to look at the different elements of a picture as well as the image as a whole and let the imagination respond as freely as possible. The consideration of universal meanings is a way of getting in touch with the water. The old analytic theories which see everything according to a fixed meaning are being left behind for this reason. In Gestalt therapy there is too much self, the person rather than the water. As Vincent Ferrini says, the 'I' cannot see itself. Both the analytic and Gestalt approaches can be helpful to people, but I need something broader. I like to go back and forth between the self and the universals. We need them both. I also believe that it is important to respond to art with art, with new stories, with imaginative interpretations which deepen the experience."

"What do you mean by too much self in Gestalt therapy?"

"I am referring to the tendency to see everything in a picture or dream as parts of the self. I have found the Gestalt approach useful as a guide to interpretation, possibly because people hunger for this kind of connectedness. The method is stimulating, in that it contradicts our routine way of seeing things and it suggests new possibilities. Yet, I think that the approach fails to acknowledge what is distinct from me. This way of interpretation is itself an expression of our era's egocentrism. I prefer interpretations which increase my ability to see the 'water.' I think that we have been so influenced by theories of interpretation that associate images with parts of ourselves, parents, childhood experiences and repressed conflicts that we require help in returning to the more natural tendency to see the image for itself."

"You seem to contradict yourself in reference to Gestalt therapy. You are suggesting that there is too much self in this approach, yet you also say that it is useful."

"I think that Gestalt therapy's original appeal came from its liberation of the self from the reductionism of psychoanalytic theory in which everything was perceived in terms of our parents, Oedipal conflicts, early childhood, and so forth. Gestalt therapy puts us back in touch with the self and this was a significant historical contribution. As its influence has grown, it is now become a problem itself. Any theory of interpretation that suggests a formula will in my opinion be short-lived. The Gestalt formula sees everything as part of the self. Now, my desire to see the water as water, and not as myself, is in some ways a reaction against the egocentrism of Gestalt theory. If I were to make a formula out of my response, it would also become problematic. I can envision a crazy scenario where we are thinking only of the water and not the other person, or of Chris's house and not him. We benefit from all of the interpretative possibilities."

"You mentioned that a method of interpretation can be useful if it contradicts our routine way of looking at things and if it suggests new possibilities."

"Maybe a goal of the interpretative process is to see more or to see things with a fresh vision. I have a tendency to fall into habits that limit my perception. I am reading *Shelley on Love*, Richard Holmes's anthology of Shelley's prose writings (1980). This passage of Shelley's describes what I see as a goal of interpretation.

> Poetry lifts the veil from the hidden beauty of the world and makes familiar objects be as if they were not familiar; it reproduces all that it represents, and the impersonations clothed in its Elysian light stand thence forward in the minds of those who have once contemplated them as memorials of that gentle and exalted content which extends itself over all thoughts and actions with which it coexists.

"I do not think that all of our perceptions are evocations of Elysium as Shelley's romanticism suggests, but he clearly articulates the eternal perceptual or interpretative principle of making the familiar unfamiliar. Poets, artists and scientists have all discovered that familiarity tends to block our vision. They are always finding ways to see things anew."

"What do you mean by your reference to Elysium?"

"One of our goals in therapy, and art, is opening to what may be unpleasant or unknown and clothed in the darkness of the underworld. 'Elysian light' has its place in therapy, too. I want them both."

"I am beginning to see interpretation as opening to the existence of a thing or another person."

"This is why interpretative systems that see everything as the self are so problematic. As I said at the beginning of this discussion, interpretation is a dialogue, a process of intersubjectivity, *between* the self and the image or another person. Of course, I do not want to deny the self, but there is so much more than me. I also mentioned how important it is to go outside of ourselves. Here's another passage from Shelley which illustrates this point.

> The great secret of morals is love, or a going out of our own nature and an identification of ourselves with the beautiful which exists in thought, action, or person, not our own. A man, to be greatly good, must imagine intensely and comprehensively; he must put himself in the place of another and of many others; the pains and pleasures of his species must become his own. The great instrument of moral good is the imagination: and poetry administers to the effect by acting on the cause. Poetry enlarges the circumference of the imagination by replenishing it with thoughts of ever new delight, which have the power of attracting and assimilating to their own nature all other thoughts and which form new intervals and interstices whose void forever craves fresh food. Poetry strengthens that faculty which is the organ of the moral nature of man in the same manner as exercise strengthens a limb.

"Once again, I discourage a one-sided romantic reference to 'the beautiful.' I also wish that these fine passages from the old writers were not restricted to the masculine. In addition to affirming the 'moral' necessity of getting beyond ourself, Shelley presents imagination as the primary faculty of interpretation. He even provides a manifesto for the creative arts therapies when he says 'poetry administers to the effect by acting upon the cause.' Does this passage on imagination suggest practical applications to you?"

"It is helpful. Shelley places imagination into the context of human relationships. I am also intrigued with his references to morality. I have a tendency to respond to the word imagination as suggesting fantasy, daydreaming, idleness and leaving the situation that I am engaged with. Shelley shows me how imagination is necessary in order to be truly in a situation with another person or an image. It seems that imagination is the faculty that I use to experience life outside of myself. Yet, I have seen from the psychotherapeutic literature that the interpretations of therapists can be widely imaginative and projections of personal fantasies, or the principles of a theory of interpretation, that seem to have nothing to do with the person or the image that they are supposedly interpreting. This is probably another reason why I sometimes react negatively to the word imagination. In the situations that I am describing, the imagination of the interpreter feeds only on itself and is not sensitive to the existence of the phenomena to be interpreted."

"This is yet another instance of the need to get outside of ourselves and our theories."

"How do we evaluate interpretations?"

"On the basis of what you have just said, our interpretations try to get as close to the experience as possible and see it for what it is. We evaluate psychotherapeutic interpretations the way we determine the value of art. Interpretations can clearly stimulate remarkable results and changes in psychotherapy. Clients generally want interpretations which express how we see them or the situation. Does the interpretation have an effect on us? Does it inspire action; offer insight and hope? Does it encourage further reflection? Does it have lasting power? Is it useful, authentic, imaginative? These criteria are much more sensible than determinations about whether or not the interpretation is right or wrong according to an 'objective standard.' I would ask whose standards are the determinants of right or wrong? Individuals, and especially clients, must have the opportunity to determine what is right for them. This is where the principle of reversal is so effective. The process of turning things around and presenting the person with the unexpected attracts attention. It take us by surprise and thus engages both the mind and the emotions.

"I perceive interpretation as a process of philosophical or poetic inquiry. This helps me to let go of the tendency to think that there is a single, empirical science of psychological interpretation. I cannot observe the internal workings of a person's imagination or memory, and even if I could see these things, I can only evaluate them from my perspective. The psychoanalyst Theodor Reik in his book *Listening with the Third Ear* (1972) described how he once asked Freud for advice about his life and Freud replied: 'I can only tell you of my personal experience.' Reik believed that psychoanalysts and therapists never have a complete understanding of themselves. The deeper we go in our psychological investigations, the more we validate the ancient slogan of Heraclitus, 'I searched myself.' Reik felt that the professionally trained therapist is someone who might simply be better prepared to investigate the inner dynamics of the self and others. It may even be argued that therapists are not always better prepared. Perhaps some of our clients will offer more useful, imaginative and insightful interpretations than us. This has often happened to me. I actually find it destructive to think that I am better prepared than another person. It puts me in a position where I must prove myself or even compete. However, I do take on the role of the therapist and the responsibilities that go with it. I always try to do my best and I evaluate my sensitivity and presence, because it is so easy to wander away. The work of therapy demands self-discipline, concentration and an orientation to others."

"Perhaps this is where the process of evaluation is to be directed."

"We return again to the theme of therapy as a performance art."

"If we say that there is no right or wrong in therapy, aren't we avoiding the ethical dimension?"

"That is a good point. I certainly do not want to be associated with the belief that everything is to be evaluated according to what is right for 'me.' Our generation and our psychotherapeutic values have gone too far in this direction. Rigid and prescribed theories or rules of behavior are as bad as excessive self-interest. They avoid the inevitable need to make decisions. Therapeutic interpretations and stories reveal the different elements and choices that are present in every situation. They help us to clarify multiple areas of responsibility. Every ethical and therapeutic judgment is for me addressed to what is right for myself, for the person I am working with, for the image or artwork, for the group or the family, for the institution that I employed by, for the community, and perhaps even the world. Psychodynamic theories function like religions in terms of ethics. They embody the lessons of history and the stories that are told to offer guidance. A guiding tradition may be as old as 5,000 years or a brief time span within one person's professional life. What constantly happens in therapy and in life is that there are conflicts between what people need and between different 'guiding traditions.' Needs often compete or clash radically with one another. This is always happening in groups. Understanding the different needs of people in groups can be difficult and complex. Many people are reluctant to say what they need, some are saying it all the time and are not as good at listening to others, and the needs themselves are constantly changing. There can never be a single, fixed answer. Health is a process of ongoing transformation guided by a sensitivity for the self, others and the environment. Therapy helps us to respond more imaginatively to the dynamic interplay. Moreno spoke about the need to create new responses to old situations. Analysis by itself may help to clarify the existing or old situation, but it does not imply imaginative and new responses."

"I do think that telling stories in response to images draws us into a closer relationship to the artworks and each other. In life, I deepen relationships with people through dialogue and the exchange of feelings. It would seem logical for this to apply to therapy, too. You seem to be suggesting that there is as much art to the process of interpretation as there is to making a picture."

"As I said earlier, we respond to art with art. This artistic dialogue is the therapeutic process. It occurs between people, within the self, be-

tween the self and art materials and so on. I am interested in interpretations that move the process along. The dialogue allows problems to
manifest themselves, and through our stories we imagine and experience
a variety of responses. If Chris is interested in hearing from you, it is a
good idea to tell him stories in response to his picture. You might suggest
many possibilities that he would otherwise never consider. You said earlier that you felt a story emerging in you. Let's try it out here."

Lisa reflected quietly for a minute. "I find myself telling the literal
story of what we have seen and discussed in the picture. . .a house on
fire, lights inside, and a fire engine with a ladder that does not reach the
house. I do not feel satisfied with this story right now."

"Your imagination is not involved. You feel the difference and I am
sure a child working with you will, too. Imagination increases vitality
and it is contagious. Whatever you are feeling will be projected to the
person with you and vice versa. This is why the interplay of imagination
and creation within your relationship to a child is so therapeutic. You
and the person you are working with are co-creators in the artistic process. Chris's picture is imaginative and it deserves an imaginative response which keeps the artistic experience going by arousing emotion. A
literal description of what you see in the picture does not do this."

Lisa felt confused and challenged me. "Some traditional therapists
would maintain that you are encouraging me to put too much of myself
into the process as opposed to being more attentive to Chris."

"The only way I know how to respond to that position is by being
analytic myself. The attempt to take 'yourself' out of a situation is a
manifestation of avoidance, a defense against intimacy and responsibility. It becomes pernicious when presented as being done for the well-
being of others. If your intent is to be sensitive to Chris and to make
something of your relationship, then I do not think that you have to fear
being yourself. Does Chris need an inanimate analyst, someone who is
cautious about being 'personal'? I believe that the classical analytic tendency of the therapist to 'lay back' in order to both further the transference process and control countertransference is well intended. But
unfortunately when the technique becomes a standard formula it dis-
tances itself from life, from risk and choice. It exists for its own sake and
not for Chris. I think you have to constantly ask yourself what Chris
needs? What can you do? How do you feel like responding? Do you
think that Chris would like to listen to stories that you create?"

"I sense that he needs to communicate with people, to exchange feelings. He can benefit from a relationship that shows him that it can be

done and how to do it. He needs to learn how to relate to people. It seems that this is where he is having difficulty."

"In order to respond to this picture imaginatively, it may be necessary to forget everything that we have said about the picture and all of the 'meanings' we discussed. Start fresh and let yourself be guided by your creative instinct for what may be useful. Take a risk, and if you do not think it is working, readjust and tell him what you are feeling. Sometimes, the best way to find out what works is to first clarify what you do not want."

Lisa closed her eyes and reflected upon what we had just said to one another. "I will give it another try. I will tell a story from the perspective of the house. This is an old building. Right now it is called 'Bob's Steak House.' In earlier times it had been a home for different families, and because it was close to the main road, a man named Bob made the house into a restaurant. Business had not been good lately for Bob, and he closed the restaurant and arranged to sell the house. All of the other old houses in the neighborhood were torn down, and new apartment buildings and stores were built in their place. This house was the only one on the street that still had a large green lawn where the children in the neighborhood could play. But lately the children were no longer coming and all of the other old and familiar houses were gone. The house got depressed. All of the new people seemed strange and rarely came to sit on the grass. The house felt that it was no longer wanted in the neighborhood. Everything inside felt empty. There was no movement other than the tickling sensation that the house got from the family of mice that lived in one of the walls and the birds that sat on the roof. All of the action on the busy commercial street had nothing to do with the house. It felt foreign, unwanted. There were no other houses to talk with at night and in the morning when the sun came up. The small tree to the side of the house was still there and it was having the same problems. In the past the house and the tree had never paid much attention to one another, but they were growing closer every day now. They were both feeling out of place within the new neighborhood.

"The house had always been afraid of fire and used to worry about whether or not the electrical wires that run through the walls, ceilings and floors were in good shape. There was a large fireplace in the old living room that the house liked to have burning, since it made everything inside feel warm and cozy. Because the house had been empty for a long time, Bob decided to let a friend of his stay there. This man had never lived alone in a house before and did not know how to take care of the place. On a cold morning in December he made a fire in the fireplace and left to go to the store. The house felt the heat rising and worried so much that one of its electric wires caught fire in a wall. The windows were bulging with light and trying to let people know that something was wrong inside. The flames began to spread throughout the house. A small fire engine was passing by after returning from the garage for repairs. It only had part of its ladder because it was not prepared for work. There was a fireman and firewoman inside. They got the hoses out. One went behind the house to turn on the water and the other one went to a telephone to call for more help because the radio in the fire engine was not connected. The small tree began to cry because it saw that the flames were hurting the house. It called for the rain to come to help. . . . That's probably enough for now."

"What are some of the things that this story might introduce to your relationship to Chris?"

"As I was telling it, I felt a strong sense of being isolated, alone and without support. The house wanted companions and it felt abandoned. It was also abused by the person who just moved in. There is a sense of helplessness to the story. These emotions are close to the life of Chris. Maybe he can respond to a story like this with compassion or insight into his personal life. It is important with Chris to leave the story unfinished. The life of the house is threatened and there is a possibility of help coming. I would like to see how Chris responds."

"The story arouses my emotions. I find myself completely involved in the drama that you have created. Therapy involves a shared sense of drama with its fantasies, problems and choices for action. It is an interactional process, a cooperative creation and an exchange of energy. You will find as you continue to work with children that after you have said a few things, they might add to the story. In this way the story embodies the cooperative creation that we want to see in therapy. It seems that when you allowed your imagination to take over, something therapeutic happened. I felt it. Although you had to go deeply into yourself to tell the story, I sensed you moving even closer to Chris and increasing your empathy for what his life might be like."

"I felt myself coming closer to Chris as I was telling the story, but ironically I had to forget about him in order to get started."

"I have heard experts in fields as varied as theatre, bird-watching and psychoanalysis say that in order to reach the essence of an experience and perform authentically, they must 'forget' what they have studied."

"Psychotherapy seems to be a continuous paradox."

"Perhaps, you are right. We have to go into ourselves to reach others and into others to find ourselves. The same applies to pictures and stories. The different elements work together and this multiplicity helps to deepen relationships. The multiplicity increases feelings and possibilities for action. All of the people involved sense that there is something dynamic happening. Our relationships with others deepen our sensitivity to the stories and pictures. Art therapy is a constant interaction."

SHARKS AND WHALES:
ARCHETYPAL IMAGERY
IN CHILDREN'S ART

"OUR DISCUSSION of symbols has me rethinking all of my years as an art teacher. I was not attentive to the many symbolic dimensions of the children's art."

"Are there any images that stand out in your memory?" I asked.

"Sharks and whales. There was a period in the 1970s when the film *Jaws* was released during which the children were constantly drawing pictures of sharks and whales. I am particularly interested in the image of the whale as it appears in children's art. Now that families here in Massachusetts are frequently going on 'whale watches,' there is an increasing tendency to perceive the whale benevolently as opposed to its old monster image."

"Films like *Jaws* and *Star Wars* activate the mythic consciousness of children. The images and stories presented by the films correspond to the deepest feelings and preoccupations of childhood. . .good and evil, life and death, animals, speed, machines, fantasy, adventure, power, danger and how close we are to being overwhelmed by forces beyond our control."

"Are these concerns unique to childhood?"

"Absolutely not, but children are closer to the mythic and imaginative realms than most adults. Their minds are more open and to a certain extent more vulnerable."

"How can you prove this?"

"They generally spend more time drawing pictures of sharks and whales than adults. They are probably closer to the mythic realm because they have more time. I do not think that children are that much different from us in terms of mythic and imaginative capabilities. They just have more time for it. They also expect it from one another and we adults encourage their imaginative nature. Animistic cultures also had more time for myth. Let's look at the pictures you brought."

"This is a picture that a seven-year-old boy did of a whale surrounded by sharks, a large and small person flying, and a figure in a boat shaped like a dragon (Fig. 3)."

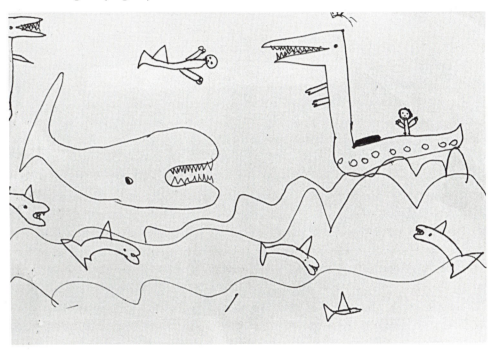

Figure 3

"Lisa, we might look at this picture from a purely mythic perspective and not discuss the child at all?"

"Why?"

"Because myth transcends the individual. It is the story of a group, a people, or the entire human race. When an individual story or picture arouses these universal themes, it becomes mythic. This picture can show us how an individual child participates in the universal story or stories. There are so many ways of approaching an image?"

"Do you think that some of the images relate to parents?"

"The whale on the left and the boat might be associated with parents because of their size and functions. It looks like the two might be squaring off while the sharks look on. But it is most important to approach them first as a whale and as a boat, to see them for what they are in the context of the child's picture."

"The whale looks menacing and capable of devouring the person on the boat. And the boat is strikingly archetypal."

"It is shaped like a serpent. The boat is suggestive of human construction and human presence in the realm of the sea, or it may represent the soul. It is a vehicle of passage. The whale is for me expressive of freedom; primal yet intelligent life. It is at home in the sea. In this drawing the whale appears to be a 'killer.' The shark is voracious, dangerous. It lives in the world below. The flying figure is a common dream image that sees everything, escapes; maybe it is part of the self that watches while action unfolds. The teeth suggest power, force and of course aggression. The sea is the vast space of life, the primal realm that is so much bigger than human existence. This might be connected to the more general fear that children have of being consumed by forces beyond their control. I see the complementary themes of aggression and companionship, safety and fear, flight and descent. I think that the child's fear of losing the parent is often a reversal of the fear of being consumed or devoured by parents. The two are closely linked. Monsters and parents are intimately connected to one another. The fear of losing the parent is far more acceptable to the child and thus appears more frequently. We have these positive and negative feelings toward parents. It is natural."

"What myth patterns do you see in this picture?" Lisa asked.

"Perhaps the story of Jonah and the whale has something to do with being swallowed by the parent and being released. If the boat and the whale are perceived as parental images, it seems that one is menacing and the other is protective. The two images are expressive of the interplay between dependence and autonomy. The person in the boat appears to be both safe and in peril. Psychosexual theory would see the boat as the mother. It carries the child and serves as an enclosure. The whale is more phallic. The perils of life and its immense, primal energy are also expressed in the picture. Non-human life forms are clearly more at home in this region. It seems that the only way the human being can deal with the sea is with the assistance of a boat, looking like a helping spirit in this picture, or through flights of imagination. The human being is not part of the sea life. The waves are large and dynamic. The sharks and whales appear to be very powerful. The human beings are not presented as possessing these qualities. I see parallels to *Moby Dick*."

"Does Melville's story corresponds to this picture?"

"It does in many ways. People have interpreted the whale as an expression of God which contrasts to the cool deity of the heavens portrayed in human form. In *Moby Dick* God is presented as a primal and physical energy. The whale is a master of regions where the human being is incapable of following. He 'dives deeper than Ishmael can go.' Melville described God as being 'indefinite' and he likened this to the experience of 'landlessness.' The divine is presented in terms of physical vitality, 'the deep' and 'harborless immensities.' Melville describes the ocean as the bottomless soul. He refers to the shark as an expression of our wicked nature. The angel is nothing but the shark governed well. In this drawing the child is engaging all of these elements and re-enacting one of our greatest mythic stories. I think the picture has to do with understanding the destructive and primal life forces that exist both within the person and in the immensity of the world."

"You seem to be advocating an archetypal understanding of children's art."

"It helps us to put the soul and the imagination back into the school experience. We have had developmental, psychosexual and cognitive theories of children's artistic expression, so why not add the archetypal which I believe is much closer to the experience of the child. They do not interpret their work according to psychological theories but rather interpret life according to their drawings. It would be interesting to ask the children which way of interpreting the images they like best. There is drama, story, myth and an animistic world view in the artworks of children. Their drawings of animals, whales and other figures are alive not only in their imagination but on the page as well. Children's drawings are loaded with soul. That's why we adults like them so much. They are expressive of what we have lost."

"Do YOU HAVE a theory of personality?" Lisa asked.

"I may have one, or a few, without realizing it. If I describe a theory of personality right now, it is likely that it will change the next time I attempt to reflect on the subject. To the extent that a theory of personality is an 'interpretation' of the person, then this theory will be characterized by the same principles that we have repeatedly observed in the interpretation of artworks: multiple interpretations and stories as opposed to single labels; projections on the part of the interpreter; intersubjectivity and dialogue between the interpreter and the subject of inquiry; the ineffectiveness of formulas; withholding meaning and letting phenomena speak for themselves; reversals and metaphoric substitutions; and just as images are formed through the specific properties of materials, then it can be assumed that people are similarly formed by their cultural and material environment. We also said that our interpretations of images are never final and fixed. They can only be further interpreted. The same applies to people. Your question is important to me, since I have never consciously operated within a particular theory of personality, nor set out to establish one of my own. I remember being impressed by J. L. Moreno's statement that the therapist without a theory has little value."

"And you do not have one?"

"Maybe I should do something about that. Theory provides direction and a sense of purpose. My orientation has always been one of avoiding identification with a single theory or school of thought. But I have been thinking lately that there may be an implied theory in my position. D. H. Lawrence said that 'art is utterly dependent on philosophy.' He felt that the artist's philosophy might never be stated and that it may be unconscious. Nevertheless, it is the theory, or better yet philosophy, that directs action. I think that we can prematurely formulate our philosophical positions in response to needs for control and certainty. Many of us are too quick in adopting the philosophies of other people. A deep and intelligent philosophy needs time to brew and take shape organically. The philosophy manifests itself through the patterns of our actions which are then subject to our reflection and organization. If I look at all of the focused studies that I have done on motivation in art; the phenomenon of therapy; cross-cultural psychotherapy and indigenous healing practices; interpretation; and the education of the creative arts therapist, I see that I have consistently supported multiple points of view. I am keenly interested in universal patterns and themes, but I seem to be coming out much more in favor of variety and multiplicity as prerequisites for human understanding. The only theory that is capable of containing human experience is the one that recognizes all of the other theories. The making of a theory is a creative act, a construction and an attempt to give meaning to life."

"You have written about the need to create an 'artistic theory of mental health.' "

"In art therapy, I think it is necessary to have theory that corresponds to the process of art. The theoretical guidance that we need can be found by direct reflection on what we do with art materials. Everything can be found in art itself. When I called for an artistic theory of mental health and therapy, I was challenging myself and art therapy to become more ambitious, self-confident and primary within the world of psychology. The deepest, most effective and lasting articulations of the human soul have always been made by the arts."

"Then why is it that artistic inquiry has been separated from psychological thought in the twentieth century?"

"One factor is the separation of psychology from the philosophical tradition. For example, psychology has no equivalent for the philosophical study of aesthetics. Our psychotherapeutic theories need philosophy and, particularly, epistemology. Theory making in its many forms must become the subject of psychological analysis. In addition to philosophy, psychology is desperately in need of history and a much larger perspective on the inquiry into the nature of the person. The creation of psychological theory also has its precedents in religion and mythology. Much of today's psychological theory is a narrow and shallow tributary from the mainstream."

"Is your theory of personality in therapy connected to philosophy, religion and mythology?"

"Absolutely. My difficulties in identifying with a single psychotherapeutic theory have to do with their denial of these elements."

"You seem close to the Jungians."

"I share many of their philosophical inclinations but to the extent that they are 'Jungians' and use a particular jargon with fixed terminology then I lose interest. I am much more interested in old and culturally universal concepts and words like 'soul,' 'will,' 'action,' 'angels,' 'demons' and 'transformations.' I am even more attached to specific images like trees, rocks, water, sun, goats, sparrows and colors. . .blue, crimson grey. I find myself directed toward names for things that are shared by different cultures and historical epochs. I am attracted to ideas that not only contain but reach out to engage vastly different phenomena. I think the operational process of opening to these multiplicities is more useful to me than the creation of a fixed theory which labels phenomena according to the way I might be seeing them at a particular time. As I said before, my interpretations will change. Again, there is a complete correspondence between how I interpret the image and the person. Dogmatic theoretical orientations are the institutionalization of the experience of their creators. It is remarkable how hungry people are for psychological dogma, for certainty."

"Are you suggesting that we cannot get beyond ambiguity?"

"When you ask this question I think of my friend and teacher, Truman Nelson. He is a novelist, a historian and a revolutionary activist. In our discussions on art and literature, he typically becomes irate about the literary values of our epoch and the tendency to celebrate the work of what he describes as 'the ambiguity boys.' Truman believes that the function of art lies in its ability to clarify the complexities of life and to transform experience. Art is the best thing we have for grasping the soul of the world. One of the functions of art is the expression of ambiguity and indecision since they are part of life. But taken in its entirety, art, and only art, manifests the range of human emotions and experience. If I am to consider a theory of personality, then I will look to art and images for instructions. They embody the varieties and commonalities of the human experience in a way that has not been achieved by any other mode of documentation. The arts, when viewed as an entirety, allow human experience, events and phenomena to reveal themselves to us. I think the depth of the arts lies in the fact that they are not intentionally or self-consciously attempting to present explanations. I would de-emphasize theory in understanding personality and emphasize a process of being open to the multiplicities of experience. Rather than encouraging a codification of psychological interpretations of the person, I encourage a process of ongoing interpretation. It is necessary to create a theory for every situation, just as we create a different artwork each time we come into contact with materials.

"Our understanding of the interpretative process reveals our understanding of the person. For example, the therapist who operates according to a rigid theory of the person will project this orientation into interpretations of images. Rather than beginning with a theory of the person, it is helpful for me to do the reverse and begin with images, and the artistic process, and then work back to the person. This way of working is consistent with the sacramental tradition in religion. The sacrament is the visible sign, the manifestation of the divine. In this respect the image and the artistic process manifest and make the person visible. People reveal themselves, their preoccupations and their depths, through art, so it seems logical to construct an image of the person from these manifestations. Since one artwork cannot embody the entirety of the human condition, it is unlikely that a single psychological theory can do this. The artist follows one work with another. There is an endless search. Satisfaction is momentary. We need many artworks, many theories and fresh interpretations."

"Do you identify with any of the twentieth century psychologists?"

"Right now I identify with Otto Rank, with his psychology of soul, his focus on the artist, his respect for Nietzsche. Rank, like the artist in our society, stands alone, in creative isolation. It seems that the best way to get to the universal, to the collective, is through our individuality. It is paradoxical. Going it alone, and of course with a few good companions, makes the multiplicities more accessible. Psychological schools of thought can be likened to tribal communities. They give a sense of belonging, coherence, explanations, comradery, but the tribe is an enclosure that restricts our understanding of what is outside its boundaries. Again, we have a paradox in how the individuality of the artist typically results in a strong motivation to relate to universal essence as a way of being connected to the world and transcending individuality. Does this sound too abstract?"

"I identify with what you are saying. I believe that you are describing the psyche of the artist. I like the way you present the paradox of how the artist chooses isolation in order to relate to the universal. In our epoch, the 'tribes' of culture and professions make it difficult to reach outside their boundaries. However, artists, particularly those who are closely involved with adapting to the marketplace, are as enclosed as any other group in our society. Do you agree?"

"It is important to distinguish between my image of the artist and the more general role of 'artists' in society. I have discovered that certain artists are the most difficult people that I have met when it comes to describing what we do in art therapy. Their idea of art is sometimes terribly narrow and formed by the trends of the contemporary art market. They have a difficult time relating to anything outside their framework. Yet, there is a clear trail though history of artists who are great depth-psychologists and transmitters of culture. . .William Blake, Emily Dickinson, Delacroix, Nietzsche, W. B. Yeats, James Joyce, D. H. Lawrence, Stanislavsky, Grotowski, Edna O'Brien, Picasso and many others. All of these artists have 'visions' that attempt to embody the essence of life and soul. Because of them art becomes what Lawrence described as a religion without dogma."

"You described how you identify with Rank because of his isolation. What do you mean by this?"

"I see Rank as an immensely important psychologist who does not have large numbers of followers. Even though he was a member of the original psychoanalytic group, he has a voice, tone and style that is distinctly his own. Within the psychoanalytic group, he is the person who had a clear grasp of the artist which he was also able to articulate in his writings."

"Do you work in complete isolation? Do you have a community of colleagues?"

"The isolation that I am describing is intellectual. It is important for me to be alone and to make my own way in the pursuit of knowledge. I do not follow a particular school of thought. It is interesting that those of us who try to relate to multiplicity, to many people and many theories are isolated. The same situation can be found within interpersonal relationships. Being close to many people seems to reinforce isolation, self-awareness. I think that this condition has been good for me in my professional and personal life. It has helped me realize how I am responsible for my personal and scholarly vitality. In my daily work I have close associates with whom I maintain an ongoing dialogue, particularly Paolo Knill. In the art therapy profession I have important colleagues in the United States, Canada, Europe and Israel. In psychology, Rudolf Arnheim and James Hillman have been valuable guides. There is also the community of artists throughout history. The company of these people is much more important to me than theory. Their ability to stand alone inspires me."

"So other people are necessary for intellectual isolation."

"The situation can be likened to how a monastic community operates."

"What do you mean?"

"For me, a monastery is a symbol of isolation. Yet, it is also a community with stable principles of social organization. The community and its rituals support the individual's inner search. The person who lives in the monastery is alone and with other people."

"What does the artistic community that you are describing do for you?"

"It gives me something to relate to and it demonstrates how to work. History and the tradition of ideas are what really matter and not an individual theory. Yet, it cannot be disputed that some people contribute more to the tradition than others. For me, the individual search is motivated by an urge to deepen my experience of life. Lawrence Durrell described how we have to make an effort if we are "to suck out the marrow of things." Most of what I am saying has been said before, and perhaps better by others. For example, in *The Tropic of Capricorn,* Henry Miller described a man who 'had no theory at all, except to penetrate to the very essence of things and, in the light of each fresh revelation to so live his life that there would be a minimum of discord between the truths which were revealed to him and the exemplification of these truths in action."

"Can you say more about how human relationships can be compared to theoretical inquiry?"

"Only that the artistic and scholarly isolation I have described is an attempt to relate more completely to life. Again, we have the paradox, with isolation deepening relationship."

"I do not understand what you mean by psychological multiplicity."

"My self is multiple and made up of varied elements and interests. In my daily life there are many things that I enjoy doing, some of which conflict with one another for time and attention. The tendency to attach an individual or single role to the person denies and avoids the multiplicity. The pleasures that some people take in repetition are manifestations of how routine keeps the underlying multiplicity in check. The same applies to dogmatic beliefs, all of which are sometimes blissful avoidances of multiplicity."

THEORY AS CREATION

"CAN IT BE SAID that you are only projecting your personal life into a theory of the person?"

"Of course, every theory is a projection or creation. But the theory that I project is one that is profoundly interested in the projections and creations of other people. As Ferrini says, 'Enter the caves of other people; there you will find me who is yourself.' Can you identify with this multiplicity in your life, Lisa?"

"I chose the art therapy profession because it will hopefully allow me to engage my many interests in art, teaching, psychotherapy, psychology, and world culture. Art therapy is giving me the opportunity to not only deepen my relationship with myself but with the world. The profession provides a container for my many interests."

"I think you have something here. Operating exclusively within the confines of a single theory limits our experience of the world which is so diversified. Yet, the profession of art therapy also provides a container. It is an expression of our historical epoch. Our professional container is an art that focuses on specific materials, images and other phenomena. The profession also provides a community of colleagues. Material things of this nature are not projections. The profession helps to deepen our relationship with people, things and the world. Hopefully, our profession will always serve us as a source of support. The profession is a container which holds varieties of people, methods and theoretical orientations. It is a vehicle that draws together diverse elements. . .people, art, soul, psychology, mythology, images, symbols, dreams, learning and healing. . .and places them into a form that is suitable to our epoch. The world must have the things that art therapy represents, and because of this I have confidence in the future of the profession."

"You seem to be raising the old issue of whether or not we create our environment or whether it creates us."

"There has to be a combination of both, an interplay. It is amazing to me how psychological theories throughout history have adopted only one dimension of a question like this and aggressively try to dominate the opposition. Perhaps this proves how important conflict is within our lives and how we need it to challenge complacency. We are the tools of our epoch. It shapes us into forms that function within a larger purpose. The strength of the whole is more than an accumulation of the parts. It is a dynamic organism composed of multiple elements that move in a variety of directions. These multiplicities need to be recognized, and my experience indicates that health demands that they have the freedom to express themselves. They might include different ethnic religious cultures living in a common geographic region or the varieties of interests that live within a single person. Terrible strife occurs when one element attempts to suppress the others."

"What do you mean when you say that we are 'the tools of our epoch'?"

"Professions, institutions, and especially individuals are embodiments of the historical epoch. Yet, the tool that is shaped by the epoch is also the instrumentality of transformation and the restructuring of the self and the world. This is the dynamic interplay that I spoke of. The world itself is a work of art that is shaped according to aesthetic principles. Rhythm is important to me. It contains multiple elements that work together and fit into a pattern. The rhythm is motion and it changes, incorporating new elements as it goes on. It can be simple and complex. For years, I have felt that rhythm is a fundamental principle of health. It touches everything, from the body's functioning to the planets. 'Soul music' is highly rhythmic. If we perceive personality as process and action and not as static entities codified into a theory, then rhythm is what holds the process together and provides the pace."

"How does history relate to psychology?"

"We embody our epochs, families and roles. This is why it is so important to think in terms of multiplicity and different options. Our position cannot be understood without history. In animistic societies history is expressed through attentiveness to ancestors and the community. Our materialisic era is more concerned with events. Yet, these focal points of ancestors and events are so universal that they seem to be present in all civilizations. It is a matter of emphasis. If psychologists were historians, they would not be so likely to embody the narrow constructs of their profession. Do you see how theories about human beings are themselves embodiments of the containers that they live within? We are what we make of ourselves with the materials of our era. Our personalities are manifestations of our process. A person is the embodiment of a particular mode of action and sensitivity."

PERSONALITY, AN INTERPLAY
OF MULTIPLICITIES

"THE EXPERIENCE of multiplicity within ourselves and within the world creates the need for a relationship to something essential. Each of us chooses what this is to be. Constant change and variation create an interest in what is universal. We may go searching in nature, religion, art, science, work, ourselves, other people or in a combination of these things."

"How do we manage this multiplicity that you speak of?" Lisa asked.

"It is interesting that you have chosen the word 'manage' in relation to multiplicity. Management and managing are important concepts in our culture. Right now, they embody the soul, energy and ambitions of this epoch. The majority of college students are now selecting management courses. Management graduate programs have expanded dramatically in the past ten years. I think that there is something to be learned from this world trend. It is difficult for me to see the society losing interest in the arts, humanities and the classics, but there is a message in the movement toward 'management.' The metaphor of management has grasped the imagination of our society. It is an active, dynamic, process-oriented concept as opposed to more passive and static areas of study. Psychology and the social sciences have also lost ground to management studies. The successful manager is described as creative, action-oriented, sensitive, cooperative and knowledgable about the changing needs of the world. It might be useful for us to see if the world of business, which would appear to be so far removed from art therapy, corresponds to the theory of the person that I am trying to present. If the theory has validity, it should be capable of application to varied situations."

"How would you do this?"

"Let's apply methods of management to the self which is a microcosm of the group, the community and the society. Our beings are a dynamic 'management' of different forces, manifesting themselves freely in a state of health. The skillful manager relates pragmatically to whatever presents itself within the field of operation. Business studies may be closer to the essence of our world today than the theoretically based social sciences, because they deal directly with diversified phenomena, with multiplicity, interaction, change. Management does not operate according to a single dogma. It reflects the multicultural reality of the world, multiple needs and products. Like art, management values what works within a material context.

"If the management metaphor is offensive or overly identified with the world of business, we can substitute it with the description of the self as an 'interplay' of multiple elements and interests. These forces are shaped by my context and my free will. The will gives shape to experience. It is sensitive to the interplay of forces in the environment and within other people. It restructures experience in response to its interpretation of what is needed to maintain vitality. So there is an interplay of dynamic forces that needs to be shaped within the person. This interplay also takes place in relationships, in therapy, in groups, and in the world at large. All of these centers of activity interact with each other in a complex interplay of dynamic action. The accurate profile of the person reveals this interplay or inter-conflict in its many forms. Just as we cannot describe a complex organization or an image with a single label or theory of operation, we similarly cannot describe the person in this way. Every attempt at description demands a theoretical response that is unique to the phenomena being reviewed. Does this image help to convey a sense of multiplicity?"

"Yes. But how do we guide ourselves through it all? The more I see, the more complex it becomes."

"This is where the trend toward management studies offers a useful insight into the psychic condition of the world. I like the orientation to action, process and transformation. As artists, we share many things with the managers. Psychology and psychiatry are problematic when they take static and self-enclosed concepts and project them onto the totality. No study of the person can approach completeness and depth without other elements of human reflection. . .art, philosophy, religion, history, science and, of course, business. Maybe business studies, because of their direct dealings with phenomena and action, are closer to the soul of the world. Keep in mind that my definition of soul has to do with physical vitality and action. Jung defined the soul as 'the living thing' in human beings, 'that which lives of itself and causes life.' In *Psychological Types* he says that if we cannot differentiate ourselves from the roles we take in life, then our inner lives become restricted. 'In such a case the soul is always projected into a corresponding real object, with which a relation of absolute dependence exists.' People in business get so identified with their roles as managers, the companies they serve, or their products that they do not see how they may be acting-out deeper psychic processes. They do not see themselves as manifesting the soul of the world. I am interested in understanding what the metaphor of management embodies. I keep coming back to the process of opening to the person before me, to myself and to images. In order to open effectively to a dialogue or to an experience, I have to let go of my preconceptions and even my theories. Opening in this way is not easy. There is always something to distract me, some voice that tries to take me away. As I said in *Educating the Creative Arts Therapist* I have found 'opening' to be one of the most essential and challenging principles of operation in both therapy and life. It is very simple, but yet I am always working on it and I predict that I will never stop trying to improve myself in this way."

"How does this theory of multiplicity relate to mental illness?"

"During acute illness the person does not have the ability to manage the interplay between the self and the world. Everything is seen from the perspective of distorted perceptions."

"How do you define the distorted perception?"

"Since every perception is a point of view, then it can be argued that the supposedly distorted image is as valid as any other. The 'distortion' can be a creative perception that is defined by its deviation from the viewpoint of people in general. Some people cleverly manage their relationship with the world from the perspective of the distorted image. Elaborate and imaginative constructions are made on this basis. My colleague Baruch Zadick in Israel told me about a man that he was seeing in therapy who would begin his session each week by talking about how all of the taxi cabs in the city were after him. Growing frustrated with this repetitious story, Baruch said that he had some very good connections with the police and maybe he could help out with the problem. The patient became angry and said that since Baruch was a psychologist, he should know better than to believe such a story. The man concretized his fears into a perspective on life that he did not want to abandon. Perhaps, he wanted to think that people were after him and thus paying attention to him. He might prefer this image to one of being alone in the world. The definition of illness can be difficult. In some cases the 'disturbed' mind may simply be a more imaginative one. I try to define illness on a situational basis, in relation to the context of the person's life, the ability to function, to find satisfaction and to give something to the world. I think it is a good idea to strive to be tolerant of those who may be more imaginative than me. Some of these more imaginative people may be living the dream in a way that I am incapable of. Have you thought about how the dream expresses multiplicity?"

"My dreams have many themes, many images that rarely follow a single pattern. In this respect the dream presents strong evidence for the multiplicity of the psyche. All of these elements do live together with one another in the dream. Their differences are not integrated into a single unity. Your description of the interplay of forces within the individual as a microcosm of the larger interplay in the world makes me realize that global conflict is an amplification of disturbance within the self. Do you agree?"

"Yes. The eternal problem is the projection of a single perspective or bias onto the world. The individual person does this, the individual theory, religion, ideology and nation. This projection, often moralistic, of what works for me onto the world as a whole is a hopeless crusade. Projection becomes prescription. In *Educating the Creative Arts Therapist* I said that inspiration is far more effective than prescription. The good leaders are the ones who are sensitive and realize that they will never be able to embody the needs and interests of all of the people that they serve. They facilitate the interplay of multiple elements within the group, organization or nation and enable it to achieve certain collective goals. I have said before that the strongest group is the one that most thoroughly recognizes and respects the individual elements and differences within it and allows them to express themselves fully. The same applies to the individual person. So, we are again working backwards here from what we have learned through experience in groups, to the person. I find the correspondence of dynamics between the individual psyche and the group to be a useful test of validity. I believe that the individual can only be understood within the context of relationships to other people and the world. There is a complete correspondence between the global and the individual. My theory of personality is an interplay between multiple elements. Identity is process, the form of the dialogue. It is an expression of my changing relationship to the world."

"And the world is always changing. Sometimes I think it is too much. Do you also experience this?"

"Yes, most definitely."

"What do you do about it?"

"I might take a rest and limit what I am doing. I have repeatedly discovered how highly focused activities and sustained relationships with particular things bring me into the best contact with the universal."

"But this sense of the universal may just be your individual projection."

"You are right. It goes round and round. The earth does not live in a single cultural container. As suggested by Melville, this world is a wondrous and sometime brutal immensity. The person can be understood only through interactions with the world. The different religions and political systems are ingenious creations. But they often desire to eliminate and consume their neighbors. All of these traits can be seen in the individual person and in small groups."

"How do we engage them in art therapy?"

"We work hard at sorting things out and finding ways to live with these multiple elements rather than have them conducting war with one another. Analytically oriented art therapy focuses on understanding the many images and voices within us. But in order to know them, we have to see their shape and physical characteristics. They must express themselves and come forward in order to be known. The images that emerge in art therapy are manifestations of this inner life. I cannot envision a depth psychology without them. We have to respect the different things which often compete with one another for time and attention and understand our projections. Stronger elements support the expression of weaker ones in therapy where we act forcely but also listen sensitively. All of these things live together in our artworks. Each has its place in a composition. Conflict, tension, opposition and contradictions give life to the artwork. They are essential to its vitality."

IDENTITY, A PROCESS
OF INTERPRETATION

"I AM CURIOUS as to how you perceive identity."

"Identity is the process of interpretation," I said. "In this respect I do not know if it exists at all as a single entity for me. It is not a fixed image or label. My identity is scattered about in the form of my interpretations of myself and those of other people, and all of these interpretations are in a process of constant change and transformation. There is always something new to be revealed and something old to be rediscovered. I might be useful and more psychologically accurate to completely eliminate concepts of personality and identity and concentrate more on the process of interpretation. Again, interpretation is a process rather than a specific entity as suggested by concepts of identity and personality. The arts can be helpful to us here. I believe that real things like portraits, stories, biographies and autobiographies are much better terms than identity. Or perhaps identity can be redefined as portraits, stories and interpretations."

"Can you give me an example of what you mean?"

"Let's begin with the portrait. Experience and history have demonstrated that if more than one artist paints a portrait of a single person within the same time period, these portraits will differ from one another. The same can be said of a series of self-portraits. Variation is guaranteed. What is consistent is the process of painting the portrait. I find this process of creating portraits to be the closest I can get to describing myself or another person. Variation is furthered by changing media. Paintings, drawings, sculpture, photographs and written descriptions all present interpretations of the person that are shaped as much by the qualities of the artistic materials as by the consciousness of the artist.

The potential for formal variations appears to be endless. Photographic portraiture would seem to be the medium that minimizes variation from portrait to portrait. Yet, our experience with photography indicates subtle but definite variations in images of people that have been taken from a fixed perspective. Lighting, environment, the time of day, the changing moods and expressions of the person, all contribute to making successive portraits, composed by a single artist, distinctly different from one another. History has shown that the same variation characterizes biographies and autobiographies dealing with a single person. It is predictable that a series of autobiographies produced by an imaginative writer will vary considerably, even if they deal with the same events. Our experience with art interpretation reveals that people will tell varied stories in response to the same image. Some interpretations will relate to the person better than others, but as I said earlier no single image will describe the complete person at a particular time. Therefore, it seems unlikely that a permanent and fixed identity or self-image is possible. In *Moby Dick,* Melville said:

> The great Leviathan is that one creature in the world which must remain unpainted to the last. True, one portrait may hit the mark much nearer than another, but none can hit it with any very considerable degree of exactness. So there is no earthly way of finding out precisely what the whale really looks like. And the only mode in which you can derive even a tolerable idea of his living contour, is by going a whaling yourself. . . .

DIAGNOSTIC LABELS

"MELVILLE'S message seems to be: 'Get involved with the thing that you are trying to understand.' Portraits are useful, but they cannot substitute for direct experience with a person. I have a difficult time in the clinic when I am asked to suggest a diagnostic label for people. I am much more comfortable describing my relationships to children and their families. I can give my opinion of how they are managing. It seems from what you have said about identity that you question the validity of diagnostic labels."

"The labeling approach to diagnosis is a projection of an attitude toward classification that desires to place everything in its proper place. It assumes that the soul can be organized like a tidy pantry with the canned tomatoes in one area and beans in another. People do not lend themselves to these tidy attitudes. A labeling approach to identity assumes that the individual has definitive characteristics that can be isolated as persistent traits. I do not think that the fingerprint, identity number or unique body traits approach fits the soul. In addition to the flux that we have been discussing, there are the non-personal aspects of our inner lives, what we might describe as more universal energies and images that do not belong to us. Labeling approaches to personality, identity and clinical diagnosis are all projections of attitudes of material possession. They attempt to sort out who owns what and to keep things in their place. It is necessary to look into what our ideas assume and where our concepts come from. I am not advocating a mystical approach to working with people in therapy. I am trying to be more accurate in my observations of people and more capable of understanding what is going on in me and in our relationship. We need ideas that are more descriptive of experience. The classification systems are themselves based on very outmoded scientific concepts.

"Labeling also assumes authority and the right of the diagnostician to make judgments. As therapists, we certainly have a responsibility to describe what we see and to make recommendations for improvement, but these clinical activities do not in any way require labeling. The soul and the life of the person are in constant movement. The use of diagnostic labels is actually one of the most anti-therapeutic things that we can do. The label serves the purpose of keeping people in their designated places. This can be catastrophic with psychopathological labels. Even positive and illustrious labels, titles and degrees can become serious obstacles to change and imaginative transformation. What most therapists actually do is help people to unfix and discard old labels. However, process-oriented clinical descriptions that use jargon and terminology that help us to understand behaviors and inner-feeling states can be useful. To the extent to which clinical language is descriptive of phenomena, I cannot argue with it. But this descriptiveness cannot attempt to classify people and place them on a pantry shelf. I am in agreement with James Hillman who believes that psychological language lacks imagination. The effort to fit what we see in a person into standard forms limits our descriptive powers. I am more interested in the broader use of metaphors, imagination and simple language in clinical descriptions. Clinical work will benefit from a more vital and descriptive language."

"In my life the labels that other people have placed on me and that I have placed on myself have been obstructions," Lisa said.

"It is good that you mention the labels that we attach to ourselves. These can be the most oppressive. What kind of labels have you given to yourself?"

"As a child, I was known as quiet but intelligent. This description of me was accurate and based on facts. The original labels were benign and well intended, but they began to rule my life. The label did not change. During all of this I had many feelings, some of which were complex and confusing, and they did not fit with the label. I was a shy child and I did not become involved in the more aggressive games and activities that other children participated in. Because I was 'shy and quiet,' I progressively began to feel that I was not aggressive. I attached this 'non-aggressive' label to myself and over time I began to act in this way. It has caused me great difficulty because I now know that my inner being is extremely aggressive. I blocked this energy for most of my life. My father has always been an outgoing and charming man. He never called me 'quiet' or 'non-aggressive' and I never felt that he used me to ventilate his frustrations. His consistent kindness was actually a problem, in that I could not turn my aggression toward him, and I increasingly turned it on myself. As a teenager and young woman, I would often act out my aggression on my father. He was safe. As confusing and difficult as it all was, this stormy period in my relationship with my father was critically important for me. It was the beginning of my taking the initiative in being more aggressive and forceful. It was often a mess, because I did not know how to do it. I was breaking out of my stereotype and probably trying to have a new kind of relationship with him, something more complete and responsive to my real nature as a person."

KILLING AND RESURRECTING
THE FATHER

"THE PSYCHOANALYTIC emphasis on the relationship between parents and children is correct in terms of tuning into one of the greatest sources of emotional energy as well as conflict. We can empirically show how parent-child relationships are the most consistently dynamic sources of energy in psychotherapy. However, I think there needs to be a distinction between the relevance of what the psychoanalysts looked at and the manner in which they interpreted the phenomena. I admire their ability to select the terrain for exploration, but I am not as enthusiastic about what they built.

"What you have described about your relationship to your father is a milder version of a theme that I have heard from many other women in my training groups in different parts of the world. They are stabbing their fathers in their artworks, drowning them, blowing them up. In general, I believe that these emotional enactments are attempts to get the father out of the way so that they can achieve autonomy. It is an emotional liberation movement as well as a desire to have a new kind of relationship with the father as you have said. The same pattern can be seen in mother-daughter relationships and between sons and both parents. It is not reserved exclusively for fathers and daughters. However, the theme is particularly strong with women, because they are not only challenging the father but all of the institutions of patriarchal society. These feminine transformations of culture are major revolutions of consciousness. In many ways they are more influential and far-reaching than some of the governmental revolutions that our society has experienced, because they have profoundly affected not only the dynamics of daily life but also the inner movings of the soul. So, it is no wonder that women are symbolically killing their fathers in the artworks that they do in my groups. We cannot separate the personal experience from the larger transformations of our epoch. Sometimes they go after me with this killing energy."

"Is the killing useful?"

"Generally, it is a good, healthy and transformative experience. I have had to learn how to embrace the killing. This has taken me many years and a number of significant failures. The disasters have taught me that the killing follows the pattern of the Dionysian myth where the maenads tore him to pieces but also put him back together again, lovingly. I am after all a male and usually in the leadership role. Children must be given the freedom to get the parent out of the way, to revolt. They do this in order to establish themselves as distinct from their parents. The fear that children have of losing their parents, of being abandoned, is reversed in the adult scenario where there is a desire to be liberated from them. I have found that people who symbolically kill their parents in therapy generally experience tremendous love in connection with the experience. Aggression and love are so deeply related. Since our society does not provide us with initiation rites for leaving our parents, we do it instinctually, blindly and sometimes like terrorists. This revolution against the parent is inevitable. In addition to our natural parents, we go through the process with mentors, teachers and role models. We have to get beyond their direct influence in order to act spontaneously. The influence and inspiration of the teacher has to become part of us. It is necessary to distinguish between what is mine, what belongs to the teacher and what we share."

"I have experienced a more intense revolution against teachers and certain men than against my father. My father has generally given me unusual freedom to be myself and he has reacted fairly well, but not perfectly, to my changes. He has not been an oppressor or even a dominating figure in my life, so I have not revolted against him. At times, I have wished that he would be more aggressive. This fighting with the father can be useful. I have had my battles with other men."

"I am convinced that we define and shape ourselves through these conflicts. I cannot imagine myself without them. If we do not have the battles with our parents, we will have them with other people. Nietzsche's death of God fantasy was an expression of his need to kill the ultimate authority figure in order to create new meanings and values. He specifically commented on how 'the new, conscious culture kills the old culture' as well as 'the distrust of progress.' This corresponds to what women say about having to consciously deal with what was done unconsciously to them, by themselves and others. Nietzsche affirms the necessity of killing culture in order to prepare the way for new transformations. The word 'killing' in this respect suggests conscious and deliberate action."

"Perhaps this theme of killing the father is one of the emotional and political metaphors created by this era," Lisa said.

"There is a definite contagion factor, and the external forms of our pathologies and liberation movements do embody the concerns of particular eras."

"This can be seen in the present frequency of 'eating disorders,' which are symptoms and actions that manifest a wide range of inner conflicts. Struggles with parents seem more eternal."

"Parents are psychologically fundamental to our lives, because we spend so much time with them and they know us so well. There are also the instinctual and social responsibilities which deepen the parent-child relationship. Yet, I think that the psychoanalytic tradition has placed excessive emphasis on the nuclear family in determining how the psyche works. For example, Otto Rank in *Psychology and the Soul* (1950) described Freud's relationship with his mentor and colleague, the Viennese physician Joseph Breuer, who introduced Freud to the possibility of treating hysteria through hypnosis and the cathartic method of talking about problems. Rank believed that Freud confused the psychodynamic impact of the death of his father with his separation from Breuer. In the foreword to the second edition of the *Interpretation of Dreams* (1909), Freud said that the death of the father was the most important event and the most significant loss in a man's life. Rank believed that this 'subjective source' became 'the basis for Freud's entire psychoanalytic psychology.' He also believed that Freud's creative contributions were more concerned with the art of interpreting dreams, subjectively, than with the creation of an objective science. I do not think that this kind of criticism lessens Freud's position. It rather clarifies what he did and makes him more of an artist. In suggesting that a fantasy of objectivity lies behind the psychoanalytic tradition, Rank is terribly helpful to all of us. This knowledge frees us from the necessity of following prescribed procedures and psychological 'truths' and ultimately increases the range of possibilities for inquiry. Depth psychology is in essence a science, or better yet an art, of interpretation. Subjectivity is its primary tool. Depth psychology is much more of an interplay between imaginative possibilities than a replicable laboratory procedure.

'Hard' science became associated with depth psychology because of its social esteem and intellectual influence at the turn of the century and throughout the twentieth century. Ideas conform to the containers and fantasies of the marketplace. Depth psychology cannot be accurately defined within the fantasy of a single psychological source.

"Let's return to Freud. I do not wish to deny the validity of his statement about the importance of his father. What is problematic is the Freudian tendency to base a theory and an entire science upon a single interpretation. My experience is always revealing how there are many interpretative possibilities. Rank believed that Freud was unaware of principle sources for his subjective psychology and masked the primary influence of Breuer on his work. He suggests that Freud's description of the influence of his father on the creation of the *Interpretation of Dreams* contradicts what was happening in Freud's life at the time. In this respect, the entire psychoanalytic edifice can be perceived as an avoidance of the real influences of the immediate environment. The fantasy of the ongoing primacy of early childhood and the nuclear family can take us away from present possibilities. Freudian psychology could benefit from initiation rites that separate the child from the parent. Hillman suggests that Freudians keep returning to childhood in order to rediscover the imagination that is absent in their adult lives.

"Rank said that psychology is 'an essentially projective affair.' He documented how the death of Freud's father was simultaneous with the separation from Breuer who gave Freud 'the key' to his clinical work. According to Rank, Freud had to separate from the influence of Breuer in order to make his own contributions. Rank used the words 'death' and 'killing' to describe what Freud did to his friend Breuer. He believed that Freud denied the 'killing' of Breuer and replaced it with the 'far less painful' death of his father. Rank felt that if Freud had focused less on his father in the interpretation of his dreams, the image of Breuer would have appeared because of his 'unsuccessful attempt to put the living Breuer out of the way.' He described how Freud did not interpret the appearance of his father in his dreams and neglected one of the principle phenomenon of dream interpretation: the appearance of one person in the place of another. Rank maintains that Freud's 'displacement into the past' of his feelings for Breuer onto his father was 'therapy and not psychology' and that it documents 'the birth of psychology from self-illusion.' He felt that Freud was intellectualizing his dream interpretation and finding an acceptable and convenient interpretation. Wish fulfillment, according to Rank, can be seen in the dream's interpretation rather than its content. Rank also believed that interpretation will always conform to the prevailing 'spiritual ideologies of an era.'

"For our purposes right now it matters little to me what the 'correct' interpretations of Freud's dreams or psychology are; whether his theories were based more on self-illusion or enlightenment. What I care about is the actual work that he did and the contributions that he made. I am interested in Rank's story, or fantasy, about Freud. I was fascinated to read his account of Freud's 'killing' of Breuer and the father figure that he represented. Rank's observations corresponded completely with what I am observing in the dreams, artworks and stories of the people in my art therapy training groups. There is the consistent theme of children killing parents. The story that Rank tells of Freud 'killing' Breuer in order to achieve his independence and rid himself of the restrictive influence of the other man fits the universal theme. Rank himself did not seem to be aware of the fact that he was doing the same thing to Freud and this makes the story even more believable."

"Do you think that this symbolic killing of the parents is a psychological necessity?"

"The fact that it is so common suggests this. But I do not want to repeat the old psychoanalytic errors and attempts to make all stories and interpretations fit into this framework. Endless variations are more likely. The universality of initiation rites and the ritualistic death enactments that are often associated with them makes me think that 'killing' childhood dependency relationships with parents is a human necessity. It amazes me how indigenous cultures do these rituals so intelligently and our supposedly advanced civilization does it blindly and violently. Parents also have to let go of their children and former patterns. The 'killing' we are describing refers to attitudes, behaviors, and habits."

"How do you relate to the sexual aspects of the Freudian interpretation of the Oedipus myth?"

"I cannot deny the physical attraction of the young child for the parent and vice versa. Our first love relationships are with our parents. They are physical and intimate relationships. Again, the initiation rites of indigenous cultures help people to clarify the relationships between children and parents and to make necessary distinctions and separations. Our culture is more confused in its practices and thus we have more confused psyches. Michel Foucault has documented our history with the problematization of sexuality. I do not want to throw away the Freudian interpretation of the Oedipal myth which is sometimes accurate and useful. However, I do want to introduce new possibilities. Con-

ventional psychoanalytic interpretations of the Oedipal myth can be perceived as an expression of the fantasies of parents and their wanting to
be desired by their children. Sexual relations between parents and children are the responsibility of parents. Explicitly sexual actions are generally initiated by parents as well as the myths that support them.

"What I am observing in my work in terms of women's relationships
to fathers has little to do with interpretations of the Oedipal or Electra
myths that suggest that they may be desiring their fathers. It may be
possible that we are all denying these feelings, but I would prefer to believe what people tell me. Rather than desiring the father as a love object, I see women trying to get him out of the way together with
patriarchal society. They are attacking what Nietzsche presented as the
old and unconscious culture. Very often, the objective may be the creation of a new and more mature love relationship with the father in which
the daughter's independence and equality is acknowledged.

"All of this is always complex and cannot fit into a single formula, including the one I may be proposing. The killing or separation is rarely
clean. There is often an accompanied sense of guilt and this ties in with
the childhood fear of causing the parents' death. Through these fears we
empower ourselves to be the imaginary directors of our parents' fates.
Others think that they want to separate from their parents, but they
really want to hold on and they fear the possible abandonment, rejection
or isolation that may occur. They have a difficult time finding the
courage to separate and live autonomously."

"Do you feel that there are degrees of killing and aggression directed
toward parents?"

"In many cases the intensity of the revolution is proportionate to the
degree of the repression that is rebelled against. Judgmental, authoritative parents are apt to get more violent resistance from their children.
But once again there cannot be a formula for the emotions. The woman
who grew up with the totally permissive, loving and supportive father
might rebel because he did not set 'limits' and expose her to the realities
of opposition that exist in the world. The same applies to men with their
fathers and mothers. There seems to be an inevitable criticism of the
parent that accompanies the emergence of the child's judgment and autonomy."

"But isn't there a tendency to blame the father and the mother for
everything?"

"Yes. And this is not only the fault of the child. Parental psychologies
are more responsible. Just as parents may fantasize themselves as the

objects of the child's desire, our deterministic psychologies have convinced us that parents are also the architects of the child's character. This is a one-sided response that once again focuses too much attention on the parents. Why don't we have complementary psychologies that show how children shape the characters of their parents. The power balance has been turned excessively toward the parents and thus the need for revolution."

"I think that I tend to project too much responsibility and power onto other people. I am trying to avoid living my life according to someone else's standards of perfection."

"This is closely related to the rebellion against the father that I have been observing in my work. I would like to describe a dream that Leslie, who is working with me in an art and dream group, presented. She is involved right now in the process of understanding her relationship to her father who is in his early eighties. She called the dream 'leaving my father's boat.'

> I am in my father's power boat speeding through a harbor which is full of buoys and mooring markers. I am afraid that I will tangle the propeller in the lines. There is a huge canvas covering the front of the boat which is making steering difficult and I am forced to lean far over the side of the boat in order to see. I decide to anchor the boat because I fear becoming stuck. I dive into the water and begin to swim. I reach the entrance to the harbor which is marked by a long stone causeway. As I swim up to the end of the causeway the water becomes calm and warm and I notice that it tastes less salty than the water I had been swimming in. Thinking there is a spring feeding into the ocean, I reach down to find the opening. At first I feel a metal pipe but then I realize that I am holding onto a person's knee. I pull on the leg and a woman's body floats to the surface next to me. She is my age and wearing a grey, fitted jacket and a tweedy skirt, reminding me of a conservative schoolteacher. Her hair is floating around her head and she is wearing tourquoise eyeliner underneath each eye which is still visible, so I realize that she has just died. I decide that I must inform the police and I swim back to shore where my car is parked. I have difficulty finding my car. I go to the wrong car and almost climb in. As I continue to look for my car, I notice an oriental man standing in the garage watching me. He is dressed in black and has long, black hair. I suddenly realize that he killed the woman and he knows that I know this. I am worried that he will try to stop me from leaving, but he just stands and watches me. I find my car and as I get in, I wake up from the dream.

"It is remarkable how her dream images illustrate the themes that we have been discussing. The images are actually more than illustrations.

They deepen my involvement with the issues because of the way they present a complex emotional situation with such clarity, vividness and brevity. I am interested in what Leslie said about the dream."

"Her first response was fear. She woke up with a clear memory of the dream which she shared with her husband. Telling the dream helped her to diffuse what she described as the 'terrifying power' of the images. During the next day she was involved with the frightening images of the dead woman and the oriental man. Leslie's husband was more interested in her father's boat and he asked her why she 'bailed out.' She said that she left because she could not see and that she felt that she was in danger. Leslie had just been married and her relationship with her father had been troublesome since the wedding. She felt 'estranged' from him and she was concentrating on her relationship with her father in her therapy. Leslie's father had always accepted her. They look alike and they had a history of supporting each other in the family.

"She made this statement about the dream:

> Leaving the boat in the dream connects to separating from my father. I was facing constant danger in the boat and I had no choice but to leave. Lately, I have been feeling trapped by some of the ways that I relate to people and these are ways that I have learned from my father. I want to be able to see clearly and to be seen for who I am. I do not want to be shielded behind a canvas that blocks my visibility and does not allow others to see me.
>
> Diving into the water suggests entering a world of the unknown, the underworld, and I feel I am going there in this journey of separation from my father. I am forever leaving his way of doing things and searching for my way. I am intrigued by the conversation I had with you about the 'killing of parents.' I felt that I had already killed my mother whose influence had always been clearly negative for me. But the idea of killing my father was unfathomable.
>
> I felt confused and alarmed by the dead woman, and her image kept appearing before me. Initially, I was appalled by my encounter with this new world of the dead woman. I realize that she could be the type of woman my father would like me to be: dressed in conservative clothing and teaching school. My life in the world has been separate from my father for many years but my inner life was still connected. By taking control of my inner life I am killing this fantasy image of me as the tweedy woman. I am killing the image not only for him but for myself, because I have always felt guilty for not being more traditional and conservative for him. The dream may be portraying that part of me that is dead for my father and me and indicating the new image, the tourquoise eyeliner.
>
> The need to push my father away is new and it is the most painful thing in my life right now. He is old and probably will not be with us

much longer. I cannot bear the thought of putting up a wall between us, but I feel this is happening now. I do not want to confront him at this point. I just want to enjoy him and learn from him in his last years. I do not want to push him away. It is difficult because I have so much rage about his role in the family and his inability to protect me from my mother.

The oriental man troubled me until I began to think of him as the person who killed the part of me that was causing my guilt. He is dark, quiet and very still. He only watches me and makes no attempt to detain me. I am beginning to feel that this man is my helper and my partner in my journey. He has killed what I no longer need and no longer want. He has prepared the way for the first part of the journey. I expect that he will reappear, perhaps in a different guise, as I continue to change during my search. I woke up feeling scared and suspicious of this oriental man dressed in black. If I had not developed a relationship with him and explored his part of the dream, I would still feel alienated from him. As a result of the dreamwork and the drawings I have done, I feel reassured by his presence and I am relying on him and trusting him as a guide. I also sense that he is the dark side of me that I fear, because I do not understand it and do not want to look at it. He might be the dark side that I share with my father. My fear is reduced when I see that this side of me can be useful.

My relationship to this dream has changed significantly since it first appeared. It seems as though the images are so strong that they are commanding me to explore them. The dream has become a new friend. The friendship with the dream parallels what I go through in relationships with people. First, I have an immediate reaction. Then we struggle to understand each other. Finally, there is a sense of integration with the dream and the opportunity for further long-term understanding. The friendship can continue for years, always revealing new things. But the relationship cannot be pushed too fast. This would destroy the open and trusting feeling that we have together.

"Leslie's experience seems to support your belief that we experience passage rites in our dreams. I identify with her passage into autonomy, becoming herself and leaving behind her old role within the family."

"Leslie has spoken to me about both of these points. She said that the ritual of her father letting her go at the marriage had a profound impact on her and may have helped to generate this dream. She was married in a church where the father 'presents' rather than 'gives away' the bride. She told me that she likes this orientation, but that in her case her father really gave her away. She talked about how as a child she wanted her parents to stay the same and to remain in fixed roles. She also had her fixed role in the family and this did not fit her changing life structure. For Leslie, the wedding ritual facilitated the restructuring that she needs in her relationship to her father. She was amused at how the minister made such a point at her wedding of saying how the church is progressive now and that fathers no longer give their daughters away. Leslie believes that her relationship with her father could not change until he gave her up, not as a material possession but in terms of their old relationship. Tribal societies are perhaps clearer in their rites of passage, because they are closer to the natural world where animals have little trouble in letting go of their children. Our psychologies are themselves neurotic, in that they cling to the parent-child relationship as an exclusive source of meaning throughout a person's life."

"While she was working with the dream, did Leslie ever doubt the necessity of killing her parents?"

"I do not think so. She was constantly engaged with that theme, and what was at first an unthinkable idea was helpful in enabling her to become more aware of her need to separate from old patterns. She said that she had to become conscious of having a new relationship with her father based on where they both stand in the present. She is separating from her father in order to get closer to him. She is letting go of her own fixed labels of who her father is and who she is in relation to him. The process was exciting for her."

"Did Leslie's picture of her dream restructure the experience?"

"Yes. I do not think that it is possible to replicate the intricacies of dreams in artworks. People often become frustrated in art therapy when the drawing does not correspond to what they saw in the dream. The same applies to representations of any life form. Art inteprets the dream in relation to where we are at the moment. This restructuring is most useful in art therapy, since it graphically demonstrates where we are with the dream at a particular time. Leslie's drawing was large and colorful. She emphasized the oriental man, the dead woman and the blue water. Her emotions were engaged with the dead woman. She focused on her hand reaching down and touching the dead woman's knee, and she surrounded this part of the picture with an intense red which she described as expressive of surprise and emotion. The second most prominent part of the picture was the dead woman's head with her hair spread and floating in the water. The reaching for the leg looks sensuous. This part of the dream is accompanied by the sensation of swimming into calm water that tastes 'less salty.' Leslie was also reaching down for a spring that she thought might be flowing into the ocean. The leg is totally exposed and not covered by the tweed skirt. Perhaps, the tweedie woman has died and she is reaching down for the passionate woman.

Leslie did not draw her father or the boat but emphasized 'the wake of his boat.' He is out of the picture for the time being, but his wake is prominently present together with the blue water that she has entered. The picture clearly corresponds to what Leslie is saying right now. She has to work with herself, with the assistance of friends and helpers like the oriental man, in order to re-engage her father. She sometimes struggles for understanding. As she said in her dream, the steering is difficult."

"Were you able to work with all the images in Leslie's dream?"

"That is a helpful question. I do not think that it is ever possible to equally engage every image. We tend to go with whatever is emerging at the moment, in this case with both Leslie and me. Dreams are rich with imagery. They are the gold mines of the psyche. I dreamt once, many years ago, of finding myself in an infinite expanse covered with gold. Dreams are like this. Because we are human, we have to select what we will concentrate on at a particular time. It would be madness to try to collect and carry all of the gold lying on the infinite plain. I do not want to exclusively emphasize gold as the object of value which might be wood, water, grain, sand, whatever the soul desires.

"For example, with Leslie's dream we did not work with the harbor full of buoys and mooring markers; her fear of tangling these lines in the propeller; the huge canvas; the anchor; her fear of being stuck; the entrance to the harbor with its long, stone causeway; the spring; the police; her parked car; her difficulty finding the car; almost getting into the wrong car; the discovery of her car; etc. Every one of these images can be a rich mine of discovery. Perhaps we will engage them in one of our later sessions, or Leslie might choose to work with another dream. It is possible that some of the images will reappear in her dreams or her art, and we may deal with them within that context.

"Leslie was inspired by the work of Kit, another participant in the training group who was working with the father-daughter theme before she had her boat dream. We activate one another and encourage the contagion of metaphors that I mentioned earlier."

"Kit presented this dream to the training group:

> I was in a beautiful condominium, lying close to the fireplace with Kenny who was my first boyfriend. I was fifteen when I met him. In the dream we were close to each other, but we did not kiss. Our faces were inches apart and this made the experience more powerful than if we were touching. His head was in my lap. It was important that he was in my lap rather than me in his. There was a shirt hanging near the fire. I was afraid it would burn, but it felt like I was in control. The

door was locked. My father burst in with a big fire extinguisher that he was shooting all over the apartment and into somebody else's house, which seemed to be more like a hotel room. There was a fire starting in the roof of a cathedral in the distance. It was the size of the small, dark spots that magnifying glasses make on paper if you hold them up to the sun. I could see the church roof with a cross, and in between my window and the church there was an apartment house totally exposed with no exterior walls. It was as though someone had ripped the walls off. It was like a dollhouse with rooms but no outside walls. Out of the window of the condominium I was looking at boats in a California bay. I could just barely see three masts through a glimpse of moonlight that was like looking through the eye of a needle. When I left the room, I saw that the other side of the house was in daylight. Through another window all of the boats were clearly visible. Outside there were many people. It was blistering hot, but there were also shadowy woods where there was a person camping. At the end of the dream I went into the forest.

"Kit called the drawing she did of the dream (Fig. 4) 'fire extinguisher.' The picture focused on her father and the large red fire extinguisher. He was drawn as a large mass of black. She started the picture by drawing the sailboats in the upper-right section of the picture that she could barely see when she squinted her eyes. She wanted to get back to the fireplace experience and then drew herself and Kenny in the lower right as two brown seed shapes that represent their heads that were almost touching. The two shapes were surrounded by an orange circle which gave a warm feeling. She said that this expressed the love, warmth and safety that she felt in being with him. The lines swirling around them express the arrival of her father. I commented on how big the figure of her father was in relation to other parts of the picture. She said that he is a large man who tends to be overweight. He was always the one who took her out as a child and she was embarrassed by his size. Yet, he was a popular man, funny and liked by everyone. Kit said he was 'always the star' and she wanted to be like him. Everyone told her what a great father she had.

"Kit's father and the fire extinguisher are in the lower center of the picture, just to the left of herself and her boyfriend. In the upper left, she drew the sailboats as seen in daylight and to the side of them she drew the forest. I spoke to Kit about the contrast between her father's entrance and her being with her boyfriend next to the fire. She experienced the scene of the apartments with no exterior walls after her father burst in. It made her feel totally exposed as though 'the walls had been ripped off.' Kit said that her father always has an excuse for entering her life. In the

Figure 4

dream he had to put out the fire which was just a tiny, brown spot on the roof of the church in the distance. She said that his arrival immediately stopped the feeling that she was having with Kenny. She said that her father knew there was something going on and he had to desperately put himself in the room.

"The fire extinguisher appeared to be in the midsection of her father's body. She said that she did not intentionally put it there, but that it is 'clearly phallic and spraying all over the place.' She said: 'It embarrassed me. It was such a public thing.' This brought her back to her childhood feelings of embarrassment that she had with her father in public. In response to the presence of the cathedral, I asked if her family was religious and she said no, but her father is presently going through a religious phase in his life. I told Kit that she seemed to know her father well and she agreed, telling me that he was always present when she needed him. I asked Kit what the problem was and she said:

> I never had a sense of privacy in relation to him. He is always finding an excuse to burst into my life. Since I started therapy I have been constantly looking at my relationship with him. I keep putting up new barriers and he finds ways to make contact with me. He will talk my language and get involved with what I am interested in. Right now he is reading books on Jung and dreams. He is one of the most sensitive

men I know. He is totally aware of his feminine and masculine nature. The problem is that he was never close to my mother and I was always his emotional anchor. I feel now that he needs to rely on me as his partner, intellectually and emotionally. I want to be able to love him but all of him, and all of his problems are pressing down on me too much.

After you asked what this dream is saying to me I thought of how no matter where I am or where I go, my father wants to be with me and he will find a reason. When he burst into my dream, I resigned myself to his being there once again and I just walked out of the room and into the color and the brightness. In the dream he is afraid of losing me to a man. He has always been gracious to the men in my life. But we grew up as a couple. I want to be his companion but as myself. He has a huge emotional pull on me. The pull comes from him and from within myself.

In our training group we were talking about how children may have to symbolically kill their parents in order to establish their independence. When you checked with me to see if 'killing' is too strong of a word to describe what has to be done, I felt that is what I need. There has to be something as strong as 'killing' to get rid of the old ways so that we can move into the next phase of our relationship. I do not have to kill something that is evil. I have to kill something that is good and loving. 'Killing' is the right word for what has to be done.

He is still my childhood hero. I do not think that this problem is something that I have to confront him with. I have to do it within myself and then I can go back home. I have been going away on many trips over the past eight years. My father is always the one who drives me to the airport or the boat and he is there to pick me up. Maybe these are initiation rites that I am creating. The traveling to other places has been helpful, but now I have to go on the inner journey to get to that place within myself where I want to be with him.

"Kit and I talked about how indigenous societies offer initiation rites that use external and public ceremonies to clearly state that things have changed in parent-child relationships. Today, we have to get it clear inside ourselves without this assistance. She said that her attempts to separate from her father have been difficult and awkward. In the dream he takes the smallest pretense of danger to her as a reason to break in. Kit said that his spraying with the fire extinguisher feels more like a release for him than protection for her. There is the paradox of how his sensitivity and attentiveness to her is at the same time insensitive to what she needs right now. Everything that she said about her father indicates that it is more her problem than his. Something within herself has to be changed and transformed. In response to Kit's frustration at how messy the separation process was, I said that it is rarely clean.

"When I said that she might have to put stronger locks on the door in her dream and walls on the outside of the buildings, she asked if I was suggesting that she should cut off her openness to her father. I said 'absolutely not.' Her house still has windows and doors. But it needs walls in this climate. This talk about walls and doors makes me think of work that I have done with my colleague, Annette Brederode, in Holland.

"I gave a lecture at the University of Industrial Arts in Helsinki about father-daughter relationships as expressed in art therapy. Of course, the topic of 'killing the father' aroused emotions. Annette was with me and she made it clear how there are many women who do not have these aggressive feelings toward their fathers. She is close to her father and described how she went through her killing or rebelling phase with him in order to establish herself as an independent person. The fact that he is such a strong and idealized character in her life made the killing inevitable. Right now, she feels that she has passed beyond the separation process. 'I killed him long ago,' she told me, 'and now I want to be intimate with him.' Other women have similarly described how they passed through the killing phase and ultimately 'resurrected' their fathers.

"In addition to being a trainer of art therapists in Holland and Finland, Annette has an extraordinary collection of bird cages. Her father is a retired surgeon. He carves and paints birds for her cages. Her colleagues who interpret everything according to psychosexual conflict with parents have presented her with many interpretations of this process. Their responses have helped her to shape a personal approach to art interpretation. When I was working with her in Holland, she told me her story about the bird cages (Fig. 5) and her father.

> I bought my first bird cage when I was fifteen. I am attracted to the mysterious quality of the cages and the romantic shapes of the old ones. Right now I have a collection of 120. Each is handmade and not one is alike. Most of them came from France and they were used in houses to have the bird as a companion. I do not like to keep real birds in the cages. I feel that they belong outside. Fifteen years after I began collecting, my father felt the cages were so empty, like abandoned houses. Without saying anything to me, he made beautiful, realistic wooden birds. Every one was different. It felt like he was filling my house. He painted the birds in colors that matched the cages.
>
> When professional therapists, psychologists and psychiatrists, came into my house, they started to interpret this hobby of mine without being asked. Artists and art therapists always enjoyed the cages for what they were. They experienced their shapes, the atmosphere and what they described as the magic feeling that they evoked. The reactions of artists were always positive. The others were putting out negative in-

terpretations. 'You must feel caged in. . . . Do you feel that you are not free?' They made statements rather than asking questions. . . . 'You collect these cages because you must feel that you live in a prison. . . . You are not open. . . . You are unable to fly out. . . . He is putting himself inside you.'

It is interesting to look back at how unimaginative these responses were. They were always literal, obvious and they gave me bad feelings. I admit that I began to believe them. After all these people were supposed to be authorities and I was insecure. I thought that there was something wrong with me and that I should get rid of the collection. When I felt better about myself as a person and as a professional, I felt good with my collection of bird cages. I saw their beauty, history and how they lived in different parts of my house. I noticed that other people enjoyed them. Now people are always calling me to buy the cages. I have set a trend. I have the largest collection in Holland and I have sold more than fifty cages during the past three years. Vincent Ferrini saw the cages as my temples. He mentioned how the doors were always open and I can fly in and out any time. Others see them as cozy, gezellig, homes. I have always appreciated their transparency. They are open. I can look through them from all sides. They are friendly and the wooden birds are like companions.

The negative interpreters said that my father was too much of a presence and caged into me. 'You hold your father inside and do not let him go,' they said. If they looked at my relationship to my father they would see that he is in me, but in a very good way. We belong together. I see him as being present in my life, in an independent way.

I respond strongly to your talking about killing the father. When my father was taken to the hospital recently, I did a series of drawings in which I felt that I was embracing him (Fig. 6). When drawing myself, I saw the face of my father in mine. It is similar to the bird cage feeling. He is in me and I want to protect him now that he is getting older. Like every healthy relationship between fathers and daughters, I killed him from time to time, but this only made us closer. Now I see that I chose my ex-husband because he was the total opposite of my father. I wanted to live my own life and make my own decisions. My father is so strong and such a wise man. I felt that everything he did was right. It was as though I could never put my finger on a weak spot. In choosing my husband, I selected someone that he would not approve of. I am only seeing this now. Right now, my father is a powerful and sensitive man who treats me as an equal and I see him as an equal. In my drawings I see that we are the same. The line of his life is crossing mine. Our faces fuse together.

Aggression against my father helped us to draw closer together. It was necessary in helping me establish independence.

"Annette's story is closer to the relationship I have with my father. As you said earlier, the intensity of the killing is probably relative to the degree of oppression."

Figure 5

"I think that Annette's poetic description of her relationship to her father helps us to be cautious about making universal judgments about the theme of aggression toward the father. We put forth the phenomena of daughters killing fathers as a means of achieving autonomy for the purpose of demonstrating alternatives to psychosexual interpretations of parent-child relationships and to document what appears to be an important pattern that is appearing in the art therapy work that I am do-

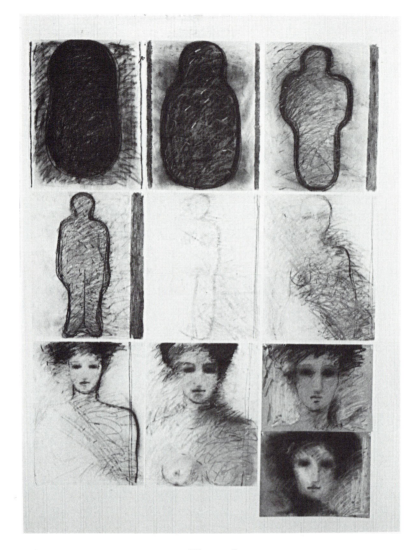

Figure 6

ing. I do not want to suggest that this is an attempted replacement of the Oedipal/Electra complex. This would amount to me trying to kill Oedipus in order to establish my own theory. Oedipus continues to be relevant but not necessarily in every parent-child relationship. The same applies with the need to kill the father."

"It depends upon where we are in our personal journeys," Lisa said. "Annette has done her work on her father and she has successfully established her autonomy and equality. She has resurrected his intimate place in her life. Leslie and Kit are in a different phase. They seem to be feeling that it is necessary to accelerate the conflict at the present time."

"From my experience it seems clear that one position is not necessarily more advanced than another. They are just different. I am always in awe of the varieties and the authenticity of the stories."

"Why are you so concerned with the killing-the-father theme?"

"Because, like other people that I have talked to about the issue, I originally rejected any reference to the word 'killing.' It was too violent and negative. By opening to the image, I have seen how it continuously manifests itself in the psyche. We are always killing something in order to create new forms. I find that it is crucial for me to be open to the transformative qualities of violent emotions. It also helps me to understand aggression that is directed toward me in my work and private life. Being the target of this aggression has been the most difficult thing for me to deal with in my work. It has been equally difficult for those who have expressed the aggression. I can be helpful and sensitive only if I understand. As Kit said, she needs something as strong as 'killing' in order to change her situation."

"Do you need to perform acts of this kind yourself?"

"There are certainly things within myself that have to be destroyed on a consistent basis. Sometimes, I can simply let them go. But with the other conflicts or problems there is more struggle and aggression. This is not only manifested within myself but also in my art. In my professional work as an art therapist, I have tried to work more with my compassion and openness to others and images. I have generally been able to save my aggression for those situations when it is necessary to protect a person, an image or myself. I am capable of being extremely aggressive to anything that threatens my freedom. This aggressiveness and killing characterized the formation of the art therapy profession. It was like a frontier town with regular gunfights whenever the group got together. Any element within an institution, society, family or individual person that dominates and represses the instinctual strivings of other elements will ultimately get it."

"You have mentioned how the theme of killing the father is consistently emerging in your art therapy groups in which there are many women. How much do you think the personality of the therapist or teacher has to do with stimulating this?"

"We cannot avoid the truths of transference and countertransference. But these concepts can be overemphasized and used as a way of avoiding other people and who we are in the present. It may be far more threatening to deal with the people before us than it is to see them as 'objects' from the past. These references to people as objects are dehumanizing, and it can be much safer to deal with an 'object' than a real person. But, of course, we evoke memories in each other and suggest connections to people who are not present. This imaginative dimension is what gives depth to human relationships. I do not want to avoid what you have just asked me in terms of my personal experience."

"Thank you."

"I have found that if I am aggressive and provocative as a group leader or therapist, I will generally arouse the aggressive emotions of the people that I am working with. They may respond with a desire to protect themselves or others, because they are afraid, or perhaps with an eagerness to take me on. There are many therapists who intentionally provoke these reactions. It is not my style. If I do it, I am acting unintentionally. Yet, I still have to deal with the reactions as openly as the therapist who chooses to act in this way. As an art therapist, I try to take on the roles of protector, listener, community builder, agent of liberation and expression, etc. I try to get myself out of the way as much as I can. I tell people that I am there to open the gate and step aside. It is against my nature to fill the room with myself. Yet, I have discovered that the more I can step aside and give freedom to others while being fully present, the more authority and respect I am given. It is my responsibility to use this authority if it is necessary to protect people and images; slow the group down; make an interpretation; suggest a change. I am a gatekeeper in a shamanic sense. If I open a path to an unknown and threatening realm or encourage others to do this, then I have to protect that opening and go in as a guide or companion if necessary. My therapeutic values are much more oriented toward images, love, companionship, compassion, storytelling and expression than they are toward aggressive provocation which we have so much of in the world. I am more interested in what we do not have and therefore need. I have also found that a safe, artistic and inspirational environment results in opening gates to demons, fears and the most threatening secrets. If I am aggressive and provocative, then I take too much space for myself and I force people to deal *with me.* This way of working can be effective for many therapists but not for me. It does not fit with my values, my deep sense of equality between myself, other people and images.

"But I cannot avoid the fact that I stimulate feelings in people."

"Whatever you do will stimulate feelings. Laying back can be as provocative as being intrusive."

"I am a man who works with many women, and because of this there may be more father-daughter issues than mother-daughter issues. There might also be more male-female themes. However, I did a training group in Switzerland in which there were twelve women and three men including myself, and a primary theme of this group was sexual relationships between women. The women in the group wanted to deal with their deepest feelings for, and blocks toward, other women. Apparently, they felt that they could do this with me, and I found myself as personally engaged with these 'women-to-women' themes as I am to relationships that include men. In my deepest work, I can go for hours without perceiving gender differences between myself and the women that I am involved with. We go to a place that does not deny gender but which removes factors that act as obstacles to complete interpersonal communion.

"Returning to your question about me provoking the theme of 'killing the father,' I am still relatively young. Every year I find myself becoming more of a father figure in the groups, because I am aging. I also have three children. I find that men in the groups are beginning to compare me to their fathers. Other men see me as a male companion and friend. The father role has generally been a pleasing one for me and less difficult than the roles I took on when I was leading groups in my twenties and early thirties."

"It would seem that the future looks good for you as you age and become more of a father. The role of the psychotherapist generally evokes parental feelings. I imagine that it is more difficult for younger people to evoke the same range of emotions and needs."

"Every year I find myself more relaxed in the work and this is good. Yet, we cannot lose the motivating edge of conflict and emotional arousal."

"I think that I have an imbalance of the conflict and arousal. I am thirty-six. The children that I am working with certainly see me as more of a mother than a peer. But I have not figured out and mastered the psychotherapeutic role, and this is my source of conflict. I have to convince myself that I can be helpful in spite of what I do not know. What do you think of this?"

"It is possible that you may be just as effective, or more effective, than an experienced therapist."

"What do you mean?"

"The comfort and relaxation that the experience factor brings does not necessarily mean that the senior person gets better results. It only means that this person might be able to enjoy the work more. I realize that the person who enjoys the work generally performs better than the person who does not. It would seem that you might try to relax as much as possible and just do the best you can and see if you can even enjoy yourself. There is a part of me which is an eternal beginner. It seems that you have to accept this in yourself and continuously seek out supervision. The supervisory process that we are engaged with has depth because of your questions and conflicts. You will find that some of your best results as a therapist will be attributed completely to your personality. People will find things in you that are not present in me. Their relationship to you will be different. You are a woman. Some of your best work in therapy will be a result of the fact that you, rather than someone else, just happens to be there at the right time."

"You are optimistic."

"You are the instrumentality of therapy together with the images and the people that you are working with. The therapy will result from the particular things that you do together. You can only do it in your own way, and certainly not mine. The key to effectiveness is staying with the work, the problems and the questions. As beginning and experienced therapists, we do the best we can and continuously seek out supervision."

"It is shocking to think that the beginner may be as effective as the expert. I wonder what the value of experience is."

"I think that experience helps us to become supervisors, teachers and it hopefully gives us the security to deal openly with the realities of effectiveness. It allows us to make honest assessments about where something is working and where it is not. Sometimes, I think that I am getting better at art therapy as I increase my experience and I realize that there are endless possibilities for learning in the future. But I think that the idea of becoming 'better' is for me an illusion and it can create a tyranny against beginners. In therapy we cannot measure ourselves against a clock like a runner. Right now, I can do things that I could not do fifteen years ago, but it is just as likely that there are things that I did well then that I cannot do now. My experience in organizations has repeatedly shown me that new, young and fresh people often bring the best ideas for transformation. The same is true with therapy. Youthful and vigorous criticisms keep the edge sharp and clean."

"There is also the fact that many newcomers change systems only to impose their point of view, or to mark out their territory as animals do."

"This can also be seen within institutions. Sometimes their changes may work wonders and at other times they are only expressing personal needs for control and ownership. The process will always be complex and imperfect, and this is perhaps why we have psychologists and therapists."

COMMITMENT TO THE IMAGE

"As I LISTEN to you describe the work of Leslie, Kit and Annette, I am seeing how there are so many ways to relate to a dream, a picture and the stories that they have told. With Leslie's dream you mentioned all of the images that you did not work with, and in Kit's dream I see how so much more work can be done with the sailboats, the harbor, the forest, the different kinds of fire, her relationships with men, control in love relationships. . . ."

"There are many possibilities for discovery within each of these dreams and then there are more dreams, artworks and stories to be told. When our training groups are operating well, there are more things and desires to engage than we could possibly ever handle with any suggestion of depth. This fecundity presents us with the necessity of selection and choice. I believe that opening to the expansiveness of the soul is one of the primary goals of art therapy. It demonstrates not only the multiplicities of interpretative response but also the varied paths of inquiry. To the extent that we are what we do, art is an extraordinarily rich mode of therapy. It taps into the vast reservoirs of imagery. Art therapy embraces talking and dialogue but offers so much more through the presence of the material image and its process of emergence. I am becoming increasingly convinced that the fundamental power of art therapy involves our opening to imagery. Soul is not invisible. It presents itself through imagery. Art integrates physical material and soul; it activates soul and takes us into it. Life can be perceived as a process of fleeting and recurring images. Art therapy makes good use of spoken language to deepen and clarify our relationship to imagery. Yet, language can be used too much. It can become a defense against the power of the image and soul. I have found that the success of art therapy is dependent upon the person's commitment to imagery. I watch myself and avoid my tendencies to hide behind words. Art therapy is a process in which one image follows the other and in which language and interpretation serve the image."

"Can you give me an example of the primacy of the image in a therapeutic situation?"

"In a recent training group a woman was distressed about a bird image that kept appearing in her drawings. She felt that the bird must have a message and she was frustrated that she did not understand what it meant. The bird kept coming back. She was nearly in tears when she asked me if I knew the meaning of the bird. I said that her obsession with the 'meaning' of the bird was an expression of her inability to experience the presence of the bird. I suggested that she simply try to see the bird, accept it, greet it and spend some time with it. I do not think that images have to always stand for something other than themselves. Her bird did not have to be perceived as a messenger, a Western Union courier. It was the message. Images do have metaphoric functions and they do bring messages. In this case, however, the woman had difficulty accepting herself and what was happening in the present. The bird ultimately helped her to realize this. She used her search for meanings, things that she could not see, as a means to avoid what was happening in the moment. The bird was persistent, it kept coming back to engage her. This experience corresponds to what the Gnostic Gospel of Thomas says about the person who can read the stars but cannot see the person before him."

"She seemed committed to her experience of the art therapy process."

"A core element of the therapeutic process can be perceived as the activation of this commitment, and the value of every therapeutic modality or profession is determined by it. Art therapy has so much to offer with its combination of artistic process, imagery and dialogue. Whether or not it can become a major psychotherapeutic modality throughout the world depends only on the ability of art therapists to establish the skills and self-confidence that will activate the commitment of people in need of services. We art therapists have to lead the way with our commitment to imagery in psychotherapy."

"The commitment that you describe in this situation where the woman asked for help in understanding the bird contrasts to the work we do in institutions with adults and children where there is little motivation."

"The professional identity of art therapy has been largely established by its ability to motivate and engage people within institutions that do not respond to other therapies. If art therapy can do this within institutions, just imagine what it is capable of within the context of depth psychotherapy with motivated people. I experience the absence of commitment with many people in my training groups and this is usually an expression of their insecurities and the fact that they give more energy to resistance than expression. Their work projects ambivalence and reluctance which can be useful to us if we engage these feelings with commitment once they appear. Conflict is one of our most important catalysts and allies. It serves to deepen the experience when we accept it openly. I am pleased that you see how the sincere request for help influences the therapeutic process. This not only determines the influence of an individual therapeutic session but also the influence of a psychotherapeutic profession like art therapy. Our future will be determined by the extent to which people desire the help we can give."

"This commitment can also be abused. People often place too much power in a therapist or in a profession."

"Art therapy has yet to confront this problem on a large scale. But we have seen it with the larger psychotherapeutic disciplines. And we all make mistakes. Perhaps the work I did with the bird image that I just described was inappropriate. I think that it is helpful to stay close to these feelings of doubt while also building self-confidence. The endless possibilities for the interpretation of imagery eliminate clear-cut standards of what is correct and incorrect. Our interpretations and the themes that we see in experience and art are constantly changing. They are simply the stories that we tell about our lives. These stories are fundamental to our human nature. We use them to express and embody soul. We also use them to experience soul. They deepen our relationships with ourselves, with other people and the world. They give meaning to our lives and to the experience of others. As with the appearance of the bird in the art that I have just described, the story is everything: the end and the means, the search and the grail. We live to tell and share our stories, our art, our sensitivity and soul. Materialistic psychological science has lost the integration of soul and matter that presents itself in art. It believes that its discoveries have validity outside the framework of the particular psychological search. Art demonstrates the inseparable nature of object and process. Within the context of art, there is little confusion about how each art object is an entity unto itself. The same applies to psychological theories and interpretations."

"Can we determine whether or not you are going in the correct direction with your interpretation of the bird?"

"I do not think that this is possible. We can only stay with it, with commitment, and see where it leads us. Tomorrow we might interpret the bird in a completely different way. Perhaps what matters is the willingness to change in relation to our assessments of what the situation calls for. History shows that people interpret images and phenomena to their advantage. This has resulted in some amazing distortions, such as historical epochs and people who have interpreted scriptures dealing with love for the purpose of serving their interests in repression. As I said earlier, I try to keep my interpretations focused on what I believe to be good for the person that I am working with, and we also consider what is good for the image."

ART AS DREAMING

"**D**O YOU SEE parallels between art and dreams?" I asked.

"The first thing that comes to mind is the way the psychoanalytic tradition associates both with the unconscious."

"What other similarities do you experience?"

"They both work primarily with images and imagination. Surrealistic art consciously made links with the dream through its representations of dream time and dream space. There is a freedom to follow the energies of imagination and the emotions in both art and dreams. They utilize the resources of creative instincts. They are both characterized by spontaneity, contradictions, emergence. What do you think?"

"It may not be possible to make a definitive psychological statement about the relationship between dreams and art, but my experience in art therapy clearly suggests that they have many commonalities. I have noticed how there is an interchangeable quality to art and dream interpretation. The same principles that we use for the interpretation of artworks apply to the interpretation of dreams. They complement one another. I have learned more about art through my interpretations of dreams, and vice versa. The meanings of both artworks and dreams are as Nietzsche says 'imagined *after* the fact.' My training groups reveal that the introduction of dream experience to art therapy places us in touch with the depths of our psyches. The soul speaks poetically through art and dreams, both of which need to be interpreted in order for us to understand what they reveal. The inclusion of dreams in art therapy furthers intimacy. The dream is generally not as defended and consciously controlled as the artwork. In this respect, dream images and energies can help to loosen up artistic expression and deepen our attachment to the images that we make.

"The fundamental differences between art and the dream is that one is volitional (art) and the other involitional (dreams). Perhaps the arts are the intentional expression of dream experience in our waking life. In this respect, art can be described as a waking dream or the physical embodiment of the dream. Artworks and dreams are combinations of images and feelings that are held together by a drive to provoke an emotional response. They desire to awaken our attention and go directly to our sensibilities, utilizing shock, absurdity, adventure, fear and pleasure. Art and dreams are an expression of an imaginative intelligence that contrasts to linear materialism. They demonstrate how the psyche does not follow a straight line but follows its own inclinations. I think that the ability to express many different things simultaneously, with no apparent relationship to one another, is one of the most distinctive features of art and dreams. Dreams have an ability to shatter conventions that art is constantly emulating; they show that depth psychology speaks a language of images. The infusion of art with dream attitudes can help it to become less self-conscious and more imaginative. Just as we have 'big dreams,' we have images in art that are more important to us than others. Dreams were the artworks that the first psychoanalysts engaged."

"Does part of the value of art therapy lie in its ability to bridge our waking lives with the dream?"

"Art therapy brings us into the animistic world. It gives us a physical experience of soul. Art makes us more conscious of our dreaming, our imagination and our ability to transform experience. I find that art keeps my senses awake, alert and open to fresh insights. History shows how art expressions are both fomentations of the underworld and ethereal visions."

"How important do you think the cognitive dimensions of art are?"

"Both art and dreams are ways of knowing that utilize images. They can be best interpreted through images, feelings, stories, imagination and poetic expression. Art therapists will gain a deeper understanding of dreams by working on their dream experiences. Their cognition of art will be similarly deepened through involvement in the creative process. Theodor Reik said that dream research remained unproductive after Freud, because psychologists were reluctant to openly deal with, and publish, their own dreams. He was upset by the way in which therapists expect patients to reveal the secrets of their souls but do not share their own dreams. Professional distance, impartiality, and taboos against self-disclosure by the therapist are forms of avoidance that sacrifice depth for safety."

"The same can be said about the absence of publications of art therapists that deal with their personal creative expression. I imagine that those who do present their work in this way are viewed as searching for attention and mixing personal expression with professional responsibilities."

"I think that we need more of this mixing. We have to take more risks. Art therapists might follow Reik's advice and reveal more of their intimate dream life and artistic expressions. I am convinced that this will deepen our involvement and knowledge of our profession. I have consistently found that art therapists who are personally involved with the artistic process are more sensitive to how interpretation is a process of projection. No doubt Reik would suggest that we study our artistic expressions as Freud studied his dreams. It is a big risk, because we not only expose our intimate feelings to the judgments of others but our artworks as well. I have done it myself on a number of occasions but I do feel awkward, since audiences are not accustomed to this kind of presentation. It is perhaps necessary for me to let go of the feeling within myself that the presentation of my art may be perceived as self-serving and egotistical. I find it much easier to present my dreams in a lecture than my artworks. Perhaps we should try to approach our artworks with the same non-judgmental attitudes that characterize the emergence of a dream. There is less ego involvement in the dream. Art's authenticity might be furthered the closer it gets to the dream.

"Every year my interests have been moving closer to the use of art as a depth-oriented psychotherapy. This may be a direction that is much larger than my personal interests. I am sure that eventually the depths of artistic practice and the depths of psychotherapy will be joined together by the movements of history. It is something that is meant to be."

"You have mentioned many times that the arts speak the language of the soul."

"The same thing has been said about dreams. I would add that artists have been great depth psychologists. In order to experience depth, there has to be an expression of emotion and this is what is conveyed through both art and dreams. Rather than talking too much about how art and depth psychology complement one another. I would like to demonstrate this when we continue to work with pictures."

ARTISTIC WILL

"I WANTED TO speak to you about the will in therapy and art," Lisa said.

"It is a terribly misunderstood phenomenon. The same is true of power. We tend to perceive them more in terms of their negative manifestations. It is interesting how they join together in 'willpower.' I do not perceive will exclusively in terms of a rational, ego-bound and individual judgment. For me will is soul itself, the soul of the world. It is a transformative energy that destroys and creates. Will is an inner wind or current that directs action and instinct. The locus of control is once again an interplay between the will of the person and the will of the world. We can say that art materials and images have a will of their own and that the process of creation is a shaping that emerges through the interaction of souls and wills. There is some truth to the stimulus-response theories of the behaviorists, but they take away our humanity and our history when they deny the will. They also obscure their contributions with this unnecessary negation. I do not see the person as something which is passively determined by the past. I am returning to the tradition of freewill and choice. The ancient nature of these principles gives them credence. The importance of will is emphasized by the writings of Otto Rank who introduces the philosophy of Nietzsche to psychoanalysis. He transforms Nietzsche's will to power into a 'will-to-health.' Rank perceives resistance as a 'counter-will' which therapy transforms, rather than overcomes, into creative expression. This artistic will is expressive of the soul and its resources. It is more than positive thinking and willful formulas for getting better and better every day.

129

"I have consistently discovered that emotional conflict is the subject matter of both therapy and art. Conflict motivates, or provides the impetus, for therapeutic and artistic transformations. It is up to us to determine whether or not we will do something creative with it. In his book *Will Therapy* (1945), Rank spoke of the 'negative origins of will.' He said that 'the will always longs for something other than it actually has.' "

"That sounds familiar. I spend too much time being dissatisfied with myself and my life situation."

"Eugene O'Neill expressed this in terms of people who are always living 'beyond the horizon.' The eternal therapeutic resolution, from the ancients to Thoreau, is the appreciation of the commonplace and the simplicities of daily life. Nietzsche's philosophy of will affirms the transformation of our emotional muck into gold. In *Moby Dick* Ahab makes this point when he says: 'Oh, now I feel my topmost greatness lies in my topmost grief.'"

"Ahab may not be the best role model. He is generally interpreted as a madman and a failure."

"Novelists are successful moralists, because their characters are not perfect. From literature and psychotherapy we discover that 'negative origins' can lead to happiness and emotional vitality. Conflict provides the irritant that moves us into action and creates the need for help, transformation, acceptance and understanding. Rank said that the 'counter-will' of resistance goes against the will of the other person or it opposes reality in general. It thus creates 'the necessity of denying this negative nature of will so that we may be able to perceive it positively and thus reverse it into effective action.'"

"The 'negative nature of will' applies to everything that we have discussed about daughters symbolically killing their fathers. The conflict with the father, the negative feeling, activates the will of the daughter. The negative influence of the father has to be overcome in order for the child to proceed to an improved relationship with the parent."

"In *Gone With The Wind,* Rhett Butler at the birth of his daughter lovingly said: 'This is the first person who absolutely belongs to me.' I think that it is fair to say that attitudes like this, as loving as they be, serve the purpose of setting up the kill. Yet if it is not this, it will be something else. Children have to transform and change their relationships to parents. Parent-child relationships suggest the inevitability and *necessity* of negative feelings in the creation of our lives as independent people. Our will originates through conflict with the will of our parents. Following Rank's insight, we can say that it originates as a counter-will against the desires of parents. This was certainly the case with my relationship with my parents. I am going through it now with my own children. It is difficult for me, and I know that it is not always pleasant for the children, yet it helps to know that this conflict is necessary in terms of the shaping of character. We learn how far we can push, when to lay back, when to rebel and hopefully how to moderate our will in terms of what is possible within a given situation. The person's will cannot overcome the will of the world, the will of nature, but learns how to navigate. Ahab demonstrates how we must ultimately submit to greater powers. The ambitious or strong-willed person, perhaps the genius, takes the situation as close as possible to the breaking point. So there is a price that we pay for raising and living with talented people."

"The will can be blind. I am intrigued by the way you use literature as a psychological source. I have to read *Moby Dick* again."

"I think that the will is much more of an instinct than a thought process. It can be our greatest source of torment. I think this happens when it turns its energy against itself or against others. Since you have shown an interest in Melville, we can use Ahab as an example.

> What is it, what nameless, inscrutable, unearthly thing is it; what cozzening, hidden lord and master, and cruel, remorseless emperor commands me; that against all natural lovings and longings, I so keep pushing, and crowding, and jamming myself on all the time; recklessly making me ready to do what in my own proper, natural heart, I durst not so much as dare? Is Ahab, Ahab? Is it I, God, or who, that lifts this arm? But if the great sun move not of himself; but is as an errand boy in heaven; nor one single star can revolve, but by some invisible power; how then can this one small heart beat; this one small brain think thoughts; unless God does that beating, does that thinking, does that living and not I. By heaven, man, we are turned round and round in this world, like yonder windlass, and Fate is the handspike.

"In the West we have this dichotomy between fate and freewill."

"Ahab articulates it well. There is a mystery to the interplay between the two that I cannot explain. I can only accept their existence and do my best with them. How would you define the will?"

"I think of it both as the process of making choices and as emotional persistence and the ability to make things happen, what we call 'willpower.' How do you define it?"

"I think that will does entail both conscious decision making and our more spontaneous drives and instincts. I also introduce the third and larger will of the world, which might even be another name for fate. The negative reactions that many people have to the idea of the will are in my opinion associated with the historic overemphasis in our culture on its volitional, deliberate nature and the attachment of these functions to moralistic principles. Our rebellion against these attitudes gets confused with the will. Even great figures like Ralph Waldo Emerson have perpetrated narrow conceptions of will. He called the will 'the coercive, ministerial power — the police officer' which resides in the human being. With all do respect for ministers and police officers, I do not think that they alone are the characterizations of will. The will may contain their images together with many others such as animals, angels, devils, artists, construction workers, cooks, housekeepers, mechanics, etc."

"How do you see the essence of will?"

"My immediate response is a perception of will as a motor, or the pumping function of the heart. It is the source of motion within the person. The will is both the propeller and the pilot. It is a transformer, a guide that shapes the act as it unfolds. In the emotional context, I perceive will as commitment, aesthetic judgment, sensitivity."

"I see how these ideas about will give us the opportunity to define its qualities that are distinguished from punitive morality. Negativistic notions of will are so intertwined with repressive morality."

"People have eternally feared the passions and the willfulness of the emotions. The notion that the will is a police officer and judge is intended to hold these forces in check. Control rather than liberation is encouraged. The will thus becomes the embodiment of a split between consciousness and passion. I believe that the will embodies all of these elements. . . .passion, judgment, liberation and control. Splits between instinct and intellect were an expression of an era that elevated mind and lowered the passions. Why can't the passion and instincts be seen as directing mind and intellect in an ethical way? The arts are only one example of this. When we project negativity and fear onto the passions, they take on these forms."

"Will is also viewed negatively by those who feel that it tries to go against nature."

"Will is nature. The creation of a dichotomy between the two creates the problem. Ambition, desire and longing are healthy so long as they are not inflexible and blind."

"Conflicts of will might be what motivate certain spiritual traditions to espouse a separation from the world and the transcendence of material things," Lisa said.

"These traditions discourage desires directed toward the material world where individual wills are believed to be in inevitable conflict with others. The denial of these things can be viewed as being provoked by the inability to deal with the conflicts of the material world. I keep returning to the belief that soul is a quality of material things. The conflicts of will and the strivings of our world are the subject matter of life. I would rather shape them than avoid them. The artist forms materials, interacts with them, transforms them. And they do the same thing to the artist. It is an interplay, a reciprocal formation. They make one another."

"So you believe in striving?"

"I certainly do. Sometimes I am like a plant or animal that finds a way to live in the desert. When we think in terms of survival and instinctual needs, will takes on a clearer meaning for me. Someone once told me after a lecture that I raise instinct to a new level. Successful interpersonal relations and artworks are formed by disciplined instincts. Perhaps, it is because I am an inherently lazy person that I need to work with purpose and enthusiasm. This may be another example of Rank's negative origin of will."

"It would seem that health involves an acceptance and recognition of the will."

"I do not think that it is constructive to deny the will. Yet, it may be equally important to be able to let go of its desires and obsessions. Rank described how it is necessary at times to surrender to the will of the other. I have found this to be one of the principle factors in domestic relationships, in my professional work and even within myself. Rank describes how when 'will conflict' is overly negative, the person becomes 'incapable of surrender and unity because he cannot get free from the consciousness of himself.' The effective interplay between wills requires the obvious give and take, striving and submission, all of which are guided by both aesthetic judgment and instinct."

"There must be a guiding and creating faculty in us."

"Right now, I think of this as the will. As an artist I know it well. It is the ability to go on, to continue and to stay with something. I see it in healthy people. They are able to moderate their desires in relation to the needs of others. I find hope and optimism in the transformative energy of will that interacts sensitively with the world. It is closely connected to love as Rollo May suggests. They need one another. Will might also be defined as soul. All of these words express an orientation, a direction and an energy. Jean-Paul Sartre is helpful to me. He said that 'Man is nothing else but what he makes of himself.' This fits with my philosophy of life as art. Sartre stresses how we are responsible for ourselves. We create our lives and our health, and they create us. Everything is reciprocal. For me well-being involves an acceptance of this responsibility for myself as well as a responsibility for the world, for something outside of myself."

"Do you feel that Rank's emphasis on the strengthening of the positive will was a reaction to Freud's suggestion that will is an illusion?"

"It would seem that Rank's close relationship to Freud provided him with an important impetus in the formation of his position. His psychology of will is perhaps a reaction to the Freud's deterministic framework. Rather than focusing on negative determinants, he supported Nietzsche's 'positive affirmations of will.' Rank said that the task of therapy is the transformation of 'compulsion of will into freedom of will.'

"How is a psychology which affirms the will useful to art therapy?"

"It is closer to the process of art and it articulates the transformative qualities of the arts. Rank's psychology of will is action-oriented and optimistic. It challenges us to do something about our condition. The old deterministic and negative psychologies of the mental health field do not correspond to what takes place in the art experience. The sublimation principle is helpful but not invented by Freud. Although he did not to my knowledge use the word 'sublimation,' Nietzsche said that if conflicts and problems are not expressed, they will be internalized. How do you perceive the will of the art therapy profession?"

"It is certainly committed, persistent, spontaneous, energetic and responsible. The art therapy profession embodies many of the traits that you have described in discussing will. It has created itself, as Sartre recommends. However, I see a definite resistance within the profession to claiming or achieving the full range of its powers and depths. There is sometimes an insecurity that holds the will of the profession back. It seems that there is a part of the profession that is willing to accept a secondary, adjunctive role in relation to other mental health disciplines. I think that we have been so good at being submissive and attentive to the will of other professions that we may be losing some of our willpower in the process. Perhaps this is a necessary part of the building process, in that art therapy is respectful of the more dominant professions and this has generated incremental gains. Yet, I can envision the depth and sophistication of art therapy that you suggest, and I hope that the profession has the will to create it."

"**A**RT THERAPY has to commit itself to what can be learned within the studio. Art therapists in training are generally far more concerned with clinical training."

"Isn't this because the task of preparing ourselves psychologically is formidable?" Lisa asked.

"There are external and internal pressures that call for psychological rather than artistic skills. There has to be a push for art and the perception of therapy as an artistic process. My fantasy for the future is the creation of art therapy studios for both training and expression. I envision free, yet disciplined environments which inspire art. I emphasize the studio because we need it more right now. I know that I desire the studio. There is not enough of it in my life. Two decades of working with graduate students and art therapy colleagues has shown me that they hunger for it too, and the phenomenon of art therapy needs the studio. If I walk into a medical environment with its chemical and antiseptic smells, my soul is aroused only to the extent that I want something else. These medical environments can sometimes be the antithesis of art. The studio summons the artist in me and the artist in art therapy."

"You seem to treat your training group as a studio."

"This direction is increasing every year in my work. It is a return to my original vocation as a studio artist. I do not think that therapy has to be separated from the studio. Art can be an acutely clinical activity. Yet, I am more interested at this point in my career in working with people who are willing to make a serious commitment to the art therapy studio. I want to go even further with image making and art in my training groups. Rather than 'analyzing images' or switching to 'talk therapy' after we make art, I am trying to expand the artistic context so that it includes every aspect of art therapy. Pictures are interpreted with more pictures. People communicate and thus influence one another with their images. Talking can be both an avoidance of depth as well as a mode of deepening. Because we have done so much with talking in art therapy and psychology as a whole, I am increasingly committed to researching the silent dialogue with art materials. As I said before, talking takes the form of storytelling within our training groups. I am interested in viewing all aspects of art therapy as performance art. This helps to heighten concentration, commitment and the effective use of time. When we talk too much as an avoidance, I find that it can be boring. I rarely experience this sense of boredom with art materials. Even when nothing is emerging I try to reflect on the process as a meditation."

"The ideas and practices of performance art fit with your description of the art therapy studio. Within the performance tradition every gesture, image, artifact and quality of the environment are part of the artwork. There is an attentive audience that energizes the person who performs. This corresponds to what I see happening in our art therapy studio sessions. How do we take it further?"

"When we begin to appreciate the totality of the art therapy studio in the way that I am suggesting, the depth of the process will correspond to the condition of our consciousness. If I am bound by thoughts or conventional studio environments that do not attend to the therapeutic, then my work will reflect this split. The first objective is to convince myself and then begin to act on the idea."

"Do you experience setbacks?"

"Constantly. They take the form of ambivalence and doubts about the validity of what I do, together with dissatisfaction about certain elements of the work and boredom. The encouraging thing is that I have found that crises and setbacks are consistently the impetus for transformation. When I begin to engage the desire 'to do something else,' I realize that I do not have to change the entire structure of my life, but perhaps I can do something different within the context of art therapy. I change and go further in the work."

"And where is it taking you right now?"

"To the studio, a place where images are created and respected. In the studio the image and the process of creation are equal to, or sometimes more important than, the human being. This emphasis is reversed in the clinic. I am not interested in a return to 'art for art's sake' or 'aesthetic disinterest.' I am concerned with the human being who is in the studio, but I think that we can benefit from this image-directed attitude which contrasts to the sometimes excessive personalization in therapy. Ironically, we experience ourselves more completely or imaginatively when we focus on something other than the self."

"You are suggesting the religious dimension again."

"Art therapy intrigues me because it is a phenomenon that is completely outside of our concept of religion and yet it answers what I perceive as religious needs. It has certainly done this for me and many of my closest colleagues. I see my work as part of the eternal emergence of soul within the contextual forms of our era."

"I am noticing how often we speak of what we need, what people need and what art therapy needs."

"Art therapy has come into existence as a response to needs. . .biological, imaginative, those of the soul. The origins of art therapy are in the studio and the lives of the artists. The artistic environment cannot be left behind or diluted in the creation of a new professional mutation. The profession of art therapy can keep the studio and perhaps even revive some of its lost relations with the soul."

EROS AND IMAGE

"A COLLEAGUE recently told me that he thought that self-expression through the arts was narcissistic."

"To the extent to which narcissism involves paying attention to the self and loving the self and life, then perhaps it is. A conception of narcissism that focuses on self-indulgence at the expense of other people to whom we have responsibilities does suggest undesirable human qualities. But what about the artist whose self-reflections are guided by a moral purpose to transform society? There are also artists who are inspired by a love of life itself. Since we are part of life, it is not a bad idea to love ourselves, too. The popularized notion of narcissism suggests 'excessive' love of self. I do not think that we can ever love ourselves enough, and the same applies to our love for other people. The pathologies that are clinically associated with narcissism manifest preoccupations with the self that are actually indications of a lack of self-love and self-confidence. If I am relatively secure with regard to myself, I can attend to the feelings of other people. Psychoanalytic concepts which describe narcissism as a regression to infantile, autoerotic feelings misrepresent the life of the infant. I have had the good fortune to have spent most of my life in close contact with infants, and I have observed how they are interested in the world around them and other people. In fact, the infant is generally in more active and direct contact with physical things than the adult. We project this autoeroticism onto them. It is adults and adolescents who have to struggle with their preoccupations with themselves. Autoeroticism is confused with the infant's need for help from other people. This dependence actually demands that the infant have contact with other people and it stimulates the use of imagination. Theories of early childhood egocentrism are established according to adult psychological standards and the adult's inability to become involved in the child's imaginative life. I think that if we could ask animals, physical things and nature how they felt about children, we might hear something very different. They might say that children are far less involved with themselves than adults."

"Can we avoid preoccupation with our personal experience?"

"I have discovered that every picture I make contains elements of self-portraiture. Even when I paint women, animals and trees I see my physical qualities in them. This does not suggest that I am preoccupied with myself. I am preoccupied with art, images, paint and other materials, and I project myself totally into this activity. To the extent that contemporary concerns with narcissism liberate us from restrictive guilt and barriers to sensation and the experience of daily life, then they are helpful. The danger in psychologies of narcissism is their overemphasis on the self as opposed to other people and things in the world. Even the new attempts to say that it is okay and healthy to love yourself can be one-sided in their revisionary zeal. Narcissus fell in love with 'the image' in the pool of water. Was he really in love with himself, or was it the water or the light reflections and nature's ability to perform these miracles? Perhaps we should re-vision the Narcissus myth as the beginning of portraiture. There are many possibilities."

"You are always looking at the other side of a story or myth."

"Images, myths, stories, the past, families and culture need to be continuously reinterpreted, imaginatively. This is what therapy is all about for me."

"I imagine that part of the risk involved in artistic performance and exhibition concerns their potential for misinterpretation."

"Artists must go into themselves in order to reach us. This is distinct from narcissism."

"I have often thought that art is a sensuous, and perhaps even an erotic, activity."

"Artists are constantly making this point. Many describe how art can be as satisfying, or more satisfying, than sexual activity. It is the sensuousness of art that distinguishes it from other forms of intellectual activity."

"Do you include art as part of the intellect?"

"It engages both feelings and ideas. Cognitive psychologists like Rudolf Arnheim and Howard Gardner dispel the old notions of art as 'regression,' 'separation from the world,' 'pure id' and so forth. Art is a form of contemplation and work which is distinguished by its sensuousness and engagement of eros. It is these qualities which make art therapeutic."

"How do you define eros?"

"For me it is very close to soul. Eros includes sexuality, love and more. I use the term to describe passionate feelings that we have about the physical world. . .our bodies, other people, nature. It is everywhere. Did you hear Rudolf Arnheim's lecture at the college dealing with sexual symbolism?"

"He said that sexuality, or any other element of life, cannot in itself be the final artistic statement. Sexual symbols are a means to making statements about life and not just sex. He said that our interpretations of erotic images can expand upon the biological aspects of sex and that 'art goes beyond the subject matter to human attitudes.' I was particularly interested in the way in which he demonstrated how indigenous art forms in all cultures use sexual images as protection against evil and as fertility charms. People in our culture tend to make literal interpretations of these images rather than contacting the deeper human meaning which is, as he said, 'served by the subject matter.' He also felt that 'automatic' interpretations of the Freudians reduced everything to sexuality and stopped here. Arnheim seems to be suggesting that we should embrace the sexual image and allow it to work on us in a way that suggests more than 'sex for sex's sake.' There is no doubt that sexual content is sometimes hidden in certain artworks, especially when direct presentation is considered to be a taboo. Freud helped us to see this. Arnheim's core theory that 'expression is directly given in the object itself' suggests that eros may be represented more by a lush drawing of a jungle with intertwined vines and flowing water than in a stiff drawing of sexual intercourse. He said that 'the shapes have an inner kinship to the behavior that is reflected in them.' "

"Do you see a contradiction in Arnheim's focus on 'the thing in itself' and his belief that 'no subject is ever the final statement?"

"The two positions complement one another," Lisa said.

"The emphasis on 'the thing itself' keeps us close to the art object. This position is enriched by the realization that the image links us to other dimensions of life. He does not separate art and reason, sensation and thought. To the extent to which eros is a generative force in all of life, then its manifestations cannot be restricted to sexuality. It is as much involved with our thoughts as our bodies. I am interested in furthering or deepening the erotic elements of the art experience. The process of going into eros generally stimulates feelings of gratification as opposed to obsessive sexual preoccupations which take us away from our immediate experience. I think that a therapeutic and artistic view of eros helps us to see what we have, whereas tormenting sexual preoccupations are obsessed with what we do not have."

"Is this what the psychoanalytic tradition refers to as sublimation?"

"I do not call it sublimation. Although the idea of sublimation is not offensive to me, I prefer the old poetic concept of catharsis or the alchemical principle of transformation."

"But the release of energy in art is not always cathartic. It can be steady and gradual."

"This is an important distinction that you are making, but I do not think the catharsis has to be climatic. A prolonged experience can offer a catharsis. The word is defined as purging and cleansing. A contemporary equivalent is the concept of ventilation."

"Why do you stay away from sublimation?"

"The psychological concept of sublimation is an adaptation of the chemical principle which deals with solids and gases changing places without turning into a liquid. I am also interested in preserving the uplifting nature of the 'sublime.' The modern psychological concept of sublimation suggests that we are getting rid of our lower impulses by turning them into something more acceptable. There is a moralistic dimension that I disagree with. Sublimation is a behavior-modification concept that stresses how sexual energy has to be 'channeled' into 'socially productive behaviors' which are not overtly sexual. Although sublimation acknowledges sexual energy and the necessity of its release, it desexualizes the act itself. Catharsis and transformation do not have these negative moralistic connotations. When D. H. Lawrence talked about 'sexualizing everything,' I think he was encouraging us to see how all aspects of experience are characterized by sensuous and erotic qualities. Michel Foucault documents how our western society has problematized sexuality. This negativity has spread to the larger dimensions of eros and our sensate experience with the world. Our puritan work ethic permeates our psychological assumptions which have associated sensuousness with hedonism and hedonism with pathology. The absence of aesthetics in the twentieth century history of psychology proves this point. Aesthetics is the science of sensibility."

"Then you see sublimation as a concept which desensitizes?"

"Right. It is part of a non-aesthetic psychology that thinks in terms of cleaning up sensibility rather than deepening feeling. The aesthetic attitude takes us into eros."

"Does the engagement with eros have to be direct?"

"I generally prefer to operate in this way and to engage 'the thing in itself.' But I cannot make a general clinical principle out of a personal preference. We know that certain phobic fears and patterns are sometimes reinforced by direct attention. In these situations we might have to reshape habitual responses with the introduction of new imaginative possibilities and metaphors. Trying something new is however a direct effort to get out of the old pattern."

"How do we engage the sexual image in therapy?"

"First it has to appear and work its way through all of the taboos against the manifestation of sexual images within our society. Eroticism, associated with the primary religious functions of many societies, is 'X-rated' in ours. In my training groups, supervision sessions and other private settings, the erotic images are welcomed and people are generally quite comfortable with them. The art therapy environments that I have been involved with tend to sanctify whatever images emerge. We are not all libertines. Many colleagues and students are deeply involved in traditional religious worship. I have consistently worked with male and female clergy, all of whom show little hesitation when it comes to engaging erotic imagery."

"Can this acceptance be extended into the public context?"

"Within the private therapeutic setting, I have experienced few conflicts with the presentation of sexual imagery. This freedom does not exist in the public sector. We have laws against the naked presentation of our bodies. The society has many different interest groups to respect and protect. Sexuality is a highly political and divisive issue in public life. I have internalized many of these conflicts and cautions. I will give you an example. In 1974, I organized an invitational exhibition at the Massachusetts College of Art called 'Images of Fear.' We invited regional artists to submit artworks and we also included some children's art. Don Burgy, a prominent conceptual and performance artist who was also a new faculty member at the college, talked to me about submitting a sculpture made from a casting of his erect penis. He thought that the male erection is the most feared image within our society. I agreed with him, thought it was a great 'idea,' but I began to feel my own fear being aroused by the possibility. Since he was a new member of the faculty of the college, I asked him if he wanted to risk presenting his erection. I was also concerned about mixing this image with children's art. I think that he shared my cautions and we agreed to present his artwork as an art idea. Off to the side of the other conventional paintings and sculptures we placed an empty pedestal with a printed statement describing his image of fear and why we were not presenting it in its physical form."

"Do you think you did the right thing?"

"We certainly did the safe thing and I do not think his statement was weakened. It might have actually been furthered by the imaginative dimension and the sensitivity we tried to show to those people in the audience who would have responded violently. I am not interested in that kind of provocation."

"Do you experience the same cautions when these images present themselves in therapy groups?"

"Not at all. As I said before, the environment is safe and accepting. When I was beginning to work as an art therapist, I was not quite as relaxed. I was interested in sexual imagery, but I did not know what to do with it."

"What did you do?"

"I responded as honestly as I could and I did not try to offer pretentious interpretations. It is always a good idea to appear humble when approaching the image. As it turns out, I generally do the same thing now. It took many years for me to discover that open, humble and respectful attitudes toward images in art therapy are the most sophisticated."

"When you make art together with your groups have you allowed yourself to make sexual images?"

"I frequently do, since I am involved with these themes. I have generally found that my work helps to liberate rather than restrict the images of other people. In terms of all of this societal or 'super-ego' taboo, the involvement of the leader can indicate what is permissible. I have been caught off-balance earlier in my career when I was not as clear about my sexuality and my intentions. If the image work is part of my authentic self-expression and my involvement with the group as a leader and a teacher, then I am on secure ground."

"What would you consider inappropriate?"

"It is impossible for me to make universal laws of propriety. Everything depends upon the context and the type of relationship that I have with the other person or group."

"This sounds like situation ethics."

"I am interested in responding sensitively and respectfully to what the context calls for. In addition to looking at the ethical responsibility of the therapist, the emergence of sexual imagery also raises issues with regard to the motivations of the people that we are working with. Is the image an expression of the person's desire to come closer to me? I do not want to sound puritanical in chastising actions of this kind. They are part of the therapeutic process and part of being human. We can get into trouble when we are not aware of what is really happening. D. H. Lawrence perceived art as a moral activity which is essentially passionate rather than prescriptive. He distinguished sympathetic and helping motives from the desire to 'merge' with everything. Merger is sometimes a disguised form of possession. He talked about 'feeling with' and 'catching the vibration' of another soul."

"Can artistic sensitivity be a guide to psychotherapeutic ethics?"

"I think so. For me there have to be distinctions between what is mine, what is yours, what we are together and what has nothing to do with either of us."

"There must be therapists who are not comfortable with explicit sexual imagery?"

"There are, but the problematization of sexual imagery in art therapy has more to do with institutional environments and ethics. I have not seen many art therapists who have trouble dealing with erotic imagery. Panic, suppression and avoidance often have much more to do with what art therapists feel their employers and the society will tolerate. One of my graduate students did her thesis on her art therapy internship in France. She was fascinated with how the French creative arts therapy program that she was involved with encouraged touch and massage as part of treatment. The American clinic that she worked in previously cautioned against touching because it was felt that the patients would 'overly sexualize' the experience. This is one area in which animals are treated better than humans. Art therapy has not given a significant amount of attention to the erotic image. Perhaps this is because most therapists work within institutions which have a history of supporting containment, sublimation and alternatives to working directly with sexual energy. If there was support for this kind of expression within society and the mental health field, art therapy will be more than happy to respond. Even if an individual therapist is open to in-depth work with the sexual image, there will inevitably be concerns about how this will be interpreted by the employer and the community. It is no wonder that many therapists stay away from a direct engagement with eros."

"Is the atmosphere the same in Europe?"

"It depends on the country. I have found that sexual imagery is far more plentiful and overt in my training groups in Holland, Sweden, Finland and Switzerland than in the American groups. I have found few differences between men and women with regard to their openness and acceptance. My learning and experience base with regard to sexual imagery has been largely European. I have not found central and northern European's to be significantly different from Americans in their fundamental sexual orientations and patterns, but as a culture they are more open with their bodies, with nudity and sexual imagery. Sexual imagery has been far more plentiful in the training groups that I have done outside America."

"Do you think it might be because the group members see you as an 'open' American and therefore present you with what you want?"

"I try not to overlook possibilities like that and the role that I am playing in eliciting imagery as a group leader. Even though I am never telling group members what to draw or suggesting themes, I am aware of my traits and the influence they may have on people. However, I have observed that the sexual images come forward when I am quite passive. It may be possible that the more I get my personality out of the way, the freer these images are. I am always working with mature groups of therapists and artists who are not making their images to please me."

"I noticed that people in our Cambridge training group influenced each other with their pictures. We were affected and inspired by the way others were working with materials and themes. Does this happen with sexual imagery?"

"That is an excellent point. In a number of my groups, there has been a contagion of eros as a result of what a single person might be doing. In one group, a woman was doing explicit and provocative erotic drawings and her work seemed to liberate the group as a whole. It was as though she gave them permission to explore a taboo subject. As a result of the entire group's involvement in the creation of sexual images, the impact was deepened considerably. It felt as though we were participating in an ancient and prolonged fertility ceremony."

"Is liberation the goal?"

"For some people it can be. Others might work more on control, acceptance or understanding. Universal sexual feelings take many different forms in the lives of people. At times our work has qualities of sex education or religion. If there is a consistent quality to the work, it can be presented in terms of respect for the subject matter and the different choices people make in relation to it. As a man my life has been enriched by what I have learned from working closely with women on these themes together with what I have learned from men with similar and different sexual orientations. I just returned from a training group outside the United States in which we worked with the sexual imagery of two women who have agreed to my use of their art for teaching purposes."

"I would like to see their pictures."

"I will show you Anna's art first. She began by making large paintings of mouths on paper. Some had huge red lips and others had prominent teeth. As she continued to paint, the mouth became a vagina and she worked on the erotic relationship between these body parts. The teeth introduced the element of aggression and the *vagina dentata* ('toothed vulva'). Anna was not as concerned with the traditional notions of *vagina dentata* and fantasies of biting off the male member. These concepts emphasize the destructive powers of the vagina, whereas her imagery was more concerned with eros and fertility. She saw the teeth as expressing the aggressive qualities of sexuality. In this first painting (Fig. 7) the vaginal opening is giving birth to a male artist-magician. Anna said: 'A female part of myself has nurtured and created an artist-magician.' She experienced her artistic creativity as an interplay between her feminine and masculine qualities. The red, male figure was described as 'inventive, playful, childlike, impish, aware, free to create and free to change.' The feminine carries and gives birth to this part of herself."

"What she said about the male sounds like a classical description of Hermes. In an archetypal sense she presents her art as an interplay between the trickster and the earth-mother."

"Anna described painting as a sexual experience in which these elements interact with one another. As we said before, she felt that art was a more satisfying form of sexuality and that creation was a process of giving birth. She went on to give a more detailed description of the masculine and feminine parts.

Female

The germ of an idea sown; slowly grows; is nurtured; develops into a more complex form; becomes defined; incubates; becomes ripe; swells inside me and needs to emerge; when it is ready it is BORN on to the waiting sheet of paper where it becomes alive in its own right—no longer part of me but still connected to me; the sense of slowly and lovingly nurturing something new and then bringing forth.

Male

Mounting excitement which needs to explode itself in a great red spurt all over the pure white sheet of paper; the need to assert myself by an act of physically projecting my inner 'juice' on to the world; the emptiness of the waiting paper needing my energy to fill it with form and color.

"It seems that the process of painting is a metaphor for the deepest concerns in Anna's life," Lisa said.

"She described how our therapeutic studio environment allowed her to paint feelings and images that she never experienced before. The pic-

Figure 7

tures that she made are completely different from the art she does out-side of the therapeutic training group. She spoke of how important the therapeutic environment was for her and how she needs to keep return-ing to it in order to release these powers within herself. Anna spoke ex-plicitly about how she is perceived in her professional life as a 'proper' and esteemed teacher. She kept talking about how she felt that it would be impossible for her to show these pictures within her home community because of the way they would shock people. They would not only be stunned by the images themselves but by the fact that she did them. Af-ter our first training group she actually threw away many of her large paintings because she felt that she could not show them to people. Yet, she loved the images and the process of making them. During the training group she painted for hours everyday without interruption."

"I imagine that the members of the training group supported her in painting these pictures."

"They really did. The women perceived her as a courageous person who was able to express things that they felt but could not paint. The men were excited by her work and her commitment and described how her images and her artistic process liberated them. Some of the women encouraged Anna to show the paintings outside of the group. But I think that she had reasonable cautions. She had found a place to express this part of herself, and of life, within our therapeutic studio and she did not have to expect the rest of the world to have similar values."

"We have many dimensions to our lives that do not merge together. It seems that Anna is finding a way to take care of the varied parts of herself. Her focused work with the male and the female suggests this. It is both an end in itself but also a metaphor for distinguishing the different elements within her life as a whole."

"She did talk about how she wants the parts of herself expressed in her pictures to become more visible. She wants them to be seen by others. In the next picture (Figs. 8 & 9), she is worshipping the male phallus and the artist within herself."

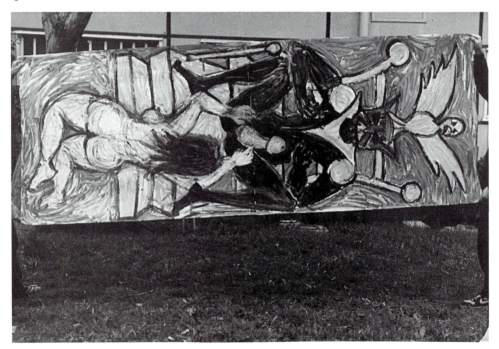

Figure 8

Figure 9

"Is this penis envy?"

"Penis adoration is not necessarily envy. The old psychosexual concepts are twisted in this respect. They are always negative and suspicious. Anna explicitly said that she 'worshipped' the penis in this picture. She was not covering up a desire to have one of her own. 'Desexualized' theories do not know how to deal with adoration of genitalia. In this picture the woman again gives birth to the man who is presented here as a king on a throne. He is wearing a mask because she wants the man to be universal and she also wanted the focus to be on his penis and not his face. He has a golden bird on his head which is presented as a symbol of personal empowerment. The throne is also yellow. Anna talked about the picture as expressing the liberation of the male penis which society has so much trouble accepting. She described how the picture is a manifestation of her desire to be seen. One of the women in the group observed how both the woman's body and the penis were colored pink, whereas the rest of the man's body was black. Anna perceived this as reinforcing her identification with the penis and its visibility. She wanted this for herself. The penis becomes a symbol of exposure. She laughed at the fact that the picture presented her lying before the penis in a submissive position and described that she is not like this in her life and is certainly not perceived as being this way by other people. 'I can worship the penis when I am having sex, but I do not want to make the coffee. I am a dominant woman.' We talked about how the portrayal of the male artist-magician figure as a 'king' supported her feeling that art was an elevated form of sexuality."

"I do not want to take us away from Anna's drawing and her experience, but I think it would be interesting to consider some of the archetypal meanings of these images," Lisa said.

"Indigenous societies perceived the penis as having an autonomous soul. These beliefs were supported by the phenomenon of the erection which seemed to operate in a way that was not always controlled by the man. Anna's painting suggests that the penis has a life of its own."

"Within indigenous cultures nudity is associated with ritual and sacred functions, perhaps because it reverses habitual behavior and calls attention to desired results. I understand that early Christian baptisms were performed in the nude to signify rebirth."

"It would seem then that this nudity is necessary for Anna's transformation rituals in the art therapy studio. In this second picture of her artist-magician coming out of the vagina (Fig. 10), new elements are introduced. He is red again and wearing the yellow bird on his head. The paint brush that he is holding in the first picture is now in both hands, and the brushes are dripping with red paint. The vagina has been transformed into a theatrical stage with yellow curtains. He is standing on a creature that Anna calls a 'worm monster.' The image reminds me of the classical representations of St. Michael with his foot on the head of the serpent. Anna made this statement about the picture:

> When the yellow curtains open the drama is performed. The artist-magician paints his forms to assert his powers over the great, slimy worm-monster. The worm is slow, sluggish, depressive, empty, dull, repressed, stinking, seething, red-eyed and held down. It wants to rule the world. The artist's face is masked and his red penis is erect. Red paint drips from his 'full' paintbrushes. The magic of the paint can

overcome the worm's tremendous power. The worm is writhing in frustration. The golden eagle on the artist's head can fly high and rise above all of the worms. The artist's energy confronts the worm's heavy power. The worm tries to free himself by devouring the artist, squashing him and suffocating him with his stink.

Figure 10

"The struggle with the worm continues in the next picture (Fig. 11). The artist is white now, partly in the vagina which is painted with brilliant red. His penis is gone, but he is holding a large brush in his left hand. Paint is flowing from the brush. The worm is more upright and menacing in this picture. I am sure that there are interpreters who will see the artist-magician as guarding the opening on the vagina against the phallic worm who is threatening to enter, but this interpretation does not fit. The worm is presented as a part of Anna that she struggles with.

In the training group we discussed the possibility of reversing her relationship with the worm. Perhaps it is a part of herself that needs love. Maybe the worm is the professional image that her more passionate artist-self is struggling with. She said:

> The white figure leaps from the woman's 'lower' mouth. The worm rears up. The magician paints his body white and is moving lightly from the inner, red wetness. Black hair grows thickly around the hole. . .curly, vital, natural growth. The paint brush in his hand is something that he rules with and uses to make magic and paintings. The dripping red paint is filled with power. The worm rears up, showing his teeth and his anger at the appearance of 'the red one.' He is furious at having his omnipotence challenged. The artist-magician doesn't fear the worm and doesn't need to stand on him now to keep him down. He believes in his brush and trusts his power to overcome the grey, sluggish mass. The worm hates the sunlight and hates change, growth, warmth and fresh air.

Figure 11

"It seems that the battle with the worm is diminishing. As Anna said, her artist does not fear the worm. The situation now seems to be one of coiled tension between the two. Both sides are alert and ready to spring. They appear to be fully engaged with one another.

"In the next picture, which is the last one in this series (Fig. 12), the artist-magician is gone. Maybe he has done his job and has transformed the situation and he is not necessary now. He might have been internalized by both the woman and the worm or perhaps he is resting inside the vagina. The worm looks far more passive. His eyes are downcast and his teeth are not visible. The mouth appears wrinkled and weak. Perhaps, he misses the energetic artist-trickster. It would seem that the worm receives his power from the relationship with the artist. Note that this is the first picture in the worm series in which the woman's entire body is shown. The worm has grown in relation to the size of the vagina which continues to be wide open as it has been in all of the pictures. To the extent to which Anna paints her self-portrait in these pictures, she presents herself as an extremely open, energetic and passionate woman who is not afraid to engage conflict. She is both mercurial and bonded to the earth; a powerful combination. I am impressed with her presentation of the male and female parts within herself. The last picture gives a sense of submission and pleasure which corresponds to Figures 8 and 9. The picture complements the earlier one by presenting the female genitalia and the woman in a state of pleasure and excitement. The picture was also done after we talked about the possibility of befriending the worm. It seems that the neutralization of the worm releases her sexual powers. Anna called this painting 'pink woman with worm' and gave this description:

> The full-bodied, fleshy, pink woman has her legs open wide, exposing red lips, and open hole, throbbing, waiting, expectant, hair flowing red and fiery. She allows the worm to see her intimate parts. She doesn't cross her legs or close them tightly to keep him away. She accepts his interest in her and throws one leg across his thick, slimy neck-body. She's a rosey pink, warm and glowing, nipples erect with excitement. The worm is silver and shining. He has become fascinated with the woman and is a bit wary, not sure he's wanted. She's abandoned and giving herself. He does not know whether he can go further toward her.

"I had the fantasy that after all of that build up, the worm turns out to be impotent."

"But Anna seems to be able to take care of herself," Lisa said. "She has both the male and the female inside herself and she activates them both and their combined procreative powers through art."

Figure 12

"I think that the series is encouraging in this respect. It expands our concept of sexuality. The series does away with many of the stereotypic psychosexual interpretations, because the sexual images are overt and not hidden. We do not have to go looking for the penis in a chimney or a tree or the vagina in a doorway or pool of water. We can actually do the reverse here and expand upon the sexual images to nature as a whole. I prefer this psychological expansionism to reductionism. We can proceed from the genitalia to other forms of life."

"How would you expand upon Anna's last picture and relate it to nature?"

"The woman's body can be perceived as an undulating landscape and the vagina can be a grotto, oasis, resting place or perhaps it is the eye of storm. Anna described the hair as 'firey.' She has already expanded to the elements of nature. The laid back position of the head can be likened to the setting sun. Maybe it is rising. The worm does not seem to know what to make of it all. He might be the sea, pressing against her shores, or the wind. His coiled position suggests that he is loaded with energy that might either burst or dissipate."

"We do not have to become fixated on a single frame of reference."

"Stereotypic psychosexual interpretations resemble adolescent sexual obsessions. Our genitalia are only one of many erotic areas of the body. Obsession on them results in a restriction of the total erotic and expressive relationship with nature."

"In mythology, objects like sceptres, candles, swords and ploughs are symbols of the penis, and rings, caves, gates, wells, conch shells and cups symbolize the vagina. How does this relate to what you are saying?"

"I see the symbols that you list as expanding upon the object and sexuality. These mythologies and early religions saw patterns of correspondence in many life forms. The people that used the symbols appear to have done so intentionally. They were knowledgeable about these parallels. The intentional use of objects for symbolic purposes contrasts to psychological interpretations which see the vulva in all circular configurations. Practices of this kind are reductionistic and impose the interpreter's point of view on the object. They are so obsessed with genitalia that they cannot see the doorway going into the cellar."

"Does Anna's series of paintings have a developmental pattern? Does it lead anywhere?"

"With Anna each picture leads to the next one with full commitment. That is the way of eros. We go on from one experience to another. When we finished our training group, there was a pervasive feeling that Anna's imagery could take many different directions in future pictures. We were left with a feeling of fertility and exuberance. On the basis of Anna's excitement about her work and the very strong support she received from the group, it is clear to me that the process was productive, or let us say therapeutic. Every year I grow more distrustful of the 'developmental' construct and the need that many therapists have to show 'improvement.' Attitudes of this kind can be useful with remediation therapies but not when we are dealing with the soul. My early publications focused on the developmental patterns in people's artwork and how these graphic changes influenced the person. That work was for the most part done with severely disturbed patients who needed help in getting from one place to another. The improvement model does not apply to depth psychology. With regard to your concern about where Anna's art leads, I often repeat a line from the film *Buckaroo Bonsai* in answering questions like this: 'Wherever you go, there you are.' As I suggested earlier when talking about Sartre and the will, we are what we do. The purpose of art as depth psychology has more to do with expressing, seeing and being seen than it does with improvement."

"It would seem that the therapeutic dimension of Anna's work involved the release of her sensuality, her demons and her expressive powers through the discipline of art," Lisa said.

"The large size of her paintings, some of them being as much as ten feet long, attests to the intensity of her involvement. The continuous series appears to have allowed the opposing elements to work things out with one another. She was keenly aware of the entire process as she reveals in her interpretations. She also appears to have been open to, and influenced by, other people. I do not know if we can ask for much more in art therapy."

"What do you see as the therapeutic element in this work?"

"I generally prefer to trust the interpretations of the artists and their descriptions of what they got from the experience. Sometimes, analysis afterwards can weaken the statement. But Anna's experience confirms a general theory that I have about art therapy's ability to release energetic powers or what we have referred to as soul. If these forces are not expressed and understood, they take the pathological form of conflicted sexuality. As I said before, the release of these sexual energies spreads to other forms of life and an open relationship with nature. One of the men in our group said: 'To be liberated is not just to be sexual. It is to be broader, more spontaneous.' Genitalia have become organs or rebellion in a world where our relationship with nature is restricted. Our sexual obsessions and pathologies can partly be explained by the way in which we approach nature. This link provides a key to understanding many of our contemporary pathologies. The next person's art that I want to show you illustrates this movement from genitalia to nature as a whole.

"The artist's name is Hadass. The first picture (Fig. 13) was done in response to two dreams that she had. This is what she said about the dreams;

In the first dream I was approached by a mysterious man in Germany who took me into a car to rape me. He turned out to be harmless, gentle and very beautiful. He was also passive and impotent. His penis was small and without an erection and to my surprise I saw that he had another one, a little bit bigger but impotent as well. There was nothing to do with him, so I left.

The second dream involves a woman who I have known and loved for many years. She is naked and has a beautiful erect penis. She is playing with herself and I play with her and she comes and I smell a special fragrance in her sperm.

As I reflect on the dream, I see the woman and the man both have one penis too many. The woman is potent. The man is impotent. For the past three years I have been living with a woman. Our relationship is very complete, except that we want a child. Here in my dream I experienced the joy of being with a woman who had sperm. The dreams suggest my erotic identification with the woman rather than the man. The macho, beastly man, the raper, is not really so strong and frightening. It is just the opposite. He was very female in his characteristics. I adore and detest this penis-man. The dream shows the feminine side of the man, that I both adore and detest, so I leave him. I should learn how to accept the male with his opposites, exactly as I accept a woman with her opposite sides. I admire the male by virtue of his penis and its strength. A woman does not have this visible erection. But with the strength comes the weakness. After the climax comes the anti-climax. I find women to be more independent and stable.

Figure 13

"The picture that Hadass did in response to the dreams focuses on the figures of the man and the woman. The man is slightly in the foreground and large. Above one shoulder she has drawn the car and above the other shoulder she drew the German swastika and a vagina. The vagina is green, suggesting fertility and nature. It is much larger than the swastika and appears to be dominant. The vagina touches the man and not the woman. Empty chairs are drawn just below the vagina. The woman's figure touches tower-like buildings that Hadass described as resembling the city of Jaffa on the Mediterranean. The shapes of the buildings are phallic. I observed how the buildings correspond to the male genitalia on each of the human figures. The building closest to the woman's legs, and in the foreground, has one tower and one window. The building in the background has two towers and two windows. Hadass said that the small yellow circle in the white square is a symbol of her presence and it is placed on the building with two towers. I experience the Jaffa buildings as including both male and female qualities."

"How did Hadass interpret the picture?"

"She was relaxed and pleased with it. I think that it was important for her to express this complicated scenario. When it was on the paper, she could study it, meditate on it and open to its possibilities. She first said: 'My male side needs to relax and be more passive, or maybe my male side needs to wake up and be more potent, strong and direct.'

"How do you relate to this contradiction?"

"I see it as expressing both sides of the coin. As I said earlier, contradictory positions can exist together in art and dreams and even complement one another. They do not have to cancel each other out. One position does not have to win over the other, or dominate. This is what Hadass's work is all about. She is exploring her male and female qualities. They are sitting next to each other. Both appear to be aroused and interested in sex. But their bodies do not touch. Their positions seem erect like the genitalia. She said: 'It's time for the sperm to come into me. When we take one penis from each figure, we are left with a beautiful couple.' But they both have an extra penis. In response to Anna's picture, Hadass said: 'Being able to show an erection is expressive of being able to show yourself before the world.' I think that this is what her picture is all about, showing herself to herself and to other people. I am personally moved by her small, yellow circle as a symbol of the self. This suggests to me that all of the things that she is expressing are much bigger than her. She is small and humble in contrast. The forces, energies and conflicts that she expresses do not belong to her exclusively. They are parts of a larger world."

"Do you perceive the picture as a self-portrait?"

"As I said before, I find that every painting has elements of the self-portrait. This picture by Hadass suggests that she is also presenting a portrait of the life forces that live within her. She is Jewish and is dealing with a German man in the dream and the picture. The horrors of the Holocaust are associated with the acts of men. The green vagina between the two figures looks to me like a power shield. I think that it is an important symbol for Hadass. It establishes a connection with the next picture (Fig. 14)."

Figure 14

"I see that she again used her small circle. This time the circle is white and it is in the middle of another circle rather than a square. It also seems to be more integrated into the picture as a whole. She has placed it in the center."

"Good observation. In this pastoral picture eros spreads to the animal, lake, fish, mountains and red palm trees. Hadass said that the donkey with its large breasts is a symbol of herself in nature and the red palm trees are an expression of her masculinity. Her interpretations focused on these two images. She said that her imagination thrives on the desert together with plants and animals that can survive there. She spoke of the desert as a mystical and religious place."

"The picture supports your idea that sexuality spread to all of nature. How do you relate to the archetypal qualities of the images?"

"The archetypal patterns correspond completely to what Hadass is saying about herself. The donkey is a universal symbol for 'the lower nature,' 'intense desire' and 'perversity.' It is not docile and quick to adapt to what the society wants and tends to go its own way. It is a willful animal and perverse. Roland Barthes in a 1975 interview said: 'Perversion is the pleasure principle. . .(it) is the search for the pleasure that is not made profitable by a social end, a benefit to the species.' The donkey certainly is not revered as one of the great benefactors of the human race. As a matter of fact, the image of the donkey, the domesticated ass, is very much the opposite. The *Heritage Dictionary* defines the donkey as 'an obstinate, sluggish and stupid fellow' and the ass as 'vain' and 'self-important.' My instinct is to defend the donkey from bias and the society's intolerance for perversion. The desert suggests solitude and the absence of society's conventions. It is remote, vast. Throughout history, visionaries have gone into the desert for inspiration. Palm trees flourish within arid climates and therefore symbolize fertility. Swedenborg saw the palm tree as signifying 'divine truths.' Note that there are many trees in this picture and they are 'above' the donkey. This composition reinforces the archetypal interpretations of the donkey representing the 'lower' nature and the palm trees the 'higher.' The upper trees are actually growing from the sky. These images correspond to the distinctions James Hillman makes between soul and spirit. He sees the search for soul as taking us into the 'depths,' whereas spirit is 'vertical and ascending.' I personally feel that these archetypal interpretations express the truth and fertility of Hadass's self-expression. The picture is loaded with archetypes: mountains, the lake, fish, house, breasts, the human animal, concentric circles, sky, ground. The possibilities in art therapy are endless, especially when we are faced with a picture of this kind. This image is a portrait of imagination and soul."

"It would seem that art therapy has the potential to introduce the sensuous into psychotherapy and mental health within a disciplined and clearly defined therapeutic context."

"Art is eros and soul as well as a sophisticated form of cognition and physical work. In order for art therapy to make an impact within the context of therapy, we have to rethink and change many of our taboos about sexuality and the sensuous. These negative obsessions strengthen the pathology."

"You seem to be expanding the definition of art therapy. I have been reading about the historic arguments in the professional literature which dispute the place of art as therapy vs. the use of art as a tool in psychotherapy. I think that this dichotomy can be easily resolved by the Hegelian triad of thesis, antithesis and synthesis. Art therapy can be both of these things and more. There are also the therapy as art positions, the artist-therapists and the archetypal perspective on imagery. Our discussions have included all of these things. With regard to eros and nature, art therapy might consider environmental artworks in which we directly engage and transform a particular setting. The framework of art helps us to be more aware of nature. I am not just talking about painting landscapes. Art therapy can also make landscapes."

"A colleague of mine in Israel, a woman, told me years ago that the good marriage satisfies the imagination. I was impressed by this statement, because like most married people I have done considerable thinking about the relationship. Six months later, during my next visit to Israel, I told my friend what a positive impact her statement about marriage had on me. She had also done some thinking about what she told me and she said that her statement was wrong. She then said that the good marriage 'improvises on the imagination.' This is what art therapy is to me. It expands imagination — mine and the groups I work with. When my imagination is directed somewhere other than my work or the relationships that I am involved with, there is a loss of vitality and soul. I am somewhere else. I have not had this problem with art therapy over the past two decades. It is always deepening imagination. This is why I have been so strongly opposed to overregulation, the prescription of training guidelines by national associations, narrow definitions and the weakening of the artistic elements of the profession. I do not want to lose our professional identification with the sensuous imagination."

"There is so much to do."

"That is what I love about art therapy."

II. Jill's Image Work

J ILL PARTICIPATED in a group that I led on art therapy and dreams. She is twenty-six years old. Her dreams are vivid and sometimes puzzling to her. A series of related drawings emerged that were themselves interpretations of the dream experience. In our two-hour sessions after the group was completed, we worked with one or sometimes two pictures. I asked Jill to begin by describing the dream and her picture. I asked what they meant to her, thus encouraging her to interpret the images. We then became involved in an extended dialogue about the dream and the picture.

FLYING THROUGH THE GREY CITY (Fig. 15)

"Would you begin by making a statement about your picture. Look at it and say whatever comes into your mind. It can be a story, a series of associations, a description of what you see or any combination of these, anything that helps to deepen our relationship with the image."

"I'm flying. I came from a farm to a dark, grey city," Jill said. "I cannot fly high enough. The people are trying to grab me and pull me down. It was terrifying. I have the feeling of trying to get up a little higher. I have diamonds in my right hand. I was going to sell them. I go into the basement window of a store. It was dark. This is where I am supposed to meet the person to whom I was going to sell the diamonds. I am safe there and just barely escaped the people who were trying to pull me down. In my waking life I was going to sell a pair of diamond earrings because I needed the money."

"Were they family jewels?"

"They belonged to my mother and my grandmother. I never did sell them. I felt guilty. It was a sleezy thing to do. The city in the dream was a sleezy place with trash everywhere."

"The crack of green in the upper right section of the picture seems so intentional."

"That is the farm that I flew from. I never liked the city. It scared me as a child. I felt like I was flying at the farm and that the world outside

Figure 15

would pull me down. The dream expresses how I felt about leaving the farm where I had lived for a year before returning to the 'grey city' to begin graduate studies in art therapy."

"The figure is wearing a pink dress. Her flesh is peach-colored and her hair is a bright yellow-orange."

"She is vulnerable. She is the only thing that is soft. Everything else is hard and black."

"The buildings look as if they are full of life, personified. If I look at the picture without reference to the dream you have described, I become involved with the windows. They arouse feelings of emptiness in me and perhaps the feeling of being looked at, or in a less suspicious sense the buildings seem to be engaged in the action. Maybe they are supporting her flight. How do you feel about them?"

"In the dream the main feeling was fear. There was a sensation of being different and the city was deserted."

"The brown figures could be doing a dance with her. It can be useful sometimes to restructure what we see in the picture. The possibility of them dancing with her is quite different from their pulling her down from the sky. Am I intruding with this interpretation?"

"Not at all. It is helpful for me to switch the story, change interpretations and look at the picture as an image, without reference to my dream."

"The way you have drawn the buildings, tilting toward and away from one another, together with the strong thrust of the diagonal, black road, creates a movement response in a purely formal sense. This is heightened by her flight with arms and legs extended and the action of the figures below her."

"She is clearly in motion. And the world is moving, too."

CHANGING SHIPS (Fig. 16)

"In this picture I am on an ocean liner with an influential teacher. He is out on the deck and comes in to tell me that there is going to be a tidal wave. I go out to look at the tidal wave and two friends from Boston pull me overboard and under the waves so that I will not drown. At the bottom of the ocean I run out of air and have to swim up. When I get to the top of the water I cannot find my old boat and some people pull me onto another boat. It felt like I was being rescued."

"What happens to this picture when you look at it without reference to the dream?"

"I see the boats as symbolic of two ways of living. The first boat, the one on our left, is red. It is full of emotion, but it is too hot. The new boat is green, which is a healing color for me. It expresses growth."

"It is the same green from the farm in the first picture."

"Yes. I see that now. The three figures at the bottom of this picture express being with people and being alone. The figure on the right, surrounded by a light blue aura is peaceful and it represents my decision to go off on my own."

"How do you relate to the ladder?"

"In the dream the ladder only came down a little bit from the surface, whereas I paint it coming down to the bottom. Right now, I see the ladder as 'help,' and I wish it could have come down to me when I was at the bottom of the ocean."

"How do you feel about the ocean?"

"It was wild on top and calm underneath. I do not think the picture expresses being under the water. Do you?"

"I see this as a two-dimensional image. When you say the figures are underwater, I see them that way. The fact that they are clearly distin-

Figure 16

guished from the water helps us to see them. It furthers clarity. Even though the figures are not 'covered' by the water in the drawing, I see them as immersed. It would also be possible to see them as swimming on top of the water with the boats in the distance or they could be standing on the shore. My tendency is to adjust my perception of the picture to your story."

"How do you see the water?"

"From a spatial perspective, I see it as the primary element in the picture. There is more water than anything else. The purple tone of the water is comforting. It seems soft and sensual, full of feeling."

"It was nice under the water. It was dark and quiet, but I could not live there. I could not breath. There is a deep feeling to the water."

"You described the red boat as too hot and maybe the water is too deep. You cannot live in either place. In the dream and in this picture you are changing to the green boat. Maybe the fact that you do not see the picture expressing 'being under the water' is another manifestation of your desire to go to a place where you can live. The three figures are illuminated. You are not alone and you join hands with your friends. It is a more nurturing and hopeful picture than the first one. The place that you are going to has changed from a grey city to a green boat. You are not being pulled down by other people but join hands with them. There is an equality of form and color between the figures, and also between the boats. I see a yin-yang duality in the two vessels. I do not think it is simply a matter of leaving one for another. Both of them seem to be in you, the heat and the comforting green. We can see the same pattern in the dark, deep water as contrasted to the illuminated figures and the grey city with the green farm."

"I agree with what you see. There is also the presence of the underworld together with the helping ship. I jumped ship. The dream and my pictures are expressions of my leaving the teacher and going off on my own. My departure was not smooth. There was an element of betrayal in it, but this was better than giving myself over to the authority of another. I am actually progressing from betrayal to self-trust here. I had to get beyond my need for a perfect spiritual father. Years ago, I felt that I needed a teacher who would actually be a guru to me. It was incredible how much power I gave to this particular teacher. Maybe it was not so much of a betrayal as taking this power back into myself. In this picture I find out that it is actually all right for me to be in the ocean alone."

"The betrayal of trust in another, which presents itself here as a dependence, riding in his boat, gives you the opportunity to trust yourself."

"I see the pattern now, flying alone, jumping ship, immersing myself in the sea, changing."

"The windows in the boats are similar to those in the city buildings."

"I did not see that before. I am surprised that they are so dark. It seems like there is nothing inside. They are all so empty. I need to accept this too."

GLOWING SQUIRREL BABY (Fig. 17)

"In the dream I am living in an overcrowded apartment in New York City. I just had a baby and it is glowing and I do not want anyone to see it, so I take it outside and I am going to put it into the branches of a tree and it turns into a squirrel. During the period when I had this dream, I was living in a congested environment where I felt that I could not show myself with people. I had just arrived in Boston and I was in a temporary place that felt crowded. I was perceived as being 'different.' In the dream, this is expressed by my not wanting anyone to see the baby, and maybe this is also a form of self-protection. It was too beautiful and spiritual. I think the squirrel also represents the new relationship that I have just begun with a man. Squirrels are wild animals that live here in the city of Cambridge. I felt guilty about leaving the baby in the tree."

Figure 17

"I see the picture as expressing adaptability. The letting go of the parent allows the baby to have a life of its own. There seems to be too much love for abandonment. The fact that it turns into a squirrel heightens this impression, since the squirrel is such a conspicuous animal survivor of this region. It is a tremendously resourceful and hardy creature."

"I am not hiding the baby, the squirrel or the relationship. I am putting them into a natural setting."

"Could the picture express a rebirth of yourself?"

"I am starting something new and finding the country in the city. I could not be as vulnerable as a baby. I have to be adaptable like a squirrel."

"The tree is lush, full of life and possibilities."

"This helps me to have the feeling of letting go. It is a happy loss. I'm imagining myself talking to the squirrel and asking him how he is doing. He says that everything is fine and that the tree is a good home. I ask him if he is mad at me for leaving him alone in the tree and he answered, 'No, I'm a squirrel.' "

SNAKE IN THE BOOKS (Fig. 18)

"I was looking at my mother's bookcase in her house. She is a clinical psychologist. Suddenly, I see a snake's tail and then the whole snake in the books, moving in and out. I realized that it has been living there in the books for years. It came down the shelves to bite me, sliding and jumping over where my mother was lying on a couch. I ran up the stairs, opened the front door and jumped into the air. I was trying to trick the snake into going outside so I could close the door on it. I was terrified going back to my mother's house after the dream. I was afraid the snake would really come out from the bookcase."

"How do you stand with the dream right now? Your drawing of the snake seems well organized and balanced. The books and the snake appear integrated. They complement each other."

"I feel as though I let the snake bite me. In a later dream I met it again and it did bite me. As soon as the snake bit me, the whole dream changed. I did not die."

"Perhaps this is a passage dream. Your dreams and pictures have consistently expressed themes of passage. . .changing boats, the farm to the city, and now the snake bite."

"How do you see the snake relating to passage?"

"I see you passing into your mother's profession by studying art therapy. You both share the common books of the profession, but she is

Figure 18

portrayed on the couch which I associate with the more classical verbal forms of therapy. You are more involved with the snake which suggests more archetypal and imagistic forms of transformation."

"I think you are right. This interpretation leads us into the next picture that I want to show you."

"But let's continue working with this picture. You said the snake jumped over your mother. She was reclining. Was she between you and the snake?"

"Yes, and she was not afraid of the snake. It did not have any business with her."

"What was its business with you?"

"It wanted to bite me."

"Why?"

"It wanted to kill me."

"Why?"

"It wanted me to come into its world and I could not go in alive."

"What is its world?"

"The snake is the keeper of all of the knowledge in the books. It is not going to just let me read the books. I am going to have to be bitten and feel the pain of learning all of the things that go with being an art therapist."

"Shamanic initiation involves symbolic death. Shamans throughout the world tell stories of becoming skeletons during their passage rites. The old self dies and the shaman is reborn with healing powers."

"I was not conscious of this dimension of the dream. It just came out of me right now as I am speaking to you. I did not realize that I had to let the snake kill me so that I could learn and come back."

"The snake is green and it continues your thematic use of green in these first four pictures. You said that green is a healing color for you. Are you afraid of being bitten by the healing element?"

"It can be painful. But it is the only real way for me."

"According to your dream, change results immediately."

"It makes me grateful for these snakes that come."

"We have not spoken about the relationship of the snake, or serpent, to the books. The two are actually brought together in your picture. They complement one another and express a cooperation as I see it between the serpent who is for me the embodiment of sensuousness and healing, and the books which suggest ideas and wisdom."

"I see the books as stiff. I feel frustrated when I look at all of my mother's books and I worry about whether I will be able to read them all. Whereas if I just know the way of the snake, then I will be a more spontaneous and natural therapist. But the books are important, because the snake lives in them. Somehow, he, and I think it is a 'he,' is the essence of the books."

"It seems that your passage into the profession of psychotherapy requires that you understand your relationship to your mother. Your dream is suggesting that you may not be able to read all of her books and that this may not be necessary. You identify more with the snake which is able to jump over her quite easily. Your mother is comfortable with the snake. As you said, 'It has no business with her.' The methods that you are selecting as a therapist are different from those of your mother. They are perhaps represented by the snake. It is after you. The two of you go out the door of your mother's house. As I said earlier, you portray the snake with a sense of comfort and balance in your picture. It is actually presented with a sense of majesty. Since the picture has been done after the dream, it expresses where you are right now with the image. The books are equally important in the picture. Your mother is not presented at all. But your snake lives in her books, in the essence that you share with her."

"The drawing does help me to see what I have done with the dream. The wisdom represented by the books is coming to me. But the wisdom of psychotherapy cannot be gained through books alone. The real knowledge is more painful, like the bite of the snake which will probably be fatal to some of my old ways."

LOSING MY PAINTS IN THE JUNGLE (Fig. 19)

"I am sleeping on a hammock. It is a beautiful feeling. I decide that I can spend the night. In the morning I wake up and discover that it has become high and I cannot get down. My mother is there by the house, but the hammock is so high that she cannot help me to get down. I have all of my art supplies with me. When I am sleeping up there, they fall down into the Amazon jungle. I go to pick them up (the height of the hammock is no longer an obstacle) and I have to walk through many snakes. There are other people who help me to pick them up. They just arrived and I do not know who they are. Then my water color palette, which is my favorite medium, is in the mouth of a beast and he is eating it. He is in a wall and only his head is sticking out. I did not draw the wall in the picture because it did not make sense to have a wall in the jungle."

"What does the jungle mean to you?"

"Going into art and feelings is going into the jungle. It is dangerous with the snakes. These were the first snakes in my dreams that did not try to bite me."

"Your dream image of the beast stuck in the wall suggests blocked creativity to me. The primal animal cannot move."

"Yes. And it is eating my water colors. I had to get the paints back. Normally, I would be scared to take something out of a monster's mouth."

"How do you feel about the house?"

Figure 19

"It is civilization and I am going so high with art therapy that my mother cannot help me down."

"Why does your mother appear?"

"I'm taking things to places where she has never been so she cannot help me."

"Do you feel that the dream and the picture express distinctions between you and your mother?"

"Yes. The feeling of not being helped is so strong. I experience two different worlds. She lives in the nice, tidy house and I am on the edge of this jungle. I would prefer not to live in the jungle all of the time."

"In your picture you place yourself right on the edge of the jungle and much closer to your mother and her world than to the beast. The high hammock elevates you from the jungle floor and the snakes. I get the feeling of being suspended. The figure on the hammock seems child-like and somewhat overwhelmed by the intensities of the jungle. The tree is a strong and vital image."

"What do you think of the paints falling into the jungle and my having to rescue them?"

"I see it as a descent into art, into action and exploration, into complexity and risk. The dream image of the beast in the wall first made me think of obstacles to expression. As I continue to work with the dream, this picture and the story that you are telling, I am beginning to see the beast more as primal expression and the sensuous nature of art. He seems to be suggesting how you can grab unto art. I experience the wall as the obstacle to expression. But the beast emerges from it with the paints. The rescue you describe may be the rescue of your creativity. The beast may be helping you. He is at home in the jungle."

"What do you think of the snakes not biting me?"

"You are going into their realm, immersing yourself in it. Your paints are 'falling' into the jungle. It is different from the world of books and ideas inside the house where the snake was not at home. How do you relate to the trees?"

"They are thick, twisted, full of vines, and, as you say, strong. Everything is growing. The snakes allowed me to pass. I still had to be careful of them. In the previous dream the snake bite was my death, a surrender. In this picture the snakes are harmless guardians in the jungle."

"I am noticing how similar the windows and doorways in this picture are to those in your first two pictures. Is this a characteristic of your graphic style, your way of constructing windows and doors, or are you making a symbolic statement?"

"I believe that it is an expression of my style. I did not think about them while I was working. But as I look at them now, it hits me that the windows in all of the buildings are black and empty. This makes me feel sad. But people do live in the buildings. I feel my soul more when I am outside. When I look at the picture from what I consider to be 'the conventional art therapy viewpoint,' the empty windows are impoverished."

"Maybe what you perceive as 'the conventional art therapy viewpoint' is stopping you, interrupting your process and making you feel empty and impoverished. The negative interpretation, which is really not your own, seems to be frightening you."

"Yes, as soon as I saw that all the windows were empty, I was afraid of what you would think of me and I panicked."

"I can distinguish you from your windows. But I am interested in both. The windows are actually one of the strongest themes in the pictures. They stimulate my imagination. They are suggestive of the interior, going in. Darkness is generally a restful element for me. The windows and doorways are clear and bold images in your pictures that provide an important compositional contrast. They give structural definition and introduce the complementary qualities of inside and outside. As I said about the first picture, they animate the buildings. We should not overlook these aesthetic functions. The windows increase mystery and archetypal meaning. There are vast possibilities for the interpretation of these windows. I do not have a need to reduce them to a single pathology."

"What a relief! I got stuck in that narrow, pathological way of looking. I was projecting negative associations onto the image rather than opening to its possibilities. The windows and door in my mother's house are dark, too. I started making windows like that when I was teaching art to children. I liked the way they drew with such simplicity and directness."

"You mentioned before that green is a healing color for you. This picture is loaded with green. Perhaps this is a healing jungle. In the previous picture a single snake takes up all of the space. Here you have many snakes which appear to be integrated into the more general movement patterns of the jungle. The trees and vines coil and bend like snakes. The entire place has taken on serpentine qualities."

"I am so relieved to get out from under the negative way of looking at the windows."

"You do not appear to be as interested in the snakes at this moment."

"No, please excuse me. I am still so involved with what I did to the windows and to myself. This is such a demonstration of how the therapeutic process works. I am amazed at the way in which the burden was lifted through a change of consciousness. The impact of the transformation is so strong, because it allowed me to 'feel' how I was creating the problem myself. You are giving me the freedom to describe the images in whatever way I choose. You are also able to let go of your own train of thought if it seems to be going away from me. I think that I am getting in touch with the authoritative, negative judge that I carry inside me. My feeling is so strong, because I am realizing that I create the negative judgments that I fear.

"It is significant that I draw my mother in blue. This is a peaceful color for me."

"You seem to have a good relationship with your mother."

"Yes. We did not really talk for years. But right now she is extremely supportive. She shows her vulnerability as a person. She raised me with a perfectionistic model that was not helpful. Now she is helping me to feel that it is natural to struggle, to be in process rather than perfect. It is such a relief to understand this and to see how I oppress myself with fears that I will not be perfect. The way in which you helped me to work with the windows makes this clear for me. I was able to watch myself through the concrete elements of the art therapy process. My instinct was to become immersed in the negative and panic."

"The fear seems related to a loss of love."

"Yes, not being appreciated and thus loved. I was afraid that you would not like what you saw in my empty, impoverished and black windows. All of this is connected to my relationship with my mother. The timing of your giving me the freedom and help in interpreting the windows in a non-authoritative way coincides precisely with what is happening right now between my mother and I. She is accepting and relaxed."

"Your mother is a consistent presence in your dreams and pictures right now."

"We are making progress together. I am coming so much closer to her but with a new freedom and autonomy. What I am learning right now is how important acceptance of the other person is in art therapy. It is also necessary to accept the image and let it be itself. The fact that there are many possibilities for interpretation is liberating. What immobilized me was the fear that something will come out of me that is going to be really bad and negative."

"Your experience of the process allows you to be sensitive to how labeling and reducing images to negative judgments can be inappropriate in therapy. I am not trying to avoid our pathologies and fears. I have found that we can go to the deepest places in ourselves, to our greatest areas of vulnerability, when we disregard both negative and positive judgments and try to accept and understand 'what is,' what we are and how we operate. Artists think in terms of 'what works.' This is a helpful way to approach therapy. When I concentrate on the windows or other aspects of a picture or dream, my objective is to assist you in getting closer to the images. We often fear that simple questions like that are directed at uncovering dark secrets. Our experiences with life, therapy and psychology have made us suspicious. The fear about the dark secret is for me suggestive of your motivation to work on yourself. The fears in your dreams are activators."

"My dreams and pictures are all about fears."

"But there is also life, vitality, tenderness, flight, wisdom, color, expression and many more elements. Do they cover over the fear?"

"No. The dreams start with a fear, but there is more than that."

"You are using the fear as a stimulus to express feelings and create art. You work with it and shape it into these images and stories."

"I would not have done anything if it were not for the impressions it made on me."

"So perhaps the fear is necessary and useful."

"Yes. It makes me do something about it."

A THOUSAND SWANS (Fig. 20)

"In this dream I was staying in my parents' house which was a castle by the ocean. A frozen swimming pool on the roof was full of swans who were hibernating. There were one thousand swans in the pool. They were in the ice, but it wasn't cold outside. There were two swans who were sitting to the side of the pool. They were beautiful and I made contact with them. I left to find a friend so that I could show her the swans. On the way, I found many jewels and amulets in the crumbling rocks of the castle. When we returned, people were walking across the pool with heavy boots that were breaking the ice. They did not notice the swans who came out from the cracked ice. Some flew away and others turned into penguins and did not fly away. I think the dream concerns hidden beauty. What do the images evoke in you?"

Figure 20

"The release of soul. The swan is often a symbol of soul. As the release occurs, some fly into the air and others stay grounded. The soul can be described as beauty which is contained, or hidden as you say, by the pool of ice. I am intrigued with the method of release, the people with their heavy boots who are not aware of what they are doing."

"The boots were important. They were work boots."

"Work has been a theme in other pictures that we have discussed."

"Work is contact with life."

"What are the people like who are wearing the boots?"

"They are like the people who tried to pull me down from the sky in the first picture."

"In the first picture they are trying to pull down the flying figure and in this picture they are walking blindly."

"Right in my castle. They do not seem to belong there, but they are breaking the ice."

"Something foreign, unintentional and unexpected breaks the ice."

"This did not bother me as much as the swans leaving."

"The swans can also be perceived as being released."

"And I am afraid to let them out. In the dream they are under ice and now I fear that they will fly away."

"Who is the little figure in the foreground?"

"That's me watching."

"The figure is barely defined in comparison to the swans and the penguins."

"They were awesome to look at in my dream."

"Are the birds more important in this picture than the figure in the foreground?"

"Yes. I do not think the tiny figure has anything to do with the way I perceive myself as a person. In this picture, the figure is only there to look at the swans and penguins."

"Although she is small, she is grounded and standing right in the middle of the picture. The swans and penguins are all moving in the same direction, to the right."

"It was important to me that the swans were flying inland and away from the ocean. If they flew to the ocean, it would seem that they were going into mysteries. Here they are going into the world, into practical things."

"You are bringing up work again and change. Let's return to your theme of beauty, the jewels, amulets and the friend."

"My sister was in the dream, too. I saw her just before the friend. She had slept late and was unprepared. She is always late. I am late a lot, too. It bothers me."

"Lateness can be a condition of not wanting to leave the place where you are and what you are doing at a particular time. Maybe your sister has something to do with your reluctance to change, being stuck in the ice until some 'blind' force breaks you lose. The boots can be perceived as blind and unthinking instincts that know when it is time to break the ice so your swans and penguins can go about their business. Your sister might represent what is holding you back."

"That's a good way to describe my sister. She has had learning problems."

"How do you relate to the jewels and amulets?"

"They were magical. The entire dream has a magical feeling. They also represent the new feelings and wonderful things that I can find within the castle of my family."

"The ice pool is also in there and the swans fly away from the castle. I moved us into a discussion of the boots and work and away from your image of 'hidden beauty' in the swans and the jewels and amulets that you found in the crumbling rocks of the castle. Would you like to return to the theme of beauty?"

"The whole scene was beautiful and I walked carefully to avoid waking or scaring the swans."

"What happened to your friend?"

"I do not know who it was. What do you think about my friend?"

"It seems that you wanted a witness, someone to share the experience with because it was so difficult to believe."

"It was unbelievable."

"I want to be careful not to intrude upon the magic of the dream and the picture."

"It was like a fairy tale."

"Is the dream helpful?"

"It gave me three things, three shocks. First, the shock that the swans induced. I felt as though they were my inner beauty and I was stunned to see that. The second shock was the breaking of the ice, and that has something to do with interacting with people and what this brings out in me. The day before this dream, I showed myself to people in a psychodrama class. They were the people with the heavy boots from the outside world. Before, I had been hiding my inner self behind a sheet of ice that they broke. I was surprised by what I showed to the people in the class. It was as though a thousand white swans escaped from my being. The self-revelation in the class was not planned. It happened spontaneously. My swan nature had been frozen and it needed other people to set it free. I was also pleased to see that at first two swans freed themselves from the ice. This made me think about the new relationship I am in. Swans mate for life and this also pleases me. The third shock was their leaving and this might have something to do with using my beauty in the world. The dream was helpful and so was your question."

GOING BACK TO THE OLD TEACHER (Fig. 21)

"It was as though I have traveled across the world to visit my old and influential teacher. He appeared in the dream as an archetypal teacher, a wise, old man. People are waiting in line to see him and someone gives me a baby to hold."

"The people on the left look like a series of couples."

Figure 21

"I did not notice that. The two people standing closest to him are holding huge blocks of ice on their backs. I thought for a minute that there might be something bad about the ice, as with the black windows. The ice is so cold. I originally thought it was to cool off the teacher. One of the women in our dream class saw the blocks of ice as coffins. I was struck by that response. It made me realize that I have to mourn the loss of this teacher. He was an important part of my life and I must recognize the feelings I have about leaving him."

"It looks like the people who are carrying the ice, or coffins, are walking away from him."

"The people who critize the teacher walked away as I did. That is really insightful. I never thought of that. I can just look at the body postures and realize that they are walking away. Your observation is helpful. They are giving him 'the cold shoulder.' "

"In this picture ice is associated with walking away, and in your previous picture the ice is breaking to allow the swans to fly away. The penguins walked away."

"Yes, ice is frozen emotion. I always think of water as emotion."

"So the emotions are in motion. . .thawing, melting, breaking up and being carried away. The smaller figures below look like they are praying."

"They still honor him."

"Do you still honor him?"

"Yes."

"The woman and the baby give me a sense of new life."

"I went back there with my new life. I am detached. I am not walking away and I am not praying."

"You are not walking away and you are not praying. You are just there with your new life."

"My God! I did not realize what I had said until you repeated it. I am not giving him the cold shoulder or worshipping him. I am independent with my new life. It's amazing that it is all there in the picture, in the characters, and I did not see it until we talked about it right now."

"How do you respond to the picture in terms of its shapes, colors and composition? Let's look at it without reference to meanings or stories?"

"It's solid."

"Is it solid, like the feeling it evokes in you right now about your relationship to this teacher?"

"Yes. I feel stronger now in my separateness from him."

"The teacher is at the top, but he is not bigger than the woman with the child. He seems to be in a sanctuary and she is in the world."

"Each figure in the picture accurately represents a way of feeling. I am still astonished that it is so clear and that I did not see it before. It is like a gestalt that just flips and we understand it."

"Much of the power of art therapy results from simply taking the time to look carefully and openly at the pictures together with another person. In art therapy we establish an environment in which there is an interest in the way the images relate to the person's life as a whole. We make it possible to explore these connections that may not be of interest to the conventional art milieu. It may not even be possible for the artist to do this alone. The second person, or the group, helps to flip the gestalt as you say. In our work together with your dreams and pictures, we have seen how effortless it can be to restructure our perceptions and gain new insights. You have observed how these insights sometimes simply emerge through the dialogue. You have occasionally stunned yourself with what you have said. As I return to this picture I am wondering if your separation from this teacher relates to your separation from your parents' and your father's influence."

"As with my family, I left in the dream and I am still coming to visit. My separation was gentle."

"No aggression?"

"Some separated from the teacher in the same way I separated from my family when I was younger. I just left and started new and completely different things which would have been considered inappropriate according to the standards of what I left. Many people separate with extreme aggression, with what you have described as psychological 'killing.' My way tends to be more passive-aggressive. It might have been easier to kill the old situation, because then I would not always have to deal with going back, facing it repeatedly and proving myself. That can be an unnecessary burden, exhausting."

"The symbolic killing has to do with consciously letting go and separating, dealing directly."

"Walking away as I did might be a way of ignoring what I am leaving. How would I do a symbolic killing?"

"In your art, your dreams and in your imagination. You can kill their influence, the old roles, the things that burden and oppress you, that hold you back."

"I never could show my aggression to my father. This makes sense to me. My life history has been one of not being able to say no, directly, to men that are authority figures. It is all so woven together. I am surprised."

THE SHAMAN (Fig. 22)

"This is a continuation of the swan dream. I do not know how to tie this one together with the other pictures."

"I would not try to make connections between them right now. The attempt to relate to the other pictures will take you away from this one. The connections will emerge on their own if you concentrate on the picture."

Figure 22

"In the dream that preceded this picture, I am in a van with my childhood orthodontist. My fiance is also in the dream, but he is walking to his car. We are leaving the Philadelphia Art Museum for my parents' house. I look out the window and see him making a blessing motion with his arms over five Muslim women who are holding babies. I know that he is a shaman. They were black American women who turned to an ancient religion to find meaning. They might be related to the magical feeling I had as a child when I saw the Black Muslims in Philadelphia."

"How do you feel about the babies?"

"I have old thoughts of fertility and love."

"What are some of the new possibilities?"

"I can't think of any new ones. The women represent a tremendous spiritual power in the city. They were on the grass next to the art museum. The museum is a spiritual place for me. I had a feeling of awe whenever I went there. In the first drawing there was nothing spiritual in the city. Now there is. The grey, depressive, chaotic and terrifying city is being transformed into a spiritual energy."

"In your first picture there is just a small crack of green."

"Now it is all green."

"It seems that the process of passage and change that begins in the first picture is continuing. Through art therapy you are returning to your artistic vocation as represented by the museum which is one of the first places where we experience feelings of awe and spirit in relation to art. You go from the museum to the grass, to the shaman, fertility, love and into the world where spirit now seems to relate to healing, compassion and nurturing."

"All of that is going on as you describe it. There is continuity expressed in the color green, the farm, the ship, the snake, the jungle and now the grass outside the art museum. But I have another feeling about this picture which is much stronger. When I had the dream, I felt that it was concerned with seeing who my boyfriend is. I was with the orthodontist who was a weird guy who had many relationships with women outside his marriage. My identification was more with the orthodontist, because I was in the car with him."

"Are you afraid of your potential to relate to more than one person? Or is your boyfriend afraid of this?"

"Both of us are. It is not good for our relationship. My alignment with the orthodontist does seem to express these fears."

"I was going to ask you about the five women."

"What do you see in them?"

"I experience them as multiple elements of yourself, all of which are now entering into a relationship with the man who is standing in the road. The orthodontist seems to be the embodiment of your fears about the multiplicity. In this picture the multiplicities are considering a permanent relationship, or family, with one man. You experience him as one but yourself as many. This is, of course, my story about your image. It is an expression of my imagination."

"I am split between the adulterous guy and the women with the babies. I like what you said about the family. I wonder what the blessing he is giving means?"

"Does it have anything to do with giving power to a man?"

"Perhaps, but in a positive way. I was surprised that the Black Muslim women respected him so much, because they usually do not like white people. I think that I am surprised by my respect for him."

"As contrasted to your feelings about the other man you were driving with?"

"The men in my past were more like the adulterous orthodontist."

"Did they give you pain?"

"I am not sure that I would give them that much credit. I gave myself the pain. They were generally incapable of giving. The world, and myself, were objects for their gratification. I have had a pattern of transferring my spiritual powers to the men that I am involved with. I need to give more attention to my swans and babies."

"This image of the five women holding babies follows the previous one where you are holding the child. In that picture you are quite distinct from the teacher. You were holding the child and not giving away your power. As I listen to you describe this dream with the five women, I begin to see the male as a figure that includes both the shaman giving his blessing and the weird orthodontist. And of course there are many more qualities such as fathers and teachers."

"I was surprised that I was riding in the car with the orthodontist and not my boyfriend. Perhaps I am closer to him than I realize. But we were all driving to the same place."

"Your parents' house, you said earlier."

"Yes. This increases the sense of family and meeting my boyfriend for the purpose of making a family."

"The dream does seem, as you say, to be focused on the soul of your boyfriend. Are the five women associated with his relationships to women or a love for all people?"

"I did feel jealous when I was painting this picture. Can you imagine that, jealous about a painting. There is more here than I realized. I want to say something about the conversation that we are having. I appreciate that when you introduced an idea that did not click, you kept searching for the click. I need some probing from you on this picture. It is a difficult one for me to work with. Those women have been a mystery to me, and I did not want to be in the car with the orthodontist."

"What did not click?"

"The discussion about my multiplicity as expressed by the women. It made sense intellectually, and I cannot deny that this is a part of me. But the interpretation did not engage me on a feeling level. They were other women and not me. What did connect was how the women respected him the way I respect him."

"It is important to hear you clarify that the women were not you. The tendency to see everything in the picture or the dream as part of you can be misleading. In all of the pictures that we have worked with, your presence is clearly defined and distinguished from other people and figures. Maybe the interpretation of art and dreams is based upon trying many possibilities until we come upon the story or theme that 'clicks.' When we are working with your material, it should click for you and not necessarily for me. I get my click from yours. It is equally important to let go of those attempts that were not working for you. Therapy can become terribly confused when therapists are overly committed to their interpretations."

"As therapists, our egos have to be secure so that we may change our interpretations and let things go. I have experienced being pushed into people's theories. I have the power to change it when I am able to say: 'No! That's not it.' "

THE PROSTITUTE (Fig. 23)

"I am in a hotel lobby and I see one of my best girl friends from junior high school. She is working as a prostitute in the hotel. She motions for me to follow her upstairs. As we walk up the stairs, she changes into an innocent blonde woman who is in one of my art therapy seminars. When we reach her room, there is a man there. She quickly signals for me to go out the back door before he can see me. The door opens to a dark stairway and there is a tough-looking man walking up. I feel scared and run past him onto the street. The prostitute joins me. She runs down the stairs after me.

"The first thing that I see in the drawing is how I made the prostitute big, red, and voluptuous looking. In the dream she was sweet, Heidelike. In the drawing, I am the blue figure behind the woman on the left. I am also the figure to the right of the bed, on the stairs."

"What is happening with the figures at the bottom, under the bed?"

"There are three men who are involved with her as she lies on her back."

"It is striking the way the bed seems to be at the top of a pyramid. The elevation gives the impression of an altar."

Figure 23

"Everything revolves around the bed."

"It is empty and that increases the drama. This seems difficult for you to talk about."

"It is. When I started to explore sexuality, my friend from junior high school accompanied me when I went out with boys. We used to trade boyfriends every week. It was as though it was innocent prostitution, thus the girl who looked like Heide. I would sometimes get into bad situations as with the man on the stairs."

"He and the red woman are larger than the other figures in the picture. They also appear to be more defined. The red woman is so strong. She walks decisively with her head raised, and her breast is prominent."

"And I look reluctant following her."

"Your head is lowered and your body does not have the same detail."

"It confuses me as to why she followed me into the street. In the dream we planned to spend time together, but we couldn't because she had a customer. What do you think?"

"Maybe you are more important to her than the man, and it seems that relationships and friendships are what really matter for you. They last. Is the picture celebrating sexuality through the elevation of the pyramid? Is there a feeling of sacrifice? Or does this picture express some of the painful and frightening elements of sexuality?"

"The pyramid emerged when I drew the two scenes of going up and down the stairs. The man on the stairs represents fear. The picture also expresses the peer pressure of sexuality. I am following the woman, who is also my junior high school friend, up the stairs."

"How do you relate to the theme of prostitution?"

"It concerns the conflict between my past and my new relationship to my boyfriend. It is all so innocent, but yet there is a threatening element and I introduce the theme of the prostitute. I go up and down the stairs. My boyfriend and I get jealous about each other's past."

"I feel like the orthodontist, probing at your sensitivities."

"This is all so sensitive, because I do not want to feel bad about my past. I do not want to treasure it or trash it. I would like to say something about the prostitute. She is an innocent Heide and a professional hooker."

"Her role with men is not clear."

"But she is in control. She can leave when she wants."

"This corresponds to what you said earlier about being able to say no."

"It does. The work with the last two pictures has been difficult, because my waking mind does not feel good about the images, but my dream mind is trying to tell me that they are innocent. When things are so emotional it is difficult to think clearly, especially if there is guilt. But staying with the images until I get a feeling of understanding helps me to be in control. If I cannot pull my life together into a story that feels meaningful, then life is always on top of me."

THE BATHTUB AND THE OCEAN (Fig. 24)

"This is also a difficult picture. I will need some help with it. The conflict in the images pushes me away. In the dream that preceded the picture, I am at the beach with my fiance, whose name is Bob. I see Rona, a girl who stole my first boyfriend in high school. I was always jealous of her. She is diving into the ocean naked. I do not want Bob to see her. He is sensitive to the situation and brings me into the beach-house, through her bedroom and into a bathroom. I am angry that he took me through the bedroom. He wants me to come into the bathtub with him, but I want to go into the ocean. I tell him that I am upset because of what happened in high school, and I do not want to have what happened in high school with Rona occur again with him. He understands this and we return to the beach and Rona is gone. There are families on the beach. We cannot decide whether we want to wear bathing suits or not. We choose to wear them because of the families. This dream is represented in the section of the picture which is to the left of the diagonal divider.

Figure 24

"The other section of the picture was done in response to a dream that I had two days later. I am in a clothing store and Rona walks in with one of her boyfriends. I strongly feel, 'Oh no, not her again.' I scream at her that she stole my boyfriend. Rona is in the midsection of the image with her boyfriend and the bottom right is me screaming at her. I am the smaller red figure in the foreground. The store changes to a mental institution and I am giving Rona pills to make it appear that she is crazy. I call the nurse and say: 'There is a crazy woman here' and they think it was me. I tell them that it is her and they let me go. The black image represents my getting on top of her to put the pills in her mouth. It is dark, like a seclusion room."

"How do you interpret the dream?"

"Rona is the archetype of 'the other woman.' In the first dream, I was frightened that Bob would like her and I was angry that he walked through her room. I also felt a strong love for him, because he understood my fear and it was not a problem with us."

"I feel a reluctance on your part to enter his tub. You said that you wanted to go into the ocean. This sharply contrasts to the containment of the tub."

"This is a big conflict in our relationship. The tub is intimate, but I was trapped in the little room. I wanted the freedom of the ocean and being outside. It is interesting how we go in cycles. At times I want to be inside and he wants to go out."

"It sounds like the great archetype of control in relationships."

"Whose needs are we going to follow? I think the dream expresses many things. . .the fear and reality of jealousy and control struggles. The bathing suit conflict expresses my feelings about ending a free lifestyle and entering a family phase; and the intimacy issue is something I have to think about more. The dream and my picture deal with my need to be both alone and together with another person."

"What do you think about the water in the tub and the ocean?"

"I have feelings of relaxation. In the 'changing ships' picture I was overwhelmed by the water and in the 'one thousand swans' the swans were getting out of the water. I was an observer."

"In this picture you do not get into the water. Bob is in the tub and Rona is in the ocean."

"I did decide to go into the ocean with Bob and then I woke up. The conflict was resolved in this dream. In the second dream I felt that I was really confronting Rona."

"Her blue figure is larger than your red, and she looks like she will not be easily overwhelmed."

"She is powerful. I think that is why I had to put her in the seclusion room where I could get some control over her. In the dream she has taken away a boyfriend who I recently left. I see this dream as expressing my need to have control over my fear of losing Bob."

"I have a strong sense of your aggression in this picture. The red around you and Rona is intense."

"I feel good about my aggression here. People do not see me as aggressive, so I was proud of my ability to act on it."

"Is there also a fear of going crazy?"

"I fear that."

"This picture expresses confinement and needs for control."

"It is interesting that the seclusion room and the bathtub scene are right next to each other. In both of these situations Rona was out of the way. In the bathroom, I did it in a more positive way by saying what I felt. My fears are what make trouble in the relationship. Bob's fears are a problem, too."

"Rona makes it clear that the fears are connected to the threat of loss. These dreams express how you not only fear losing Bob but also your freedom. You are fighting these fears."

"Rona represents independence. I am sedating my independence and locking it in the seclusion room. She is also the woman who goes from man to man. I do have to lock that in the room."

"She appears with your former boyfriend."

"I feel like I am beginning to know this picture better. I was constantly going blank with it. It helped when you kept asking questions. I find it hard to look at frightening things, especially when I have two desires that contradict each other: to be in a close relationship and to be alone. I am also afraid of how committing myself creates something precious that I can lose. It is circular."

"I have an interpretation that I would like to offer. Are you interested?"

"Yes."

"The clothing store where you meet Rona and her boyfriend suggests external appearance, whereas the mental hospital, and especially the seclusion room, convey a sense of internal conflict. In the dream, you fight the fear in yourself that is represented and evoked by Rona. You try to convince the nurse and yourself that she is crazy, and you leave her behind in the hospital. I see this dream, as difficult as it may be for you, as a manifestation of health because it clearly expresses conflict in the language of images."

"I fear my inability to keep a relationship going. I am afraid that it will fall apart. If she is the fear, then I do want to get rid of it. Maybe sedating the fear and locking it in seclusion room are not the healthiest ways to deal with it."

"The images in this dream express the intensity of your fear. They serve you well and do not need to be judged. Whether or not your response is 'healthy' can be determined by what you choose to do in reaction to the dream."

"Do you think that expressing the fear helps to change it? Or does it just make it bigger?"

"Fear feeds off itself and the fear is probably amplified right now because it is open and burning. We are throwing fuel on it by expressing it. What's the alternative? Is it good to repress or avoid the fear? You have to decide."

"If I avoid it, it will keep coming back."

"I agree with you. In my experience with fear I have found that we give it power. The conflict somehow or other serves a purpose for us. We often create our fears. This explains why they stay with us for such a long time."

"I might be able to let go of the fear if I could accept being alone."

"What purpose does the fear play?"

"It protects me from really trusting another person."

"And it keeps you from becoming more vulnerable and setting up the conditions where you can really be hurt. So now we come back to your question about whether expressing the fear has value?"

"My question was an act of hostility directed toward you. You were coming too close."

"How do you feel now?"

"I feel upset, scared, because right now in my life I am trusting and I am vulnerable and I do not know what is going to happen."

"What is it like now to express the fear?"

"It is helpful to talk to someone outside the relationship and receive a perspective on it. I am realizing what my defenses against my own fears are. When Bob wanted me to come into the bathtub, I said no. But he gave in and came to the ocean with me."

"We have to submit sometimes in relationships. Does it feel right to you that one person, or perhaps both, have to submit or moderate when the battle of wills occurs?"

"I never realized it before, but I always thought I could do things my own way in a relationship. I got angry when I was thwarted. This is such an accurate representation of what happens in relationships. How do you relate to this picture?"

"The couple is drawn with considerable care. They are in the center and surrounded by all of these other issues."

"I never saw that until now."

"You told me that it was Rona and her boyfriend. As we talk, I experience her as you being possessed by this Rona fear. I keep going back to the clothing store. How do we use clothes? We wear them on the outside of our bodies. They are involved with our appearance to the world. They protect and cover us. I also connect the clothing store to your uncertainty in the previous dream about whether or not you will wear clothes on the beach. You interpreted this as presenting the choice of becoming involved in a relationship that has family possibilities. Now the woman is standing in a clothing store with the man."

"That makes sense. If I have the courage to get the clothes, then maybe I will be capable of fighting off the fears. I see the picture as expressing phases in a relationship. The movement is clockwise, beginning with the bathtub where I am scared of the intimacy and I act rebelliously and 'freely' as a way of going against the fears. Then I confront the fears and put them away in the hospital. Perhaps they will get some help there since I leave them with the nurse. The movement returns to the center with the couple."

"In the hospital you are suggesting that it was Rona's problem. You also tried to leave it there. I associate this with your question about why express the fears in a picture. I think you have discovered that it is your conflict which is represented by her image. She assists you in finding the nature and origin of this fear. It is important for me to understand a situation as best I can. Otherwise, I act blindly. Fear might continue to accompany my understanding, but I am less likely to let my reactions to the fear blindly damage a relationship. I have learned that the negative influence that situations have on me is often proportionate to the amount of energy that I give to them. I am a person who reacts instinctually to most situations, so it is difficult for me to resist the bait. I have to continually discipline and adjust my instincts. I have found that a considerable amount of agitation and discomfort might be necessary in order to motivate the transformation of will. Working with a problem through images, as you have done, gives a sense of self-confidence as opposed to panic in response to the fear."

"It amazes me how today I have the same thing going on inside me and it is represented clearly by the picture which was done three months earlier."

"That is why this is such an important picture for you. And it is an image that you resisted opening to. It also shows how the presence of the image in art therapy works. Because it is with us in a physical form created by you, it is more difficult to avoid. The picture helped you to stay with the fear."

"It was easier for me to face the swans or the feeling that I was right in relation to my teacher. I did not feel as good about the fears expressed by this picture, so it was hard to face."

FINALLY GETTING AWAY (Fig. 25)

"In this dream I was in my new apartment and I thought I was going crazy. I saw Bob sitting on a couch and he kept switching from having a

Figure 25

beard to not having one. The floor was a Hopi sand painting that was being painted constantly. It was continuously changing. 'Mr. Clean' was in the room, and no one saw him but me. Bob and Barbara, the woman who lived in the apartment before us, were there and they did not believe that I kept seeing Mr. Clean. Then, I went outside and the police were chasing me because I was crazy, and a woman in my art therapy training seminar gave me a bike to get away with. It grew to be about thirty feet high. I barely made it under a bridge. Then the dream changed and I was in an abandoned elementary school playground with my father and a ten-year-old girl. The police were still chasing us and our only escape was to fly. I flew with the girl. We had magic sticks and I taught her how to flap her arms and hold the sticks. We flew into the sunset and the sky was full of birds. It was a peaceful feeling.

"Sometimes I wonder if I am crazy. But I think it has more to do with poetic perception. The wood floor in our apartment could look like a Hopi sand painting. That day was the first time I saw a photograph of Bob when he did not have a beard. We had been cleaning the apartment. Barbara had left the place in a filthy condition. Bob was angry, but he did not feel as committed to cleaning as I did. He was more involved with moving things. Thus, I was the only one who was relating to Mr. Clean.

"I don't know what the police chase was about. When my friend gave me the bike, I felt that I was being assisted. She is a fine therapist and a person who I trust. She said that I am not crazy and she gave me the bike so I could get away from that feeling. I am not sure about the bridge. I feel that it is some kind of transition, and I almost hit it because the bicycle is so high. I do not understand the school. I love the image of teaching the little girl to fly. It is expressive of taking care of the child in me and helping her to be free. Flying expresses this freedom."

"You have selected this part of the dream as the subject matter of your drawing."

"I drew the other images in my journal, but I did no work them into larger pictures. I focused on this one because of the happy mood. What do you think about me feeling that I am crazy?"

"Within this dream it is connected to being alone with perceptions that are different from those of other people. There is a continuity to the 'crazy' theme in your last two pictures. In the previous one, you described how you tried to make Rona appear crazy in the hospital. So, it seems to be associated with fear and perhaps with being alone, having people turn against you, and maybe this is what the police are all about. They are the embodiment of the fears and crazy feelings that are 'chasing' you. I cannot help thinking that the police might like you. You have not done anything to offend them. Maybe they are trying to tell you something and help you. The fearful or guilty part of ourselves always jumps to interpreting the police as being against us when in reality their primary functions are protective. They might be telling you that it is not good to run away. The huge bike, that almost does not make it through the bridge, might be saying that you are making too much of it all, 'blowing it out of proportion' as we say. The running away might also be dangerous, and 'crazy' as you present the experience in the dream.

"But for now let's respect your running from the police and see them as a manifestation of the fear that people are against you. This ties in with the dream sequence where Bob and Barbara were not with you on the cleaning issue. You walked out of the house and then the police appeared. Rather than having anger and negative feelings toward Bob and Barbara, you substituted the police. The craziness might come from not being direct and clear about your fear and aggression. Then the friend appeared, a person who is with you. She is someone who helps you to go back into your childhood at the elementary school with your father. That is where you sense freedom and complete acceptance by the sky and the sun. But the elementary school was abandoned, suggesting to me that it is no longer a place for you. It is something of the past and maybe it is telling you this. The adult relationship with Bob has the beautiful Hopi changing floor which is also magical and it seems to suggest that so much is possible in your house, the place of the present. But there is also the cleaning and decisions about who is going to do it."

"It seems that whenever Bob does not recognize my feelings about a situation, I turn to my father. What you said about childhood acceptance helped me to see it. I cope with things sometimes by flying away and by trying to convince myself that I am happy when I am not really dealing with things."

"Your first picture expressed flight of a different kind."

"I never realized that I started with flight. The first one was a flight of courage to attain something I desired. This one was a flight away from not being accepted. But there is a positive dimension to my teaching the child to fly and be herself."

"In the first picture the brown figures are trying to pull you down, and in this picture the police are after you. If we reverse your first response to the brown figures as we did with the police, they can be seen as helpers who are trying to take you down to earth. They are the color of the ground. When talking about 'the thousand swans,' you likened the people whose boots broke the ice to the brown figures in 'flying through the grey city.' The people with boots break the ice and release the swans. You mentioned how pleased you were that they flew inland as opposed to flying out to sea. You felt that the inland direction represented an orientation to practical things rather than mysteries. I do not see the sea as less practical, but I respect your interpretation which articulates your desire to be involved with practical things. These sometimes rough and worldly people, who you seem to feel negatively toward, may be allies. They are not esoteric. I view all of the pictures together as expressing your soul. If we continued, we would see more. There are many images and interpretative possibilities."

"I am discovering how spending time with the pictures and the dreams in a way that really penetrates into the world of the images results in my seeing things differently. New interpretations emerge, and they generally have more emotional depth."

"Maybe this dream can be helpful in revealing how the flight away from something is not always an expression of freedom. It may be an avoidance of conflict."

"I have been doing it for years. That's me. When do you think the flight is a manifestation of freedom?"

"When you do it for the sake of the experience itself. Right now, I have the feeling that we should respect your picture of magical flight. It may convey multiple messages, and I do not think that it can be reduced to a single positive or negative judgment. It is common for a painting and a dream to express opposing themes. They embody paradox and show all sides of the coin. Your title, 'finally getting away,' suggest a sense of relief in getting away from it all. I see a connection to the second picture where you 'jumped ship' in order to establish your independence from your spiritual teacher. In that picture, you spoke of your need to let go of the need for a 'perfect spiritual father.' In this picture, you fly away without your father. I sense that his presence in the dream signifies a real sense of support and protection that he gives you. This is something that I respect and admire and do not see as an expression of an infantile need. The police were still after you when your father appeared. The interpretation you have just given suggests that flight may not be the best way to deal with the problem that motivates you to run away. Within this context the flight takes on a negative tinge, in that it becomes avoidance. I do not want to question the beautiful feeling that you had in flight. Maybe your flight away from responsibility was transformed into a new sense of responsibility, manifested here by helping another, a child. I sense an acceptance of the parental role, as suggested by the presence of your father."

"Maybe these decisions can be as simple as the magical flight. I do perceive my father as a responsible and good parent. This picture could have been upsetting, but it has been somewhat easier to face than the two previous ones. What do you think accounts for this?"

"You are becoming more comfortable with the issues. This picture contains the same conflicts, but you worked them through, for now, in the previous pictures."

"You emphasized 'for now.' "

"I have found that resolutions are rarely permanent. They are temporal and exist in the present."

"Why is that?"

"The resolution takes place within this particular context. It fits this moment and is not always interchangeable with others. Every situation demands a new and fresh response. Therapeutic transformations are like artworks. They are sequential. Once we get a taste for it, we desire more. The process must be ongoing if it is to stay alive. I think that this is what we are after in both therapy and art. It is a process that adjusts to what is needed in our lives."

"I like the idea of not fixing an image with a single positive or negative meaning. You said in our dream class that giving the dream or picture a single fixed meaning 'shuts it off.' Labeling does this. Dreams and pictures can have many meanings. When I have a dream, I often say 'I know what that means!' but in truth I am never sure. This image work helps me to be much more aware of what is going on in my life. The alternative would be to just let the dreams slip away in the morning. By saving the dreams that I had strong feelings about, I can see the transitions that I am going through over time. As I look at all of the pictures as a group right now, I feel closer to some issues and more distant from others. The first two pictures of the city and the ships feel like a long time ago. They express a transition that is finished now. The two art therapy pictures of the snake and the jungle represent something that I am gaining control over. The pictures look flatter now. They do not call out to me in the same way. The squirrel pictures feels very close. I just put it in a silver frame. When I look at the picture, it gives me strength. It expresses independence and it touches my love. The picture flows and it seems alive. The spiritual teacher and prostitute pictures also look flat. The issues that they represent are not gone, but they are not as important right now. The shaman still glows. Just this morning I was feeling the same dark mystery about Bob. The swan picture is alive, because the process of letting the swans come out of me is still happening. I can feel how I ice up and I need people to 'break the ice' as they did in the dream. I am not upset about the images in the bathtub and the ocean picture. Today, I feel close to Bob, and when I look at the section of the picture of the two of us and the tub, it feels loving. It is more difficult to connect to the other parts of the picture today."

"This demonstrates how interpretations of the same image change over time."

"Before this work that we did together, I thought that a picture or dream has one interpretation which stays the same. Now I realize how our responses are determined by what is happening in our lives at the time. When we did the more in-depth work with this image, I was upset about the issues connected to the picture. It is fascinating to have it so clearly demonstrated how we respond to the image in relation to how we feel at the time, and as you said, this process is ongoing and always changing. The last picture of flight reminds me how negative interpretations can be pushed on me, and how in the past I believed them because I did not trust how I felt about the picture or the experience. You showed me how the flight can have many meanings and that all of these can exist together. I do not have to gravitate toward the most negative and painful interpretation in order to grow. I have experienced so many therapists both in my experience as a client, and in my clinical observations, who focus exclusively on weaknesses. In the past I felt as though people were poking until they found where the pain was and they could begin to work with that. It sometimes felt like I was being pushed too fast. Because we worked with dreams and my drawings, I began by being honest, open and exposed. There was no need to poke. There were times when you did push when I was stuck. I needed this in order to open to all of the emotion."

"Why did you gravitate toward the negative and painful interpretations?"

"I thought, and still think, that they contain the truth, but there is also a need to remember that there are many truths. I have experienced a liberation with this. It is a relief to see that there are many possibilities and choices. I do not have to get stuck with a positive interpretation that denies the pain or a supposedly true, negative and painful one that denies my inner strength. What feels good is the fact that this is not simply 'positive thinking' or an avoidance of the negative. Everything is expressed in the last flying picture which seems to have many interpretive possibilities. My first instinct was to have a happy ending, flying off into the sunset. It is amusing now, because I will eventually have to land."

III. The Art Therapist's Art

I AM IN agreement with Theodor Reik who said that it is important for psychoanalysts to work openly with their own dream experience. Art therapists have to do the same thing with their art. Only through this type of investigation will art therapy manifest its psychological and artistic depth. We art therapists contribute something different and more intimate when we reflect upon our personal experience with art. Some might disregard this type of self-analysis because of its 'subjectivity.' I have found the self-analysis of art therapists to be more direct than their analysis of another person's art which is equally subjective and 'once removed' from the process of working with materials. As helpful as the art therapist's interpretations of another person's experience may be in therapy, they do not bring us as close to the phenomenon of art as the art therapist's self-interpretations do. Reik believed that this also applies to the interpretation of dreams.

I selected three art therapists as resources for my research: Louis van Marissing, an instructor and coordinator of art therapy training at The Akademie De Kopse Hof in The Netherlands; Klaus Boegel, an instructor of art therapy at The Akademie De Jelburg in The Netherlands; and Helen Landgarten, professor of clinical art therapy at Loyola Marymount University in Los Angeles and a senior art therapist at the Cedars-Sinai Mental Health Center.

Helen Landgarten has been informally discussing these issues with me for years. More recently, I have worked closely with Dutch art therapists in investigating the artistic expression of art therapists. Dutch art therapy training programs place more emphasis on the student's personal artwork than we do in America. Both Louis van Marissing and Klaus Boegel have been active in furthering the artistic identity of the art therapist.

I have chosen to conclude this book with the words and images of Helen Landgarten. Her art, clinical work in art therapy, published writings and achievements as an international educator are a source of inspiration to me and our profession. Since I was first exposed to Helen Landgarten's art, I have been intrigued with the idea of researching how her life as an artist relates to her art therapy practice. The dialogue with her in this book is the beginning of what should be a more comprehensive study of her work.

LOUIS VAN MARISSING

Louis participated in art therapy training groups that I gave in Amsterdam and invited me to De Kopse Hof in Nijmegen which is one of the four creative arts therapy professional training academies supported by the Dutch government. He traveled to the United States for further consultation. In Cambridge, we discussed his ideas about the relationship of the art therapist's personal artistic expression to clinical practice. We worked with a series of drawings in the journal that he was carrying with him. Louis told me that he made the pictures without thinking about what he was drawing. The images just appeared.

"Art therapists generally do not envision real possibilities for living as artists. I believe that most of our colleagues feel that if they become involved in the field of art therapy, they have to let some of their personal art go. Much of the excitement in art therapy is concerned with our work with other people. As a profession, we do not arouse as much excitement about the art therapist's identity as an artist. In this respect, we have been different from studio art programs where people are enthusiastic about going into the studio and pursing careers as visual artists. I do not think this split has to exist. I believe that we can have both. The future depth of our profession actually demands that we address the artistic expression of other people and ourselves."

"I try to work this way with my art therapy students," Louis said. "They will need the artistic process to deal with their personal lives as well as their profession. One of the goals of the art therapy education that we do in Holland is the making of a real connection between the artworks of the students and their personal lives. Otherwise, they are working with, and talking about, things that they do not know from within. I am not as concerned with the 'artistic values' of their work as I am with the connection that they feel with the artworks and the process of art."

"Why not values?"

"In my work with students I find it important that they go through a process of re-evaluating values and norms. The art achieves a higher quality. When they are influenced by standards of how they 'should' make things, they forget that they have their own way."

"What is the higher quality that you said the work achieves?"

"When the impulse to work and the acts of shaping fall together, the material takes the form which has to emerge. There are no disturbances, which I describe as thoughts that it should be another way, or 'I cannot do this. . .the others are much better than I am.' "

"How do you describe and assess quality? Is it authenticity, depth, soul, energy?"

"Yes, energy, soul and authentic images are descriptive of quality. When I see these images, I feel the energy of the person who made them. It is the energy of that particular person and not something else, like norms of what 'should be.' Quality also relates to the image having its own way of appearing. It does not need a story or an explanation. It has an independent existence. I find that it does not matter whether a person looking at the pictures sees the same story as the person who made it. The image stands on its own."

"Are you against telling stories about images?"

"No, no, I like to tell stories about images and hear stories about images."

"How do you feel when you hear people tell their stories about your images?"

"It is nice to hear, because people have different reactions to the work. There are people who are really telling their own stories and their state of mind at that moment. They have many associations, and the drawing or painting is only a trigger which allows them to come out. Some people are tuning in more to the image and they associate more with what they see and they try to communicate with the painting. They try to level with the picture. Their reaction is like a dance. They go close and then distance themselves and try to find words and stories that fit the image, as though it is a dance partner. And other people attempt to see me in my image."

Louis continued to describe how people respond to his art. "Sometimes it is astonishing what people say about my work. They may be so close that I say, 'How do you know?' They might give me words and reactions that I cannot find myself. And there are situations where it is totally their story. I will say, 'Nice, but this is not my story.' "

"Can these associations which are not related to your feeling about the work be useful?"

"Yes, it is an intriguing opportunity that an artwork offers to its public. When I finish a work and show it to people, they are allowed to have their personal response, to make their own painting."

"There is an exchange of imagination."

"Yes."

"How important is it to show your work to other people? In art therapy groups there are more viewers, witnesses, more responses. I see two major elements in art therapy: making the image and sharing it with other people. Art therapy with one person or with a group complements the isolation of the artistic process through dialogue with other people."

"I think that it is important for people to receive reactions to their work. Their personal connection and feeling for the work can be deepened by the varied reactions of other people. People in therapy often stick to their own reality and think that it is the only possible way to deal with the facts of life. When they hear others react, it becomes possible to look at the artwork, and themselves, in different ways."

"Responding to art provides an experience of the multiple realities of the world. You are suggesting how the reactions of others assist us in the therapeutic restructuring of a problematic situation. It is useful for me to learn about your way of doing art therapy. You take me outside my story and into yours, and perhaps this expands mine. What do you think the fundamental elements of art therapy are?"

"The shaping with material comes to me immediately," Louis said. "It is a dialogue in which we try to do something with the material and see what happens. There is then another level of reaction. This dialogue is concrete. I can see it and other people can see it at the same moment that I am doing it, whether I want it or not. All they have to do is look across the table at the work. I cannot deny what I have done. The scratch on the paper is there. The dialogue is elementary and it uses the senses in an important way. In the shaping process the dialogue has to do with making contact."

"Contact with something other than yourself?"

"Yes, and also with myself. It is a dialogue between inside and outside. In art therapy we deal with common acts of daily life. . .nailing, scratching, putting things together. We do these things just the way we prepare a meal, clean the house, write with a pen. Art therapy uses the same movements to create forms. There are confrontations with inner and outer realities. Feelings, thoughts and impulses come up and they are manifested in the material. We can see, feel and smell the results of the acts of shaping. These confrontations give the person the message:

'You are here. You have made this. You can tell all kinds of stories about it, but the only fact that cannot be denied is that you did it.' I think that this doing, the act of shaping, brings together what many people have lost. They can trust their inner motivations to do something that has results. They can look at it and make the choice about whether or not to go further. It is difficult to describe clearly what the healing element in art therapy is. I think it is somewhere in the process of shaping."

"How does the therapist work?"

"The therapist has to create a climate in which the process can happen. The art therapist has a role, which can be compared to the public which looks at an artwork. Like this public, I have as an art therapist my own feelings, thoughts and associations. The crucial difference lies in the fact that the art therapist has a responsibility to the maker of the artwork. I have to be aware of my relationship to the person, the process and the image and deal with all of these things. It takes a great deal of training to be in tune with both the maker and the products and to be at the same time with myself and to make these contacts again and again."

"Perhaps, the therapy lies in making his threefold contact with the image, the maker and yourself."

"Yes. And because this threefold contact is so complex, it is necessary for art therapists to have trained intuitions."

"Is it important for you as an art therapist to stay involved with the art process? There are many prominent art therapists who seldom make art."

"I cannot be without making art. It is more than being addicted. Art is a state of being. I can work as an art therapist, because I have this base of making my art. It is difficult to say things about people that I do not know, but I think it is necessary for art therapists to feel the connection with their own process in art. I think it is not enough to have had the artistic experience somewhere in the past. The process of shaping provokes a wide variety of feelings. The art therapist has to know the successful moments of shaping as well as the horrible and demotivating moments that the process has. It does not always work. There is sometimes a big fight to establish concentration and to get into the mood to do something when I do not know how or what. There is confusion all around and I know the only way is to go into the material. But which material? I might try something and it does not work. It is falling apart or falling from the wall. And this is only the beginning. As I go further in the process, other problems present themselves. When I am painting, the process might be going well and I get enthusiastic, choose a color, and it is the wrong color. It is horrible. This can happen at the end of the painting as I go out of contact. I can cause this to happen by being overly enthusiastic or too conservative. If I try to conserve what is there, I do not take risks. Although risks are necessary, there has to be a balance. I can do too much or too little. It is not always fun to be creative."

"It may be possible for the person who is not making art to be a successful art therapist. I see some people who are doing it in this way. They maintain their sensitivity even though they are not doing their personal work. You are convincing in emphasizing how it helps us as art therapists to deepen our empathy with not only the person but the artist process, what you describe as the 'shaping.' You make the point most effectively when describing the struggles and failures of the artist."

"People can do good work with clients without maintaining contact with their personal art, because as art therapists we need more than experience and knowledge of the artistic process," Louis said. "There are other qualities that are necessary. It is difficult to split them from one another. The art therapist who is not making art then depends more on other psychotherapeutic skills such as the ability to listen, observe, open to the other person, respond, and so on. If a person can really concentrate on people and what they are doing, then it is possible to understand what they are experiencing in shaping and showing their pictures."

"You think that art therapists who are not involved in their personal artistic process can be in touch with the shaping by concentrating on the other person. But you seem to be saying that you feel more like an art therapist by making your own art."

"It helps me to use more of the qualities that are in the medium of art therapy. I am searching for what makes art therapy art therapy. Otherwise, it is just like all of the other therapies."

"I like the way you use artistic language like 'shaping,' 'showing the work' and 'dialoguing with material' to describe what art therapy is. You express what I perceive as the Dutch tradition of placing a primary emphasis on artistic material. The profession of art therapy has to become more involved with these artistic concepts. Art therapy in the United States can learn from you and your colleagues in The Netherlands about how we have to go further in discovering how the many qualities of the artistic process can be applied to therapy. This research can only be done through deepening our personal involvement and exploration with materials and art making. The depth and range of our insights will correspond to what we are experiencing in our lives. The art therapy profession needs to explore and refine all of its qualities as you suggest. How do you approach art interpretation?"

"We are working to make people aware of what they see and how they react to pictures. We are encouraged to have many different reactions. We train our students to be open to their own responses, those of the maker and those of the group. Rigid interpretations are discouraged. Interpretation has to develop from the threefold contact with the image, the maker and the therapist. They have to communicate with each other. For example, in my picture (Fig. 26) the finger is pointed up. Someone might say it represents my going into the world."

Figure 26

"Let's talk about the picture."

"My first reaction is, 'Well go, if you want to go there.' He is pointing there and the other one is looking. 'Go! Don't hesitate. Don't look at me.' "

"Do you identify equally with both figures?"

"I like the guy in the background more. He is really interested. He says, 'Okay, of course that is possible.' The other one is so demanding. He looks and thinks about whether or not he will do it. He does not rely on himself. He says: 'Am I allowed to go up?' Whereas the other one is not demanding and thinks: 'Ah, that is a good idea. Why not?' "

"There seems to be more stress in the figure in the foreground."

"Especially between the eyes. He is frowning. It makes the energy heavy. 'Oh, it is not easy to go up.' "

"What does the mouth express?"

"The upper lip is stiff."

"Is there a tension between his chin and his shoulder?"

"I associate now to a pimple that I have on the side of my face. It reacts to tension and sometimes grows too much. This week when I was giving a lecture the pimple began to bleed, even though it was covered by a bandage."

"Is the pimple useful?"

"It can be. It makes me aware of what is happening, but I would rather have it leave. I do not think it fits my image of myself. But this association to the pimple was not with me when I made the picture. The movement in the figure has to do with going to that place. It has to do with stepping out. 'Go! Do! Don't hesitate!' He is the worrier who also dares to say 'Go.' The other figure is not a worrier, but he does not take the initiative. He is saying 'Oh, that's a nice idea,' but the larger figure in the foreground has to point. I can see both within myself. I like the figure in the background, but I identify more with the man in the foreground."

"He looks more like you, and he is larger."

"But I also have the other man in me. 'Let's see' or 'Don't bother. Let's not be overorganized.' This man accepts that things can go wrong."

"He looks relaxed as he stands there with his hands in his pockets. What about the space in the picture, the trees and the hill?"

"It looks body-like."

"The space is open. It is not cluttered. And how do you relate to the trees or bushes, the grass?"

"The grass is growing everywhere and there is no problem. The tree on the right has hard times. It is growing there, but it is not easy. I do not know about the other one, but this one does not have easy karma in his life."

"The other tree seems to be a little bit behind the hill."

"Yes, and therefore I do not know as much about him. He has it easier. Perhaps there are less expectations behind the hill. There is this romantic feeling that life is always more beautiful behind the hills. This is the way I am viewing life at this moment."

"And you described the other tree as having a difficult time growing. It's life is not easy. It is not concealed by the hill."

"It is growing and it is fruitful. There are seasons, but it is generally tough to stand there on the hill. This is the heavy side of life."

"The man in the background is not wearing shoes."

"I often make my figures without shoes. The fact that he is dressed is something for me."

"Why is he dressed?"

"It fits his character. He is common and from daily life. This is the fellow you meet in the street."

"With a loose fitting and open shirt. The other figure is not wearing clothes. Is he common?"

"No. This is interesting. He has a great deal of conscious awareness. He knows a lot. His energy is in the head, from the eyes up."

"This is where you said the tension was earlier. You do not present the lower body of this figure as you do with the other, and perhaps this accentuates the tension."

"Yes, because I cannot imagine a figure under him. I would be lost in drawing it. Since I drew the picture from the tension in the head. I cannot draw a body. The anatomy would be confused. When I draw with a feeling for the place from where the body's energy flows, then I can do a complete figure."

"Do you mean that the body is a flowing and sensitive thing that does not fit with this tension?"

"Yes. When the energy comes from my center there is no problem. But when I have to think about it, the flow stops."

"The arm of the man in the foreground is stiff. There is a tension in the hand, in the pointing, in what you describe as the command, 'You must go here.' He is pointing in one direction."

"But he is also taking the initiative. There is a positive with the negative. 'Move! Act!' "

"In the next picture (Fig. 27), we have the two men again but with their complete bodies. The black man is smiling and does not appear to be tense. This picture contrasts to the one we just discussed."

"My first reaction is the question as to what kind of landscape they are in. It is stony or desert-like, a strange place to meet. I added the tennis ball formed like the yin-yang as an afterthought. The ball is just there. I do not know where it came from. The white figure is looking to-

Figure 27

ward it and he says: 'There is a tennis ball, but I do not know where it came from.' The arrow suggests movement."

"Do you have a story for this picture?"

"The black one is caring without nursing. It is also important that he is not giving full attention to the white man. He is not saying, 'Oh, what are you dealing with?' He is looking out. Other things are happening. The condition of the white man is not the only thing. The white man is not bothered about what to do. He is just hesitating. Something is in action and he stands back, saying, 'My gosh, what next.' He is not really stuck. He realizes something."

"Is this the same hesitation to go up the hill that you described in the previous picture? The black figure resembles the man with his hands in his pockets in the first picture, the man in the world who can accept whatever happens."

"Yes, they are alike. They have fewer problems."

"The white man in this second picture is more introspective. His gesture in holding his hand to his head reinforces this movement inward. He is also being held by the black man but appears to be thinking only of himself or of his own thoughts. He resembles the man with the pointed finger in your first picture. His elbow is pointing in the same direction as the other man's finger. The elbow and the finger are located in approximately the same part of the picture's surface. The white man in the second picture does not appear to be frowning and his stance is relatively relaxed, but the positioning of his right arm and hand do suggest some tension. The two pictures seem to be dealing with a similar theme. You carry it from one picture to the next."

"But the man who is pointing in the first picture has more problems than the white man in this picture. This man is more connected to himself and his environment."

"And his entire body is presented."

"Yes, that is a relief to have your body with you."

"He is also in contact with the other man. What is going on between them?"

"I do not know what they are doing. I am sometimes with another person and say to myself, 'What am I doing?' or I begin to think or worry about something that is not present. Maybe this is what the tennis ball represents, not being there with the other person."

"His body is present, but the mind is somewhere else. His hand and arm express both. The hand seems to be holding him there with the other man, whereas the elbow points away at the tennis ball and his face is looking away."

"He is stepping out of the present."

"Do you identify with the black man, too?"

"This is my, what we call 'gezellig' in Dutch. It is translated as cozy, but it is more than that. We have a whole culture about gezellig. First, we have to chat a bit to make things gezellig and then we get started. It is part of relationships, visits and social things. It has to be gezellig. If I am only business-like, the situation becomes too pushy."

"Does the word mean intimate?"

"Somewhere between cozy and intimate."

"So, the black man is expressive of your experience of gezellig? Do you identify with one man more than the other?"

"No, they are so together."

"What is your relationship to the tennis ball?"

"It is thought."

"How do you feel about the landscape, the rocks?"

"When I look, I see structure on different levels. The rocks can also be soft, like bodies."

"The rock in the right/middle of your picture looks like a penis."

"It is flesh-like and very much like a penis."

"We can see many things in the rocks."

"I see the backs of people. They are rocks, but they are also bodies."

"I can see grass now, Louis. It is softer. Maybe they are at the place that the man in the first picture was pointing to. He went up and this is what he found"

"It is not lonely at the top."

"But he is saying: 'What am I doing here?' He has arrived, but he cannot seem to enjoy it. His mind is somewhere else."

"Yes. I know this in myself. Is that all there is?"

"Let's look at your third picture (Fig. 28)."

"Two fellows again. This picture is associated with a playing card and it is nice to put one guy upside down. It was good to put the 'queen' symbol together with those two guys. They have such different atmospheres, one hanging by the hands and the other by the feet.

"Do you have a particular reason for including the 'club' symbol?"

"It brings good luck and it looks fertile, like seeds."

"How does this picture relate to the first two pictures? There is the repeating theme of two men in different positions and expressing contrasting attitudes."

"Again, one of them, the upside-down man in this picture, is more concerned with problems. The other is swinging. The upside-down man is not involved with real problems. He only thinks he is."

"Your yin-yang tennis ball in the second picture is consistent with the polarity in all three pictures between the carefree, swinging man and the worried man who hesitates, has a difficult time being present and perhaps creates many of his problems. The worried man looks like he is having a difficult time in this picture."

"He is trying with his hands to get a grip and flexing his feet to get a hold. It reminds me of acrobats. On one hand it is nice to dare to be upside down, but it is also frightening. He can fall down. The image is expressive of taking risks and this guy nearly panics doing it. But he is not alone. The picture combines upside down with swinging freely. They are doing it together."

Figure 28

"It seems that the 'hanger' is reaching for the swinger.'"

"Yes. He is saying, 'Are you still there?' The one who is hanging by his hands is looking good in his body, in his sport shorts. He is well shaped. The other man is not dressed well and he is not very beautiful. He is 'Mr. Nice' and more like the fellow looking up in the first picture."

"But the mood of the athletic man who is hanging by his hands is more like the black man in the second picture and the fellow looking up in the first picture. Mr. Nice is in trouble for the first time in this picture."

"There is a switch. I realize as I speak to you that I had more sympathy for the common man in the first drawing and for the black man in the second drawing."

"I do not think that you have given up your concern for this character type in the third picture. He just finds himself in a more difficult situation."

"Yes. He has the courage to hang upside down, even though he is not beautiful. The jogger can swing and that is nice. But it is not really interesting."

"Are there themes that you see in all three of the pictures?"

"Staying or leaving; hesitating or stepping forward; tension and relaxation. My work often expresses a theme of whether or not I will choose for vitality and inventiveness."

"In each of the pictures one figure engages us in the dilemma of choice, and he is complemented by the other figure who is just there and relaxed."

"I have to allow myself to enjoy swinging. It is also a state of being, nothing more or less. I can do that. And I can choose. This work with my drawings illustrates what I said earlier about art therapy. I made the pictures months ago, but I can easily go into them again here. The energy is there. If we work with the pictures again next week, I might have another story. When I talk about the pictures with another person, we might have a completely different conversation."

"This is a helpful point. I agree that interpretations are influenced by our relationships to the people we are working with. How do you feel about our conversation?"

"I feel invited."

"Gezellig?"

"Yes, at ease. What we are doing is demonstrating a way of working in art therapy. It is important for me to be at ease in my work. It makes the common things valuable. In this atmosphere we can go to what is really worthwhile, what I feel, what I want and what my life is about. It is enjoyable to discover things about myself in the pictures."

"You express this theme of being at ease in the picture. But I do not think you want to lose the tension."

"Otherwise, it is like mud. The tension has to be there to give shape. Now we are back to the dialogue with material, shaping and connecting, the impulse to work, struggles with the material, authentic expression. We art therapists have to speak clearly and close to ourselves. We cannot be afraid to go into ourselves and the work."

KLAUS BOEGEL

For years I have been thinking about how the phenomena of performance art relates to art therapy. Both art therapy and performance art came into existence at the same time. Yet, there have been few attempts to connect them to one another. I believe that the two are interchangeable as suggested by my previous research on how shamanism relates to art therapy. I have always viewed the totality of my art therapy experience as an artwork, and I have described therapy itself as a performing art. The practices of performance art are sympathetic to an integrated approach to all of the arts in therapy, in that they both respond to the need to give coherence to fragmented art forms. I believe that performance art is a response to the same social and therapeutic needs that stimulated the creation of the art therapy profession.

The work of my colleague, Klaus Boegel, in The Netherlands has helped to deepen my sensitivity to the performance dimension in art therapy. Klaus gave me copies of two books, *Boegel & Holtappels Untersuchengen* (1980) and *Tigermann* (1980) documenting his history of performance artworks. These books challenged my vision of art therapy. *Tigermann* was especially provocative. In this book and the performance that it documents, Klaus uses his body and total being to express his animal nature. My experimentations with shamanism seemed timid and bourgeois in comparison. Klaus's use of his body, sexuality, aggression and sensitivity made me realize how performance art takes risks that are not present in other art forms. The performance artist is a contemporary manifestation of the shamanic risk-taker; the religious and radical artist who uses the self as an instrument of awakening. Klaus is especially bold in the way that he uses his body as the artistic material. His art makes me aware of how I hide and protect myself for fear of being labeled exhibitionistic, seductive, bizarre.

As with other performance artists, Klaus has brought the element of psychological risk into the physical realm. Some of his performance pieces have been dangerous, reminding me of the shaman who goes to great personal risk within both initiation rites and in healing ceremonies. Within settings where therapists and teachers have responsibilities for people other than themselves, the performance dimension of art therapy has to be introduced sensitively and with respect for what the person and the institutional environment will tolerate and support.

These valid professional cautions make personal artistic explorations like those of Klaus Boegel even more essential to art therapy. If we are to expand our professional frontiers, we have to begin within the studios and laboratories of ourselves, where there is full consent. Within this experimental context, we can proceed to a deeper understanding of the artistic medium and ourselves. Personal artistic investigations become research. Experiments like those of Klaus Boegel are especially useful to me because of the way they challenge my personal limitations and the limitations of our profession. I have encouraged him to bring his performance work into a more direct relationship with the art therapy community.

Klaus and I met in Amsterdam to discuss his performance art. I was especially eager to hear more about *Tigermann*. My interest was an indication of how personally helpful I find that performance. I had kept the book on the coffee table in my office throughout the year after first meeting with Klaus in The Netherlands. Rather than focusing on one or two photographs of his performances as presented in his books, Klaus wanted to talk about the work as a whole.

"I cannot talk about one image or photograph from a performance. It is more. It is a total experience. The photograph is a form of documentation, a memory or image that is left over after the event. These images have their own lives or qualities which can be quite distinct from the performance event. When I started to work in this way, I felt that I needed a new start, a new medium. I had a long background in painting, sculpture, theatre and film. I wanted to get totally involved when I was making art. Contact with my body was important to me. I felt it as an instrument that I needed to engage. I also wanted contact with people.

"There were several periods to the emergence of this work. It started in isolation in my atelier. The first performances were done alone with Heiner Holtappels and without an audience. We felt that our art was split from life. We wanted to bring art and life into a closer relationship. The first works were a form of research. Our early performances were focused on arrangements of our bodies in relation to one another. We proceeded to more extreme forms, like becoming Siamese twins in a single white suit that we created. There was a dialogue between ourselves and outer conditions. We were concerned with how external things affected our emotional responses. We tried to put our conflicts into our art. In one piece, I wrapped myself into a body cast which expressed how I get stiff and immobilized in response to tension. When searching for areas where people express themselves by their body posture, we found photographs of catatonic people in old mental hospital books. In performances, we tried to imitate the expressions that the people were making. We had difficulty holding the expression for a few minutes, where they could hold it for hours. When I was born, the umbilical cord was wrapped around my neck. For years this fear kept returning. I constructed a performance that took me into this fear. I put my entire body into a plastic bag until I passed out in five or six minutes."

"Is the performance a form of emotional confrontation?"

"Yes. We wanted to bring our psychic material out and into a form and an image. We wanted to experience how far we could go in our experiments. It was always a process of going into a completely new area that we did not know."

"Is it sometimes self-destructive?"

"People have said that about performance art and they have responded to our works in this way. They say that it is not art because it is not building something up. I disagree. The performance is a form of purification which gets rid of destructive images and feelings. It is a form of self-healing which goes right into the heart of the problem. Rather than painting a picture about it, we do it."

"We might find that it is better to affirm the therapeutic value of destruction in art than it is to deny it."

"This depends upon how we view destruction," Klaus said. "If I want to reach new areas of experience, then I have to destroy some of the old images and ways of feeling and acting. Destruction is part of restructuring the image."

"What is it about performance art that arouses these negative images of destruction?"

"Performance is a direct way of expression. It touches people in a different and deeper manner than a painting. The feeling goes directly from one person's body to another's. In this respect, it eliminates the safe distance that exists when we look at a painting, drawing or even a film."

"When you use your body as an instrument while other people watch, their bodies become involved."

"I have observed how people have corresponding reactions within themselves to what I am doing."

"Since performance sometimes has a difficult time existing and being recognized within the world of art, how do you see it operating in art therapy? How can we become involved in adventurous and risk-taking events when the subject is another person to whom we are professionally responsible?"

"All of my early performances paralleled my personal therapeutic process. I found it to be a marvelous way to express myself. It was therapy, art and totally connected to me. I felt a release together with strong feelings of satisfaction and achievement that accompanied my being able to handle this form of art. The performance work began as an artistic response to my therapy. It deepened the experience. I felt the power of dealing with images. It was useful in clarifying my emotions and thinking. This is how my belief in this way of doing therapy began. In my work as a creative therapist these beliefs guide what I do. I am always using ritual and trying to get people involved in a direct way with their bodies."

"Can you give an example?"

"There are so many different ways. We might focus on the voice, moving, breathing and feeling our bodies. In a group we made a totem pole with wood, leather, metal and other materials. We then put secrets into the pole and created a ceremony in which we danced around the pole and celebrated our ability to open up. Some of us told our secrets to other people. Others burnt them."

"Is this theatre?"

"No, because we do not play roles."

"In some theatre forms we play ourselves."

"I feel this art form to be the most complete form of expression. We can use visual things, materials, movement voice and words. I see performance art as a focusing. It depends upon how we look at drama and theatre. We have some traditions in theatre which overlap performance art and others that do not. It is not a clearly defined area. There are unlimited possibilities."

"Why has performance developed within the visual arts?"

"In the United States musicians used the visual art scene and museums as a way of presenting their experimental way of making art. Musicians, dancers and visual artists were collaborating and through the influence of dancers, the body was seen as material for art. In Germany, performance originates in the Bauhaus School where they went over the borders between the disciplines. The Bauhaus experiments have roots in all of the arts. Performance is a new, integrated art form."

"Your performances are visually oriented. You construct objects and environments, transform the appearance of your body and then record the events with photographs and video."

"I am not concerned with visual means by themselves. For me, they are part of the performance. By using objects and environments, the performance becomes a total experience. An appeal is made to the various levels of perception of the spectators. In some performances I use environments and objects to create a special atmosphere or sometimes they function as the gate between two worlds: the everyday reality of the spectator and the reality of the performance they are confronted with. The performance artists that I know choose this art form because of its directness in communicating with people. The fact that it only happens once is an important characteristic that distinguishes the work from traditional theatre."

"Do the spectators increase the focus and discipline of the event?"

"On the one hand, it is extremely artist-centered and concerned with the person of the artist who is looking at and interpreting the world. On the other hand, the spectators are often the sounding board of the performance. An exchange of experiences takes place between the performer and the audience. I am convinced that this dimension increases the therapeutic power of the performance."

"In my art therapy training groups, I have noticed how important it is to have other people listen and watch attentively as we tell our stories and show our work. The spectator aspect clearly deepens the experience for everybody. I view the totality of what we do in these training groups as performance. Some participants have consciously introduced the performance dimension to the groups. There is a definite heightening of emotion when performance takes place consciously. I have found that the process helps us to go more deeply into our feelings and become more authentic as opposed to how the old theatre cliches suggest that it is only playing a role, which is not truly ourselves. Yet, there is always an edge that we have to maintain with regard to preventing stereotypes. I fear the institutionalization of any method that we use in our groups. How do you use performance in art therapy training?"

"We do many experiments with performance and approach it as one form of expression that can be used in therapy in addition to painting, clay and other materials. I find that it is becoming increasingly respected in our school. At first, I was only talking about my experience with this art form. Right now, it is included in our discipline of the 'visual arts,' and performance can be studied as part of our professional art therapy training.

"We are working with a man who goes through periods when he has difficulty integrating his ideas and his way of living. He had a tendency to fall into parts that do not connect. For example, he has strong emotions which he sometimes has difficulty expressing. This makes him feel separate from the world. In our school, art therapy students have to do a final examination in a medium of their choice. He chose performance as his medium. For months, he worked to find his theme and a form for it. At times, he felt he was losing himself again in the process. He had difficulty keeping the focus and choosing an image or form that fit his theme. Through this searching he came to the symbol of the pyramid which helped him to be centered and focused.

"He built the pyramid with an inner chamber out of stones. It was important for him to choose the right place at the school for it. The pyramid was elegantly constructed, with each piece fitting together precisely. His goal was to see how the pyramid worked on him. He slept in it on a very cold night in January. It was the night before his day of examination. In his examination the next day, he started with a simple ritual of playing on a gong and he ran his wet hand over a clay figure—the pelvic area of a woman—which he had made before. He also did large paintings of male and female sexual symbols. He then took us to another room in the academy where he made a circle in the room with small stones where he shared other large paintings dealing with sexual images and his relationships to women. He felt ashamed of these images, but he did it and liked it very much afterwards."

"Your experience with performance art and its impact on your students demonstrates how the art therapist's personal involvement with art relates to therapeutic practice. If you did not do this work yourself and believe in it, it would not be applied to therapy."

"I had to do it first in order to offer it to other people as a possibility. It cannot be done out of books."

"How did the faculty at De Jelburg respond to your first performance experiments?"

"They did not respond. Some were polite and interested. Three or four teachers out of sixty responded."

"How do you communicate with them about the work?"

"When I was hired at the academy, I had to present my art. I showed my first performance book and said that this is a part of me that I have to show. I found out later that the book almost cost me the job instead of making me famous.

"I did the *Tigermann* book as a more personal piece. It was a live performance and a slide show. I went out on a balcony in the middle of the Hague at rush hour and shouted as Tarzan. Many people came and I climbed down a rope, went inside the house, where I sat on a swing in a display window and read a Tarzan comic book from the supermarket to the people. There was also a slide show and a woman was lying down painting her nails and looking very bored. It was a crazy time. At the academy I hung the *Tigermann* book on a chain in the faculty lounge. Only the three or four people that I mentioned contacted me about the book. Students saw the book and came to me about it. I feel that it had an impact on them. They liked the way I took the risk and went contrary to the way things are done at the school."

"Was it liberating?"

"Yes. I am often asking them to show their secret parts, so I think it was time for me to do it, too."

"Were there moments when you were embarrassed?"

"Yes. Tigermann is extremely personal and not as analytic as the earlier works. It is related to my sexuality and my vulnerability. We are not usually showing these things in life, especially at school."

"You became an animal."

"I dealt with primary and often blocked emotions and instincts. It is about my basic life power. I use the old sexual image of Tarzan in a playful way. I enjoyed collecting small tigers, pictures of Johnny Weismuller and other Tarzan artifacts. I re-animated this Tarzan character in a personal way and felt its power. There were many feelings, but the most basic one was the identification with the animal in me. I had an urge to go into it together with a fear of losing myself and being swallowed by it. Is control still possible when I follow my instinct to surrender? Desire cannot be satisfied. There is always more. My engagement of the animal feeling was also an 'anima' experience which was characterized by surrender, receptivity and dependence. My awareness can block the experience with its moral conventions. Yet, I will always be a victim of instincts until they are integrated, made conscious and visible. *Tigermann* explores these complex emotions and mysteries."

"Would you recommend this for art therapists working in clinic?"

"If they want to be admitted, they might choose this form of art. First, we might consider doing it for ourselves and then see where it takes us in the therapeutic work. I have found it useful to see how I am still involved in the Tarzan image. In the past, I was trying to find out what the deeper personal meaning of this image is. Right now, I am still engaged with the animal but less with the Tarzan image. I am more involved with the pure meaning of the animal's instincts and primary emotions. The *Tigermann* piece was a vehicle that I used to transport myself into this deeper point."

"And you transport those of us who are willing to explore this territory with you."

"That is the way art works."

Figure 29. (From Boegel, K.: *Tigermann.* Courtesy of Den Haag Publishers, 1980).

Figure 30. (From Boegel, K.: *Tigermann.* Courtesy of Den Haag Publishers, 1980).

HELEN LANDGARTEN

Helen and I met at her home in Los Angeles, where we were surrounded by her paintings, etchings and sculpture. The two-dimensional pieces range in size from large canvases to tiny prints. When I asked Helen which pictures she would like to work with, she told me to choose whatever interested me.

"How do you relate to being both an art therapist and an artist?"

"I see them as two separate careers that do not match," Helen said. "You may not agree with this. For me, art therapy is extremely pragmatic and the art that I do is the opposite. I pull the art out from a place that I am not conscious of. It is one thing that I do not think about. In art therapy, I am always conceptualizing, thinking of goals, what media to use. . .my head is working all the time. My art can be described as a 'primary process' that is complemented by my background and knowledge of art, by considerations of space and color. My work is not preconceived. I do not make preliminary sketches. This would be more like art therapy. In therapy I am more rational and in my art I just let go."

"As art therapists we may in fact experience this polarization, but the total process of art therapy may be conceived as inclusive of both clinical thought and letting go. You are addressing differences of professional responsibility. When we are making art, we are thinking and there is a responsibility to art itself."

"I feel a great responsibility to be certain that my approach to the other person is therapeutic. I have to determine what the problem is and establish short-term and long-term goals. When I am painting, I do not think. I just act. I do not have a responsibility for anybody, not even myself. It is a time when I can be totally free and not have to give to another person. Maybe this is why art is so meaningful to me. . .especially at this point in my life."

"You are perhaps defining what art therapy is for the people we work with. When we are acting as art therapists we are taking on the responsibility of providing the experience you describe for the benefit of others, as opposed to focusing on ourselves. Why is art so meaningful for you right now?"

"I have spent many years taking care of others. I have worked at Cedars Sinai Medical Center for twenty years. I worked as the director of an art therapy graduate program since 1971. I am giving to students, faculty, patients, and to my family. I am creating new ideas. I am giving all the time. That's my job and I like doing it. But as I hit the mid-sixties, it is time for me to evaluate what I want. Being an artist is a narcissistic indulgence, yet I want to pursue my work at this point in my life; to relax and return to something that I did before and still feel strongly about. Art is being alone. I went into art therapy because I did not want to be alone. I worked primarily as a professional painter from 1956 to 1972. Later, as an art therapist I kept up my painting until 1980. I had my first exposures to art therapy in 1965 and I started at Cedars Sinai in 1967."

"You were successful as a painter. Were there many other women exhibiting with you at the time?"

"There were some. Frankly, at that time, I signed my work H. B. Landgarten, because I did not want to be identified as a female, just in case there might be prejudice and jurors who did not want to let women into shows. I surrounded myself with a group of women who were also artists, and we entered juried shows together and exhibited together. I had my support system. As my work in art therapy expanded at both the clinic and the graduate training program, I found little time to be an artist. I always had the energy and I never went dry; I never had such problems. Whenever I had the opportunity to get before a canvas, something always happened. There were always images. I did not have to store them up while I was being creative in another area. Except for summers, there was not enough time for art. There was a period of five years during which I did very little painting, sculpting or even small prints. Last year, I painted a great deal and the summer before that I was involved with painting over old works. Previously, I had a purist attitude. I worked for three hours, made a painting and never allowed myself to go back into it. I think that I was afraid that I would lose the spontaneity. This is one of the advantages of my paintings. They have a spontaneous atmosphere. Nevertheless, I found that I could go back and change all of the things that I did not like, and I did not spoil any of the works. The pictures were from all of the stages of my career. This correlates with where I am in my life. As I got older, I felt that I had a chance to rework some things. It was a gratifying feeling. Some of the pictures had been hanging around the house and stored away in the studio. I would say, 'I hate that arm. It looks bizarre. Why did I put it in such a position?' I was able to repair things that I really did not like. It was wonderful. I wanted a record of what the painting looked like before so I took 'before-and-after' pictures.

"During the five years, in the early 1980s, that I did not paint I had a dreadful fear that I had lost my talent. There was always a desire. There simply was not enough time. I thought that I would have to re-educate myself. Other art therapists have shared this fear with me. When I went back to painting, I think that I did my best work. So we don't lose our talent or our techniques and the sense of color. My last two paintings are the ones that I like the best. They are lighter, brighter, freer. They also have less people in them."

"You seem to be returning to the theme of being alone. Art therapists are always describing how they go into the field in order to be with people. Now you are saying that it is important to be alone."

"A professional artist is alone in the studio all day long, whereas the student is still in an art community. When I was painting alone in my studio I loved what I was doing, but at the end of the day I realized that I had not communicated with anybody. I was only communicating through my art. The art only has an inner voice. I am only dialoguing with myself. I felt selfish. I wanted to do something for the community. There was a dual motivation. Now, I have been with so many people everyday, with students, faculty, people at the clinic, and the outside world through presentations where people are always asking me questions and calling on the phone. I have to be by myself again. I feel inundated by constant contact. It is exhausting. I am not withdrawing or quitting. There is a better balance now, during my leave of absence from the university, between the community work and my art. Maybe this is the way it should be in life, with young people giving their greater energies so that older people can pull back."

"I understand what you mean when you distinguish your work in art therapy from your personal art. You are helpful in making these clear distinctions. When you are alone in your art studio it is different from your work in a mental health clinic with a family or an individual person. But to the extent to which you are an instrumentality of both art and therapy I see you going between environments. I know that your studio and the clinic are physically separate; however, it may be possible that you are what you are as an art therapist because of what you are as an artist."

"I agree with you. The two go together. I am me wherever I am. But when I am in the clinic, I cannot afford to take care of myself. I do not allow myself the time for fantasy, because I have so much work to do."

"I do not see the need for separation from your identity as an artist. Your knowledge of materials and long experience with art and your expertise must have a significant impact on your sensitivity to what other people make."

"From that perspective you are totally accurate. I do have a knowledge of the media. I used to teach painting to adults. Art therapists have to acquire a technical knowledge of materials. It does effect how the art tasks are designed. Matching media to the objectives, or the sessions, is of primary importance."

"You have more than technical knowledge."

"But I do not know if the 'more' makes it better."

"Does the person who has technical knowledge as well as the ability to paint with vitality and soul have a broader range of art therapy capabilities? Can a person with an in-depth understanding of the media give more?"

"Maybe it has all come so naturally to me that I have not thought about it in this way. I might be using my artistic skills without knowing it. I may in fact be transferring what I know about artistic media to the process of therapy. As an artist I am always dealing with juxtapositions, conflicts, space, color and how they go together. I can also have them fight with each other. It is possible to apply these principles to the people that we work with in art therapy. What is their inner space? What are their conflicts? How can we help these conflicting elements to complement one another? For instance, if I make half of a picture yellow and the other half purple, they are going to look terrible together. But if I put on a touch of yellow along with the purple, it is exquisite. I may be using these equivalents in therapy without thinking of them. For example, how do I get people to complement each other? Too much mother and too little father can cause fighting and may not be good. If we have a lot of father, mother may be more submissive or the whole picture may be the other way around. There might be ways for them to complement one another. It is possible that I am using a formula that I have never thought about before."

"What you are saying shows me how you do operate as an artist in both your studio and the art therapy clinic."

"I am hard on myself. When I was not painting during those years and when people asked me what I did, I did not say that I was an artist. I never called myself an artist until I exhibited in professional shows. It is a special word."

"I do not think that our personalities are single, unified entities. This may be a helpful way of understanding all of the different things that you do, which do not always merge together. I am intrigued with the role of the successful artist in our profession."

"There is a parallel between my artwork and my self as an art therapist. I see my paintings as strong. People who did not know me, when

I signed my paintings H. B. Landgarten, always thought a man did them. The strength came through."

"What do you mean by strength?"

"They're powerful. The brush strokes are wide and free. The images are clear. I am able to make a figure in space jump out toward the viewer. They are spontaneous. This is what reviewers have said about my work. These traits also characterize my work as an art therapist. I do present myself with some authority. There is a decisiveness in my art and in my art therapy work. Although I am always thinking about what I am going to do, I work spontaneously. There has to be a flexibility. Someone may have been sad last week, but today there may be a very different issue, so preplanning would be of little use. I find both fields, art and art therapy, to be challenging in this way. There has to be an honesty in both and an ability to come out. It would be interesting to investigate the images of other art therapists to see if there is a similarity between their art and their style in treatment. If it is true, then there is a great significance to this principle of the artist as an art therapist. As you said, we are the same persons as we go into both areas."

"These are the beginnings of theory that comes directly from art. Art therapists can benefit from more reflection of this kind. Yet, I am sure that you agree that there are many great artists who would make terrible therapists. I do not want to romanticize the artist but rather encourage an even more pragmatic and accurate theory of art therapy that corresponds to the process of art. It seems to be a good time to begin working with your pictures."

"Yes, let's do that."

"This picture (Fig. 31) is hanging in the most prominent place in your house. When was it done?"

"In 1965. It is an important picture for me. I have refused to sell it many times. It is an intimate image. My mother died and I did not say, 'Now I am going to do a picture of her.' I have many artworks, paintings and sculptures that just turned out to be my mother. My brother and sister would come in and say 'That's Mom!' and I was absolutely unaware of this. In the case of this picture, I saw my mother in it after it was completed. I see a woman in space and she is coming out of the picture frame. There are two things that most people will see: the strength of the woman and loneliness because there is so much surrounding space. I was dealing with my own loneliness for my mother, missing her. My mother was a powerful lady. As she got older, the mountain started erod-

Figure 31

ing and that was difficult for me to watch. I saw her as a mountain. She was solid and strong. My pictures at that particular time were concerned with my mourning process. There is no doubt about it."

"And you did not know that you were doing it?"

"That's right. There were only two pictures that I worked on consciously while my mother was dying. One of them was of an older woman with grey hair who was with a child. Most of my pictures take about three hours, but I worked on that one for a much longer time. There was a magic connected to it. I felt that if I kept painting the picture, my mother would stay alive and if I ended the picture she would die. So, I stretched it out. When I look at the picture now, I see myself, my mother and my child. It was a portrait of generations, but it was even more concerned with termination and loss. When my mother died, I remember going to a funeral home. It was bizarre. In Hollywood, when we went to pick out a coffin they had them all lit up and in different colors of satin. It was a spectacular thing and upsetting. I did two paintings of that scene and I threw them away immediately. But I did keep an image of my mother in bed just before she died. She shrivelled up within an hour and I have a picture of her in bed, having changed somewhat and my hand was reaching out to her while she was dying. That was a helpful picture because it was a part of letting go."

"You have said that the core of therapy has to do with separation and loss."

"I am noticing how virtually all of the cases that I am working with are concerned with separation and loss. Many therapists refuse to deal with it because it is so painful. Too many of us have losses that we have not dealt with. As I look back on this picture of my mother, I do not feel lonely anymore. It arouses emotions in me about her dying, but I like the picture. I like the strength and the space. I find it comforting. The face does not look like my mother, but the body is definitely hers."

"The face has a peaceful quality. It appears accepting."

"There is resolution."

"The left hand is powerful and the body seems to lean toward us with the eyes looking down. The two candles are strong. They are an important part of the picture."

"My brother looked at the picture and said 'You are doing mother again. She is lighting Friday night candles.' I rarely analyze my own pictures. A therapist might say that the candles represent consciousness, or a traditional aspect of my mother, that I carry on. Yet, in this painting, I might have put the candles in as a way of filling up the space."

"The motive is often structural in art, and the interpretation is what we see now, the story that we tell in response to the image at a particular time."

"I begin with a white canvas; suddenly, I find that I have a woman and a window. And then I develop it a bit more. I might then back off and say, 'I want her to come out more.' I never said, 'I'm going to go and do a woman.' I never do conscious structuring and sketching before. Many people do. This is what I like about art, the mystery. The image surfaces by itself, especially in my etchings. I never know what will happen next. It is a thrilling adventure."

"What is the object next to the candles?"

"I really do not know. It looks like a flower."

"It is an important part of the picture, in that it seems to belong. I would miss it if it were taken away."

"The stem goes with the horizontal line of the floor. I probably put it there because the space needed something. I put things in because the picture needs it, like the mountain in the background. If I were asked to give a title to this picture, I would say 'woman in the interior.' "

"For me, the picture is expressive of something that is going on inside her."

"I feel connected to this picture. It has been hanging in my living room for twenty-one years. Aside from what has already been discussed, it contains an existential loneliness, and many of my pictures portray this feeling of being alone, quiet and retrospective. The people look like they are thinking. They are not stiff images. Right now, I feel identified with the retrospective aspect. I like to reflect in this way. and I am able to do it in my art. Painting is meditation, a self-hypnosis. It is the one time I am completely connected to myself. I do not have to think about anything else. I am not even thinking about the painting and that's where the excitement is. I get right into it with the brush and my hands. I get filthy. I don't understand how people can stay clean when they paint. It is all process. I back up, look and discover that I have a picture. I start to think about corrections when I am standing at a distance. Self-hypnosis occurs only in the process. When I look at a picture afterwards, I do not have fantasies or free associate. I do not think about what it means. If I like something, I feel good about it. The paintings are like old friends. They are part of my physical and psychological environment. I hate feeling displaced. I have only lived in three houses during my life. I like the sense of comfort. My paintings are comfortable to me."

"You are a maker of spaces, sanctuaries."

"I rarely speak about my paintings. It is like opening up my closets. In the past I did not want to share these private things with many people, and I was careful about who I invited into my house, because they were looking into my closets when they saw my work. I would call the pictures *Man, Woman, Interior.* I did not want to give away any more information, because I had already given away so much in the picture. I am more detached from it all now."

"What do you mean by giving away?"

"I feel as though I am giving away my secrets. When we exhibit our art, we are letting people look into our souls. Over the years I have found that some people look into my soul when they look at my pictures, but actually people only look into their own. I learn so much about people that talk about my paintings. This concept helped me to feel better about showing my work, because they do not really know me at all. They use me as a mirror to talk about themselves."

"And the pictures have a life of their own."

"I hope so."

"In the picture before us, the window and the candles are as strong as the figure. The candles repeat the vertical lines of the window, the mullions. How does this reluctance to talk about yourself relate to art therapy?"

"It is a dichotomy. I do not want to disclose myself, but I am helping other people do it. Maybe it is the voyeuristic part of me. Every therapist has a bit of that element."

"In your writings you have described how you do not always tell people what you see. Perhaps your personal privacy helps you to respect this in other people. You might be giving them the safety that you want for yourself."

"So much of what we do in therapy is a matter of timing. Is there sufficient trust? The more trust we have in one another, the more we can say. In fact, I am interested in the pictures that you have chosen for us to talk about. You have picked three pictures that I think are very powerful. They happen to be related to events. The fourth picture is not related to an event."

"I selected pictures that seemed to relate to one another thematically."

"I think it is interesting, because here in my home I have many pictures that contain masses of people. I have others that are landscapes, some of which are soothing and others that are full of energy. As you look around, there are also the birthing images and yet another theme of birds and then there are moon symbol pictures. You chose four solitary figures."

"It is interesting, because at this time in your life you are saying that you have to be with yourself again. I need it, too."

"There are themes that run through all of my paintings: landscapes, groups/masses of people, moon symbols, the bird and the solitary woman."

"It would seem that they satisfy different needs that are recurring."

"The image of the soaring bird came just before I started treatment. It is called *Pandora's Box.* I had a dream that everything was going to fly out."

"That is an interesting image for therapy. Where do the groups come from?"

"They all just emerge. The masses of people have been done in the past ten years and they relate to what is going on in my life, to my career as a professor, a practicing art psychotherapist and program director. In the last two years I have been painting more landscapes with practically no people on the canvas. Since I have begun to free up my time and myself, I won't be surprised to find the bird image emerging once again. She is always soaring upward. Although, I have also had birds that have tangled with one another. The bird is clearly an aspect of myself and I sure like her. She is flight and freedom."

"It is important to hear you distinguish the different themes in your art. I view the individual person as a pantheon with varied qualities and needs."

"With this second picture (Fig. 32), I just did it with no cognizance of what it was. I kept looking at the painting and thinking about it when I was finished. Usually, I just do it and it goes on the shelf. This one was done during the time when my daughter was going to get married. The woman is the forefront is walking toward the viewer. She is wearing a veil. In some ways she is a bride and in other ways she is not, but she looks sad. I did not realize until this moment that this is a separation and loss picture. My daughter was marrying a man who was not Jewish. You

Figure 32

can see the image of the cross in the background formed by the aisles. The child is my daughter. The image in the front is my daughter, but it is also myself. It is a contemplative picture in which I was dealing with my feelings about my daughter getting married, feeling good and feeling the loss. When children get married they move out of the house. We do not see them everyday. This is the way it has to be. I was dealing with these emotions without knowing about it. The figures emerged and it is only afterwards that it dawned on me what the picture is about. Maybe you have something when you try to connect my personal artwork, to what I do as an art therapist. In my paintings I am dealing with loneliness, separation and loss, and isn't that what I help other people to do? And I did not know that my last book was dealing with separation and loss until it was finished."

"Perhaps your process as an artist is manifested in your clinical and scholarly work, too. As you mentioned earlier, the image surfaces by itself. You go into the work and see the themes afterward, when you stand back to look. This way of working increases the freedom of the images to express themselves."

"My sister once told me that my pictures are depressing, and that I must feel depressed and alone. People that know me understand that I am gregarious and I have many friends. I am not a depressed person. One of my artist friends said isn't it wonderful that we have a vehicle for expressing these feelings and this is why we are not depressed. I have a place to express parts of myself that are not seen out in the world. I am fortunate to be able to express so many things that are a part of me but which are not a part of my daily outside living. We certainly all feel lonely and we have these existential feelings of depression and loss, and aren't we lucky to be able to ventilate them in our art and go on being cheerful people. My friend was helpful in saying this to me. I shared it with my sister and she felt better and agreed with it."

"If there is such a thing as 'anima' as described by the Jungians, then these pictures might help me to get in touch with my feminine nature, my interior. I identify with these women and the mood of reflection. I see them as 'holy' pictures which are not at all depressive. I enjoy looking at them, at the solitary figures."

"The Jungian analyst I worked with said the same thing."

"As I look at the picture of your daughter's wedding I think of your passage rites, not so much your daughter's. I experience you moving through life."

"Life transitions are expressed in the artist's work. When the parent dies, the child is next. My earlier pictures are sweet, images of mothers with children, and that is where I was at the time. As I have gone on, I have integrated what was happening in my life into my artwork. They are passages."

"The space in this picture looks more like a gallery than a temple or church. For the artist the gallery is a sacred place."

"I never noticed that. You are right. When I did the picture, I probably said to myself, I have to fill up the space and I just stuck the pictures in there.

"I call this next picture 'the rock lady' (Fig. 33). It was exhibited in a gallery along with several nationally known women painters, sculptors and potters. I was also asked to place it in a feminist show and refused. This is one of my favorite paintings, and it was inspired by a specific person. I went to visit a woman friend who lived in the desert. We went swimming. She was a big mother-earth lady, with a powerful body and mind. I was fond of her. The desert mountains were formed by sheets of

Figure 33

rock. Throughout the day I was looking at her with the mountains in the background. We talked about the masculine and the feminine and their juxtaposition. As I looked at her in the water I thought that she was as strong as the images of the vertical rocks which I associated with masculinity. When I came home, I painted this picture and I have given it two titles, 'Rosa,' which is her name, and 'the rock lady' because she was a boulder in every way, physically and mentally, solid as a rock. There is a strength in this picture that feels good. She is so solid that I could kick her and it would not hurt and I know that she will continue to exist."

"Do you identify with her strength? Are you a 'rock lady'?"

"Very often, I think I am. The 'rock lady' is strong. Those thighs are solid. The rocks are on the bottom of the picture and the body is presented as an abstract, shaped by the rock formations which are carried through from the landscape to the figure."

"The external strength of this picture complements the more inner directed moods of the other pictures we have looked at. Yet, the reclining 'rock lady' appears to be introspective. She can be open and strong at the same time."

"She has those traits. I am sure that there are people who would say that they do not want to tangle with a 'rock lady.' My mother was a 'rock lady.' I compared her to a mountain before. These women are strong, dependable, comforting. They do not give double messages."

"Images of the mother, the daughter, the mountain, the 'rock lady' and yourself flow together in these pictures."

"Women are wonderful to paint, but I did not want to exhibit within the context of the feminist movement. I do not identify with it. I am more interested in personism. I seem to have managed just fine, in spite of the obstacles that might have been there because I am a woman. I like the challenge of it.

"In the next picture (Fig. 34) there is a person in a contemplative mood. It is a young person. I have never thought too much about what she is thinking. I could make up a story now and so could you. Yours would be just as good as mine. Again, the figure just keeps emerging, and I continue to be interested in the figure in space. The other three pictures that we worked with deal with events, and I felt considerable emotion when talking about them because they brought back memories and feelings dealing with separation and loss. I do not associate these strong emotions with this particular figure. I do not even see her as being lonely. I placed her in the corner with a white shirt in order to feel her body coming out. There is a sunny quality about this picture. It is

Figure 34

not as intense as the others, not as heavy. It does not force a feeling into the viewer."

"This woman appears to be looking out the window, away from the viewer, where the other figures are looking toward the viewer."

"Yes, maybe the looking away decreases the intensity. She is restful and I like her for this. You have done a good thing for me, Shaun. You picked a series of pictures that present a single figure, a woman, and all of them are related to one another. If I contemplated more about my work, I am sure that I will find more connections. I have resisted becoming more conscious of meanings behind my works while they are in the process for fear of restricting them. I am doing it now with you, but I do not want to do it while I am working."

"Many artists have expressed this fear. I have not found it to be a problem. Reflection does not seem to restrict the flow of spontaneity. The more I know about my images, the more I look at patterns. The only way we can really understand patterns is after a considerable number of years of painting. I cannot help relating what you say to art therapy where we do have an almost sacred sense of process."

"You are right. I never thought about it that way. The sacred process for me relates again to the revered word 'artist.' Michelangelo and others were not people for me. They were Gods. It took me a long time to call myself an artist. I had an artist's bank account, and any time that I felt that I was not an artist I would reassure myself by looking at that bank book. I needed validation. It is a humility which most people do not see in me. I am humble when it comes to art. When you said 'sacred,' it struck a bell."

"You are not the 'rock lady' in relation to your art."

"I can be very vulnerable there."

"Me, too."

"Don't you think all artists are this way?"

"This helps me to understand what we are working with in art therapy and to respect the artistic process."

"I do not always think of therapy as an artistic process, because so many of the people that I work with do not paint. When I worked with Lori, a patient who is described in my first book, it was truly a creative awakening. But I do not have many cases like that."

"Have you ever thought about doing therapy with artists?"

"In my experience they have been the most difficult clients. I have found that they are overly aware of 'the art' and they first have to prove what good artists they are, although this is the last thing that I want to focus on. We have to get over the initial resistance to digging in as opposed to showing how talented we are."

"As we talk, I am becoming increasingly aware of the vulnerability connected to art. This is one reason why our profession has so much depth. It gets close to this vulnerability. I feel it now. The tone changes as we talk about the pictures. Your images express these feelings."

"They are coming from inside me, from my feeling states. I am opening up the doors and the closets. My work as an art therapist is more external."

"As an art therapist I try to combine these two places."

"You do that more than I do. I am working right now with people who are more capable of sharing feelings. If you and I were working everyday under the same circumstances, I do not think that we would be that different. There are different environments, expectations and commitments. Whenever it is useful to share myself, I do it. Art is for me the most intimate experience I can have. When I talk about my art, it is the closest encounter that I can have with another person. If you talk about your work, it is not the same thing. It is on the level of what you describe as soul. We are not touched intellectually, unless we are dealing with minimal or conceptual art. We are talking about art that expresses tenderness and intimacy."

"This is why I describe art as depth psychology. We need art to get into the depths."

"In art therapy, people are giving us intimate parts of themselves without even knowing it. Art gets us right down to the nitty-gritty and fast. As you say, we can know the intimate and depth experiences of others because of what we have been through in art. It is tunnel work, which is much different from verbal work. I do not know where the tunnels are going. We might come out in China or in my backyard. It is a narrow passage and we are going underground. We open up an inch at a time when working on ourselves. There are the images that come out of me; yet, you see something in them that is an expression of your life. We create something together and I see things that I never thought about before."

BIBLIOGRAPHY

Arnheim, Rudolf: *Art and Visual Perception*. Berkeley and Los Angeles, U Cal Pr, 1954.

Arnheim, Rudolf: *Toward a Psychology of Art*. Berkeley and Los Angeles, U Cal Pr, 1966.

Arnheim, Rudolf: *Visual Thinking*. Berkeley and Los Angeles, U Cal Pr, 1971.

Arnheim, Rudolf: *The Power of the Center*. Berkeley and Los Angeles, U Cal Pr, 1982.

Arnheim, Rudolf: *New Essays on the Psychology of Art*. Berkeley and Los Angeles, U Cal Pr, 1986.

Barthes, Roland: *The Grain of the Voice: Interviews 1962-1980*. New York, Hill and Wang, 1985.

Boss, Medard: *Psychoanalysis and Daseinsanalysis*. New York, Da Capo, 1982.

Donoghue, Denis: *The Arts Without Mystery*. Boston, Little, Brown, 1973.

Ferrini, Vincent: *Selected Poems*. Storrs, U of Conn Library, 1976.

Foucault, Michel: *The History of Sexuality, Volume 1: An Introduction*. Translation by Robert Hurley. New York, Pantheon, 1978.

Foucault, Michel: *The Uses of Pleasure: History of Sexuality, Volume 2*. Translation by Robert Hurley. New York, Pantheon, 1985.

Freud, Sigmund: *The Interpretation of Dreams* (1909). New York, Basic, 1956.

Freud, Sigmund: *The Basic Writings of Sigmund Freud*. Translated by A. A. Brill. New York, The Modern Library, 1938.

Grotowski, Jerzy: *Toward a Poor Theatre*. New York, Simon and Schuster, 1968.

Hillman, James: *Re-Visioning Psychology*. New York, Harper and Row, 1975.

Hillman, James: *The Myth of Analysis: Three Essays on Archetypal Psychology*. New York, Harper and Row, 1978.

Hillman, James: *Archetypal Psychology: A Brief Account*. Dallas, Spring, 1983.

Hillman, James: *Inter Views*. New York, Harper and Row, 1983.

Holmes, Richard, Editor: *Shelley on Love*. Berkeley and Los Angeles, U Cal Pr, 1980.

Jung, C. G.: *Psychological Types*. New York, Harcourt, Brace, 1923.

Jung, C. G.: *The Basic Writings of C. G. Jung*. Edited by Violet Staub De Laszlo. New York, The Modern Library, 1959.

Kwiatkowska, Hanna: *Family Therapy and Education Through Art.* Springfield, Ill, Charles C Thomas, 1978.

Landgarten, Helen: *Clinical Art Therapy.* New York, Brunner/Mazel, 1981.

Lawrence, D. H.: *Apocalypse.* New York, Viking, 1982.

Lawrence, D. H.: *Fantasia of the Unconscious* and *Psychoanalysis and the Unconscious.* New York, Penguin, 1986.

McConeghey, Howard: Archetypal art therapy is cross-cultural art therapy. *Art Therapy, 3:*3, 1986.

McNiff, Shaun: *Art Therapy At Danvers.* Andover, Addison Gallery of American Art, 1974.

McNiff, Shaun: On art therapy: a conversation with Rudolf Arnheim. *Art Psychotherapy, 2:*2, 1976.

McNiff, Shaun: Motivation in art. *Art Psychotherapy, 4:*3-4, 1977.

McNiff, Shaun: From shamanism to art therapy. *Art Psychotherapy, 6:*3, 1979.

McNiff, Shaun: Art therapy in the classroom. *Art Teacher,* Spring, 1979.

McNiff, Shaun: *The Arts and Psychotherapy.* Springfield, Ill, Charles C Thomas, 1981.

McNiff, Shaun: Working with everything we have. *American Journal of Art Therapy, 21:*4, 1982.

McNiff, Shaun: The art therapy intensive. *Art Therapy, 1:*1, 1983.

McNiff, Shaun: Angels dancing on the head of a pin. In *The Therapeutic Efficacy of the Major Psychotherapeutic Techniques,* J. Hariman, Editor, Springfield, Ill, Charles C Thomas, 1983.

McNiff, Shaun: Art and religion in psychotherapy. *The Bulletin of the National Guild of Catholic Psychiatrists, 30,* 1984.

McNiff, Shaun: Cross-cultural art therapy. *Art Therapy, 1:*3, 1984.

McNiff, Shaun: The artistic soul of psychiatry. *Journal of the Canadian Art Therapy Association, 2:*2, 1986.

McNiff, Shaun: *Educating the Creative Arts Therapist.* Springfield, Ill, Charles C Thomas, 1986.

McNiff, Shaun: Freedom of research and artistic inquiry. *The Arts in Psychotherapy, 13:*4, 1986.

McNiff, Shaun: A dialogue with James Hillman. *Art Therapy, 3:*3, 1986.

McNiff, Shaun: Pantheon of creative arts therapies: An integrative perspective. *Journal of Integrative and Eclectic Psychotherapy, 6:*3, 1987.

McNiff, Shaun: Research and scholarship in the creative arts therapies. *The Arts in Psychotherapy, 14:*2, 1987.

Melville, Herman: *Moby Dick: or The White Whale.* New York, The New American Library, 1961.

Miller, Henry: *Tropic of Capricorn.* New York, Grove Pr, 1961.

Moreno, J. L.: *The Theatre of Spontaneity.* Beacon, New York, Beacon Hse, 1973.

Nehamas, Alexander: *Nietzsche: Life as Literature.* Cambridge, Harvard U Pr, 1985.

Neitzsche, Friedrich: *Human, All Too Human.* Translated by Marion Faber with Stephen Lehmann. Lincoln, U of Nebr Pr, 1984.

Neitzsche, Friedrich: *The Birth of Tragedy and the Case of Wagner.* Translated by Walter Kaufmann. New York, Vintage Books, 1967.

Plato: *Great Dialogues of Plato.* Translated by W. H. D. Rouse. New York, The New American Library, 1956.

Plato: *The Last Days of Socrates.* Translated by Hugh Tredennick. Baltimore, Penguin, 1954.

Rank, Otto: *Psychology and the Soul.* Philadelphia, U of Pa Pr, 1950.

Rank, Otto: *Will Therapy* and *Truth and Reality.* New York, Knopf, 1950.

Reik, Theodor: *Listening With The Third Ear: The Inner Experience of the Psychoanalyst.* New York, Arena Books, 1972.

Richter, Jean Paul: *Horn of Oberon: Jean Paul Richter's School for Aesthetics.* Translated by Margaret Hale. Detroit, Wayne State U Pr, 1973.

Robbins, Arthur: *The Artist as Therapist.* New York, Human Sciences Pr, 1987.

Ross, Steve: *Artist Therapist: Bringing Order Out of Chaos.* New York, American Association of Artist/Therapists, 1984.

Rubin, Judith: *The Art of Art Therapy.* New York, Brunner/Mazel, 1984.

Sartre, Jean-Paul: *Being and Nothingness: An Essay on Phenomenological Ontology.* Translated by Hazel Barnes. New York, Philosophical Library, 1956.

Sartre, Jean-Paul: *Existentialism.* Translated by Bernard Frechtman. New York, Philosophical Library, 1947.

INDEX

249